AA004292

CENICS 2017

The Tenth International Conference on Advances in Circuits, Electronics and Micro-electronics

September 10 - 14, 2017

Rome, Italy

CENICS 2017 Editors

Alie El-Din Mady, Senior Research Scientist, United Technologies Research Center (UTRC) – Cork, Ireland
Timm Bostelmann, FH Wedel (University of Applied Sciences), Germany
Sergei Sawitzki, FH Wedel (University of Applied Sciences), Germany

Printed from e-media with permission by:

Curran Associates, Inc.
57 Morehouse Lane
Red Hook, NY 12571

Some format issues inherent in the e-media version may also appear in this print version.

Printed by Curran Associates, Inc. (2017)

International Academy, Research, and Industry Association (IARIA)
412 Derby Way
Wilmington, DE 19810

Phone: (408) 893-6407
Fax: (408) 527-6351

petre@iaria.org

Additional copies of this publication are available from:

Curran Associates, Inc.
57 Morehouse Lane
Red Hook, NY 12571 USA
Phone: 845-758-0400
Fax: 845-758-2633
Email: curran@proceedings.com
Web: www.proceedings.com

Table of Contents

CENICS 2017

Forward

The Tenth International Conference on Advances in Circuits, Electronics and Micro-electronics (CENICS 2017), held between September 10-14, 2017 in Rome, continued a series of events initiated in 2008, capturing the advances on special circuits, electronics, and micro-electronics on both theory and practice, from fabrication to applications using these special circuits and systems. The topics covered fundamentals of design and implementation, techniques for deployment in various applications, and advances in signal processing.

Innovations in special circuits, electronics and micro-electronics are the key support for a large spectrum of applications. The conference was focusing on several complementary aspects and targets the advances in each on it: signal processing and electronics for high speed processing, micro- and nano-electronics, special electronics for implantable and wearable devices, sensor related electronics focusing on low energy consumption, and special applications domains of telemedicine and ehealth, bio-systems, navigation systems, automotive systems, home-oriented electronics, bio-systems, etc. These applications led to special design and implementation techniques, reconfigurable and self-reconfigurable devices, and require particular methodologies to be integrated on already existing Internet-based communications and applications. Special care is required for particular devices intended to work directly with human body (implantable, wearable, ehealth), or in a human-close environment (telemedicine, house-oriented, navigation, automotive). The mini-size required by such devices confronted the scientists with special signal processing requirements.

The conference had the following tracks:

- Design, models and languages
- Electronics technologies
- Reconfigurable Architectures, Tools and Applications
- Cyber-Physical Security

We take here the opportunity to warmly thank all the members of the CENICS 2017 technical program committee, as well as all the reviewers. The creation of such a high quality conference program would not have been possible without their involvement. We also kindly thank all the authors that dedicated much of their time and effort to contribute to CENICS 2017. We truly believe that, thanks to all these efforts, the final conference program consisted of top quality contributions.

We also gratefully thank the members of the CENICS 2017 organizing committee for their help in handling the logistics and for their work that made this professional meeting a success.

We hope that CENICS 2017 was a successful international forum for the exchange of ideas and results between academia and industry and to promote further progress in the field of circuits, electronics and microelectronics. We also hope that Rome, Italy provided a pleasant environment during the conference and everyone found some time to enjoy the historic charm of the city.

CENICS 2017 Chairs

CENICS Steering Committee

Falk Salewski, Muenster University of Applied Sciences, Germany
Chun-Hsi Huang, University of Connecticut, USA
Marc Sevaux, Université de Bretagne-Sud, France
Vladimir Privman, Clarkson University - Potsdam, USA
Diego Ettore Liberati, National Research Council of Italy, Italy
Julio Sahuquillo, Universitat Politècnica de València, Spain
Sergei Sawitzki, FH Wedel (University of Applied Sciences), Germany
Manuel José Cabral dos Santos Reis, University of Trás-os-Montes e Alto Douro, Portugal
Bartolomeo Montrucchio, Politecnico di Torino, Italy
Petr Hanáček, Brno University of Technology, Czech Republic

CENICS Research/Industry Committee

John Vardakas, Iquadrat Informatica, Barcelona, Spain
Laurent Fesquet, TIMA laboratory | Grenoble Institute of Technology, France
Christian Wögerer, PROFACTOR GmbH, Austria
Miroslav Velev, Aries Design Automation, USA
Ivo Stachiv, Institute of Physics | Czech Academy of Sciences, Prague, Czech Republic / Harbin Institute of Technology | Shenzhen Graduate School, Shenzhen, China
Amir Shah Abdul Aziz, TM Research & Development, Malaysia

CENICS 2017
Committee

CENICS Steering Committee

Falk Salewski, Muenster University of Applied Sciences, Germany
Chun-Hsi Huang, University of Connecticut, USA
Marc Sevaux, Université de Bretagne-Sud, France
Vladimir Privman, Clarkson University - Potsdam, USA
Diego Ettore Liberati, National Research Council of Italy, Italy
Julio Sahuquillo, Universitat Politècnica de València, Spain
Sergei Sawitzki, FH Wedel (University of Applied Sciences), Germany
Manuel José Cabral dos Santos Reis, University of Trás-os-Montes e Alto Douro, Portugal
Bartolomeo Montrucchio, Politecnico di Torino, Italy
Petr Hanáček, Brno University of Technology, Czech Republic

CENICS Research/Industry Committee

John Vardakas, Iquadrat Informatica, Barcelona, Spain
Laurent Fesquet, TIMA laboratory | Grenoble Institute of Technology, France
Christian Wögerer, PROFACTOR GmbH, Austria
Miroslav Velev, Aries Design Automation, USA
Ivo Stachiv, Institute of Physics | Czech Academy of Sciences, Prague, Czech Republic / Harbin Institute of Technology | Shenzhen Graduate School, Shenzhen, China
Amir Shah Abdul Aziz, TM Research & Development, Malaysia

CENICS 2017 Technical Program Committee

Kelum Akurugoda Gamage, Lancaster University, UK
Adel Al-Jumaily, University of Technology, Sydney, Australia
Mohammad Amin Amiri, Malek Ashtar University of Technology, Islamic Republic of Iran
Amir Shah Abdul Aziz, TM Research & Development, Malaysia
Timm Bostelmann, FH Wedel (University of Applied Sciences), Germany
Hamza Bouzeria, Constantine - 1- University, Algeria
Khalid Bouziane, Université Internationale de Rabat, Morocco
David Cordeau, XLIM UMR CNRS 7252, France
Javier Diaz-Carmona, Technoligical Institute of Celaya, Mexico
Alie El-Din Mady, United Technologies Research Center, Cork, Ireland
Diego Ettore Liberati, National Research Council of Italy, Italy
Laurent Fesquet, TIMA laboratory | Grenoble Institute of Technology, France
Patrick Girard, LIRMM, France
Petr Hanáček, Brno University of Technology, Czech Republic
Houcine Hassan, Universitat Politècnica de València, Spain

Copyright Information

For your reference, this is the text governing the copyright release for material published by IARIA.

The copyright release is a transfer of publication rights, which allows IARIA and its partners to drive the dissemination of the published material. This allows IARIA to give articles increased visibility via distribution, inclusion in libraries, and arrangements for submission to indexes.

I, the undersigned, declare that the article is original, and that I represent the authors of this article in the copyright release matters. If this work has been done as work-for-hire, I have obtained all necessary clearances to execute a copyright release. I hereby irrevocably transfer exclusive copyright for this material to IARIA. I give IARIA permission or reproduce the work in any media format such as, but not limited to, print, digital, or electronic. I give IARIA permission to distribute the materials without restriction to any institutions or individuals. I give IARIA permission to submit the work for inclusion in article repositories as IARIA sees fit.

I, the undersigned, declare that to the best of my knowledge, the article is does not contain libelous or otherwise unlawful contents or invading the right of privacy or infringing on a proprietary right.

Following the copyright release, any circulated version of the article must bear the copyright notice and any header and footer information that IARIA applies to the published article.

IARIA grants royalty-free permission to the authors to disseminate the work, under the above provisions, for any academic, commercial, or industrial use. IARIA grants royalty-free permission to any individuals or institutions to make the article available electronically, online, or in print.

IARIA acknowledges that rights to any algorithm, process, procedure, apparatus, or articles of manufacture remain with the authors and their employers.

I, the undersigned, understand that IARIA will not be liable, in contract, tort (including, without limitation, negligence), pre-contract or other representations (other than fraudulent misrepresentations) or otherwise in connection with the publication of my work.

Exception to the above is made for work-for-hire performed while employed by the government. In that case, copyright to the material remains with the said government. The rightful owners (authors and government entity) grant unlimited and unrestricted permission to IARIA, IARIA's contractors, and IARIA's partners to further distribute the work.

Evaluating Heterogeneous Architectures based on Zynq AP SOC for Real-Time Video Processing

Fanny Spagnolo, Stefania Perri, Pasquale Corsonello
Department of Electronics, Computer Sciences and Systems
DIMES - University of Calabria
Arcavacata di Rende, Italy
e-mail: f.spagnolo@dimes.unical.it, perri@dimes.unical.it, p.corsonello@unical.it

Abstract—**Embedded systems are known as valid candidates to efficiently support image and video processing algorithms. Their high flexibility, speed performances and low power consumption are mainly due to the joint design of their software and specific hardware portions. The Zynq All Programmable System on Chip, that integrates ARM processor and high performance programmable logic resources, is nowadays often preferred to the more traditional realization platforms, such as Application Specific Integrated Circuits (ASICs) and Digital Signal Processors (DSPs). In this paper, we evaluate two different design strategies, each with its own Zynq-based support platform, giving to the designers useful hints on how to identify the best design choices for the target application. The first support platform presented here also makes use of an embedded operating system (OS); it significantly limits the required design efforts and time-to-market. The second architecture is realized without the OS support, and of course reaches much higher performances than the former, but requiring higher development and verification times. Both platforms exploit a hardware accelerator for the function of interest. As a case study, a simple but complete image processing architecture has been designed by using both the above platforms. Performances measurements revealed that an approximate speed improvement between 4 and 52 times could be obtained with respect to an all-software implementation.**

***Keywords–Embedded Systems; Image Processing; Zynq*.**

I. Introduction

In the last few years, the development of even more complex and computationally intensive video processing algorithms has been made possible due to the ever-increasing technology progress. Many of these algorithms are adopted in a large variety of applications where real-time performances play an important role. In these cases, software-oriented implementations, running on general purpose CPUs, might not satisfy the tight speed constraints. Faster and more efficient implementations can be achieved with the aid of hardware accelerators that allow exploiting proper computational parallelisms. Embedded systems are a well known approach to speed up image and video processing algorithms by conjunct software/hardware special designs [1]. Such heterogeneous architectures allow trading off the advantages offered by the flexible software and the high performance hardware portions of the design [2]. Nowadays, among several possible realization platforms, the FPGA-based is the most interesting one. Its reduced design efforts and time-to-market make such an approach more appreciated than those based on ASICs fabrication [3]. The lower power dissipation and higher speed performances attainable by using such realization strategy make it preferable with respect to the DSP-based counterparts [4].

Usually, designing an embedded system for video processing, the designer must take into account that most algorithms perform both pixel-level and frame-level computations. Due to their higher computational complexity, pixel-level processing have a great benefit by the inclusion in the embedded system of a dedicated hardware accelerator. On the contrary, frame-level elaborations often process only few frame descriptors. Thus, they do not represent a bottleneck for the overall application. In this case, a pure software implementation can be easier, more flexible and does not compromise the system performances. It is then clear why, in order to conjugate the high-speed capability of a hardware implementation with the flexibility provided by a software design, heterogeneous System-on-Chips (SoCs) based on FPGA have been recently recognized as the most promising approach [5].

However, hardware-software (HW/SW) co-design shows several challenges for the designer. Not only the application has to be partitioned into software and hardware tasks, but also the communication between them has to be efficiently managed.

In this paper, we evaluate two different design strategies for the design and the implementation of real-time embedded systems for image and video processing based on a FPGA SoC. Each of the two designs presented here has its own strengths and weaknesses. The former shows an extreme flexibility and a moderate performance, whereas the latter requires more design efforts but allows much higher speed performance to be reached. As a case study, a complete image processing architecture, which includes image capturing from a webcam, Sobel filtering and output visualization on a monitor, has been implemented. All experiments have been performed by using a Zedboard equipped with the Xilinx Zynq XC7Z020-CLG484 SoC. Performance measurements revealed that the frame rates of such designed embedded systems range between 4 and 52 times the frame rate attainable by a pure software counterpart. The rest of the paper is organized as follows. In Section II, a brief background and the most relevant state of the art related works are reviewed. The first evaluated architecture is introduced in Section III, whereas Section IV describes an example of application to perform fair comparisons. A different design approach is then investigated in Section V. Finally, some conclusions are drawn in Section VI.

II. Background and Related Works

The essence of embedded systems design is implementing a specific set of functions in order to accomplish constraints on performance, costs, emissions, power consumption, etc [6]. Figure 1 shows the typical architecture of a generic embedded system. In general, one or more programmable processing units (CPUs) are used. Depending on the application domain, the embedded systems can have external memory blocks, communication interfaces and several I/O peripherals. While CPUs are traditionally software programmed, custom application specific circuits accelerate more time consuming processes. The first preliminary design step is the efficient HW/SW partitioning of the target application. It consists of splitting the application into computational tasks to be executed either by software routines or by hardware modules. Depending on this partitioning, speed performances and design complexity can be traded off. The generally used approach is to profile the application by means of specific CAD tools [7] in order to indentify its computational loads. Speed performances can be optimized allocating the processing of the most time-consuming tasks to custom hardware accelerators. The remaining non-critical tasks are executed by software routines running on the host general purpose processor. To avoid communication bottlenecks, in a similar approach, the host processor and the hardware accelerators must exchange and transfer data to each other with high throughput and low latency.

The emerging approach based on heterogeneous programmable SoCs is stimulating many application fields [8]. In this section, a group of significant related works are briefly reviewed.

A prototyping environment for heterogeneous CPU/FPGA systems is described in [9], in which a host machine is coupled to a Xilinx Virtex 6 FPGA through the PCI Express Bus. As shown in [10], the limited bandwidth of the communication bus reduces the achievable performances.

A Cadence virtual platform modeling the Xilinx Zynq-7000 SoC is adopted in [11] to implement an Adaptive Cruise Control Unit. This virtual prototyping environment allows using the SystemC language for the portable implementation of software and hardware modules, thus

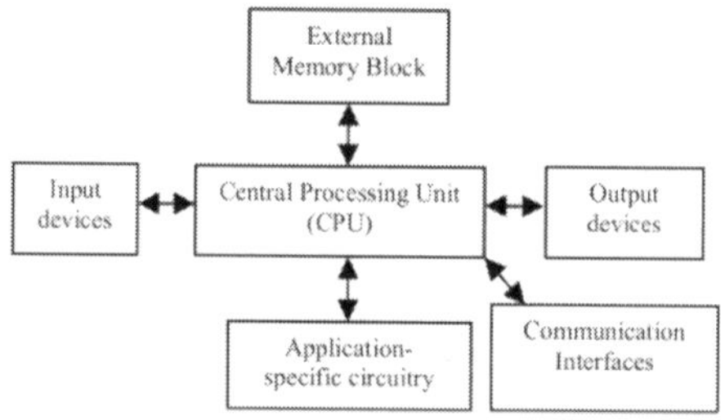

Figure 1. The typical structure of an Embedded System.

avoiding VHDL designs and speeding up the simulation of the overall system. A similar approach is adopted also in [12], where a very high abstraction design approach, based on the use of OpenCV and SystemC, is proposed as an efficient strategy to design embedded systems.

A study about the portability of the OpenCL programming model is, instead, presented in [13]. OpenCL is a framework for targeting heterogeneous platforms based on the C/C++ language.

This approach allows a HW/SW co-design that is independent of the adopted hardware platform to be obtained. Thus, the code can be easily re-targeted to different platforms. In [13], experiments conducted by using the Altera SDK for OpenCL (AOCL), however, demonstrate that the same test code performs differently on different platforms, thus requiring specific optimizations.

In [14], several real-time image processing algorithms are implemented on a Zynq-based hardware platform. This study exploits a task partitioning of the target application based on performances improvements. Linux operating system is hosted on the ARM CPU inside the Zynq to easily manage the video acquisition by software routines. An efficient communication strategy between hardware accelerators and the host CPU is realized through the AMBA Advanced Extensible Interface (AXI).

With the main objective of reducing the time-to-market of the developed system, the approach described in [15] exploits the Xillybus IP core to guarantee a fast communication between hardware and software components of the overall system. To this aim, the communication is managed by software thanks to some useful functions included in the Xillybus library.

In the next section, we evaluate such an approach as a generally valid support to design heterogeneous embedded system architectures for real-time image processing. The Xillinux open source operating system is hosted on the CPU and it manages the communication with the hardware implemented into the FPGA portion of the Zynq chip as a regular peripheral.

III. The Xillybus-based Platform

The main target of the platform described below is to furnish an efficient hardware support to develop real-time

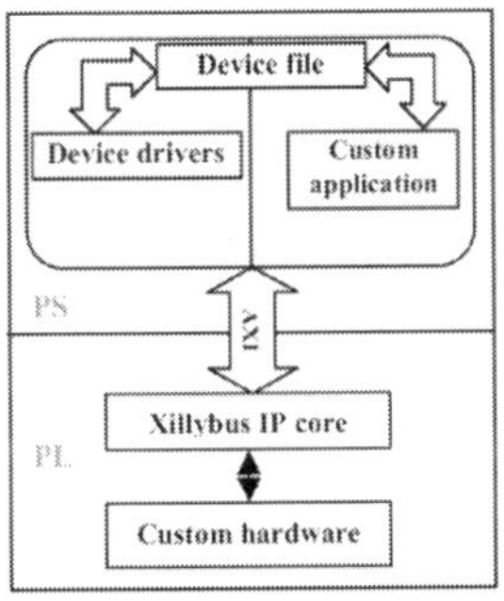

Figure 2. Xillybus-based platform. The PS section hosts the OS components, whereas the PL section implements hardware accelerators and Xillybus IP core.

image and video processing applications in embedded systems, with reduced implementation time.

The platform evaluated in this section is structured as depicted in Figure 2. The Zynq processing system (PS) consists of a dual core ARM Cortex – A9 processor, while the programmable logic (PL) is based on the Artix-7 FPGA fabric for minimizing power consumption.

The ARM processor is able to host OSs such as Linux, Real Time Operating System (RTOS), Windows, etc. The Zedboard is also equipped with 512 MB DDR3 memory and a 256Mb 4-bit SPI Serial NOR Flash memory. The latter supports speeds up to 400Mbps and hence it is suitable for storing boot loaders and kernel of one of the above OSs.

The system detailed below exploits a set of precompiled sub-systems, namely the Xillybus package, able to facilitate the communication tasks between the PS, the external peripherals and the accelerators. The Xillybus package makes also available the Xillinux open source OS that is a complete graphical Ubuntu 12.04 LTS-based Linux distribution, well suitable for rapid development of mixed software/logic designs [16]. It is a collection of software tools that supports roughly the same capabilities of a personal desktop computer running Linux. Xillybus distribution comes with two different synthesizable cores: the XillyLite IP core that allows a simple direct address/data transfer; and the Xillybus IP core that allows data streams to be transferred to/from the custom hardware accelerator [17].

The designed architecture is illustrated in Figure 3. It can be observed that a XillyLite core is used to access a block RAM, whereas the Xillybus core is adopted to transfer data from the PS to/from the custom hardware accelerator [18]. All IP cores are also connected to the PS by an AXI-Lite interface.

When connected to the Xillybus IP core, the hardware accelerators can be accessed by the PS like a common peripheral, which communicates with the OS through specific device drivers.

The interface between the software drivers and the software application is represented by the device files provided by Xillybus. These files can be opened, read and written like any files inside the user space application, so it is possible to implement a high level abstraction for PS-PL communication.

The PS manages the data transfer to capture the frames from a webcam through the USB port and to store them into the DDR3 external memory. Other memory accesses, related to the data transfers to/from the custom hardware accelerator, are governed by the Xillybus IP core through the high performances ports in the PS section. The acquisition operation is easily implemented in software by using video libraries and camera drivers. Whereas, the PL was used to hardware implement the following components:

- The Xillybus IP core that communicates with the PS through the AXI full and AXI Lite interfaces;
- The XillyLite IP core that communicates with the PS through the AXI Lite interface;
- The custom hardware accelerator;
- Two FIFOs, used as input and output interfaces between the Xillybus core and the custom hardware accelerator;
- A VGA controller connected to an external monitor that displays the output of the custom hardware accelerator stored in the DDR3 external memory.

In the designed architecture, the processor works as master during the configuration of the VGA controller, the XillyLite IP core and the Xillybus IP core. This configuration corresponds to a control signals transfer, needed to inform the hardware IP cores about the image resolution, the DDR memory addresses etc.

Each data transfer through an AXI interface occurs as summarized in the following:

- In a read process, the slave device address is sent by the master interface over the read address channel. Then, the addressed slave interface sends the corresponding data over the read data channel to the master.
- In a write process, the master interface sends the slave device address to which the data is to be written and corresponding data. On successful write at the slave interface, the slave sends a response over the write response channel to flag the transfer completion.

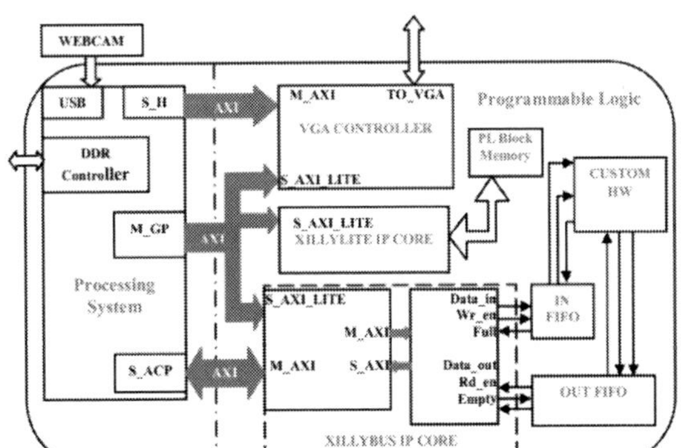

Figure 3. Architecture used within the ZedBoard to evaluate the Xillybus-based platform.

An AXI Interconnect IP core multiplexes the access by the master to the three slaves and the Xillybus IP core acts as an interface between the PS and the custom hardware accelerator. This architecture can be easily customized to perform virtually any image and video processing algorithm without re-design either the top-level architecture or the interface modules required to acquire input images/videos and to display/store the resulting frames.

Data transferred to/from the PS from/to the hardware accelerator flows through the input and output FIFOs, as shown in Figure 3. FIFOs can be configured according to the applications requirements, but they must comply with the constraints of the device drivers provided by Xillybus. As an example, the Xillybus drivers can be configured to transfer 8, 16 or 32-bit data words so the data width of the FIFOs must be set accordingly. The *wr_en*, *rd_en*, *full* and *empty* control signals manage the synchronization between the Xillybus IP core and the hardware accelerator.

The complete data flow implemented within an embedded system designed by using our platform is described in the following:

- The PS converts the RGB frame, captured by the webcam, into the 8-bit grayscale format and, subsequently, it transfers the pixels to the external DDR3 block memory. The frame is transferred from the DDR3 memory to the PL through the Xillybus interface. This operation is performed by the software routine running on the PS, which communicates with the Xillybus drivers through the available "open" and "write" functions applied on the specific device file, as shown in Figure 4. Then, the pixel transfer from PS to the Xillybus IP core occurs through the high performance S_AXI_ACP port. As a response, the Xillybus IP core activates the write enable (*wr_en*) signal of the input FIFO.
- If the input FIFO is not empty and the hardware accelerator is ready to receive the input pixels, the read enable (*rd_en*) signal is asserted and a stream of pixels is sent to the hardware accelerator.
- When valid data is available on the output port of the hardware accelerator, the latter asserts the write enable (*wr_en*) signal of the output FIFO, which receives a stream of data produced by the user-defined computational logic. The output data stream continues until the output FIFO becomes full. If this condition occurs, the output FIFO asserts its *full* signal and the hardware accelerator temporarily stalls the transfer.

```
int fdw;
unsigned char *buffer;
//Open Xillybus interface to transfer data from PS to PL
fdw=open("/dev/Xillybus_write_device", O_WRONLY);
write(fdw, buffer, sizeof(buffer));
//Close Xillybus PS-to-PL interface
close(fdw);
```

Figure 4. Use of "open" and "write" functions in the software routine.

```
int fdr;
unsigned char *buffer;
//Open Xillybus interface to transfer data from PL to PS
fdr=open("/dev/Xillybus_read_device", O_RDONLY);
read(fdr, buffer, sizeof(buffer));
//Close Xillybus PL-to-PS interface
close(fdr);
```

Figure 5. Use of "open" and "read" functions in the software routine.

- The software running on the PS invokes the "open" and "read" functions of the Xillybus driver, as described in Figure 5, so data stored in the output FIFO is transferred to the DDR3 through the S_AXI_ACP/Xillybus connection. In hardware, this operation corresponds to assert the *rd_en* signal of the output FIFO.
- The output image is finally transferred from the DDR3 to the VGA controller that is connected to an external monitor. The PS is involved in this operation only to send the control signals to the VGA controller through its M_AXI GP port. Pixels to display are transferred from the DDR3 to the VGA controller through the high performance S_AXI_HP port of the PS. The latter is not involved during the data transfer so it can run the next software routine.

In the proposed design support platform, the Xillybus IP core and the custom hardware accelerator work with the same clock, so the write/read operations to/from the input and output FIFOs occur at the same rate. The clock is produced by the PS with a frequency of 100MHz, which is the highest frequency supported by the Xillybus IP core [19]. The usage of synchronous streams is the preferred choice when tight synchronization is needed between the software running on the PS and the hardware implemented in the PL. However, in order to increase performances, multiple clock domains can be adopted if the hardware accelerator can run at clock frequencies higher than 100MHz. In such a case, asynchronous FIFOs with different input and output clock frequencies have to be employed. In particular, the write (read) operation into (from) the input (output) FIFO is performed at the Xillybus clock rate, whereas the write (read) operation into (from) the output (input) FIFO is performed at the clock rate of the hardware accelerator.

IV. The Case Study: A Sobel Filter Implementation

As an example of application, the above described design platform has been used to implement an embedded system which filters digital images. The 3×3 Sobel filter [20] is hardware implemented and applied to 320×240 pixels frames captured by the external camera. Image filtering has been chosen as the case study since it has a computational complexity sufficiently high to highlight the advantages offered by the HW/SW co-design over the all-software counterpart.

The hardware accelerator has been developed with the Vivado High Level Synthesis (HLS) tool that allows describing the hardware circuit in a high level programming

TABLE I. RESOURCE UTILIZATION.

Sobel accelerator			Custom FIFOs			Xillybus IP core			VGA Controller IP core			XillyLite IP core		
LUTs	FFs	32K BRAMs	LUTs	FFs	32K BRAMs	LUTs	FFs	32K BRAMs	LUTs	FFs	32K BRAMs	LUTs	FFs	32K BRAMs
212 0.4%	172 0.1%	1 0.7%	90 0.1%	96 0.1%	1 0.7%	3011 5.6%	2690 2.5%	1 0.7%	499 0.9%	779 0.7%	1 0.7%	67 0.12%	94 0.1%	0 (0%)

language (C++) and converting the code into a synthesizable RTL description. Input and output interfaces of the custom hardware accelerator have been configured as FIFOs, in order to guarantee the compatibility with the two FIFOs connected to the Xillybus IP core. The FIFOs have a data width and a depth of 8 bit and 2048 words, respectively.

Table I summarizes the overall FPGA resources utilization of the implemented architecture. The number of the total used look-up tables (LUTs) is very limited, about 7% of the LUTs available in the XC7Z020-CLG484 chip; the number of required flip-slops (FFs) and 32Kbyte block RAMs (32K BRAMs) is even lower (3.5% and 2.8%, respectively).

The software application, running on the PS, exploits OpenCV library functions [21] to manage the input frames captured by the USB camera. The input pixels are converted from the RGB to the 8-bit grayscale format and transferred to the DDR3 memory. The software application is responsible for transferring the pixels to the Xillybus IP core, retrieving the output pixels from the hardware accelerator and storing them to the DDR3 memory. Finally, the software application starts the data transfer from the DDR3 to the VGA controller. Figure 6 shows two output video frames obtained by the implemented architecture.

To measure execution time of each task, the appropriate software timing library has been used. Since the data transfer through the Xillybus can be performed by varying the number of bytes transferred at each write/read function call, we evaluated the execution time as a function of the bytes packet size. As depicted in Figure 7, the total execution time drastically decreases when the packet size increases. But, the minimum execution time of about 118.3 ms is reached for a packet size of ≈5000 bytes and it is maintained until 9600 bytes.

Figure 6. Some input and output video frames.

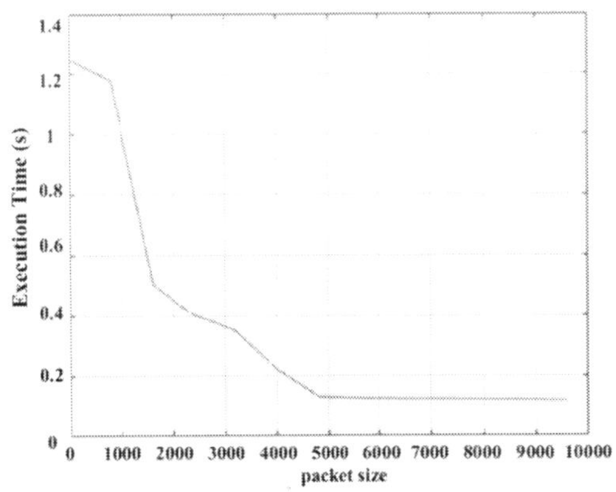

Figure 7. Execution time vs. the packet dimension.

TABLE II. EXECUTION TIMES.

Hardware Sobel filter	Software application	Communication	All-software Sobel filter
2.3 ms	100 ms	16 ms	490 ms

This result suggests to adopt transfer of ≈5000 bytes each, because this also limits the depth of the input and output FIFOs.

Table 2 shows the timing breakdown that is split into three main contributions: the hardware processing time (Sobel filtering), the PL-PS communication time ("write, "read" and "open" of the Xillybus driver) and the remaining software execution time (RGB to grayscale conversion and data streaming from/to the DDR3 managed by the PS) per frame.

As expected, the software execution time represents the highest contribution, mainly due to the OpenCV functions for the management of input frame, the format conversion and the output frame visualization. The hardware processing and the communication between PS and Xillybus IP core account only for the 15.5% of the overall execution time.

In order to estimate the speed-up obtained by the custom hardware accelerator, a pure software routine performing the same Sobel filtering has been characterized. The latter has been executed by the ARM processor hosted in the PS, which operates at a 666.66 MHz running frequency. Measurements reported in Table 2 show the benefits obtained by the heterogeneous design approach. A gain of about 4x has been achieved.

Even though a direct comparison between our results and those reported in [15] cannot be performed, due to the different user application, a brief discussion is appropriate. In [15], a Xillybus-based platform performing the Harris

Corner Detection function on 512x384 images has been implemented and evaluated. When the PL is clocked at 100 MHz and the 32-bit Xillybus software interface is adopted, the total communication and hardware processing time is about 15 ms. The latter is approximately 3.3ms lower than result reported in Table 2, which instead has been obtained adopting the 8-bit Xillybus software interface. If the 32-bit Xillybus software interface is used in the architecture of Figure,3, the communication time is reduced correspondingly.

V. THE VDMA-BASED ALTERNATIVE

The high level design approach used above employs a ready-to-use communication solution between hardware and software components. Due to this, it significantly reduces design efforts, the development time and the hardware design expertise required for realizing a complete embedded system for video processing applications. Of course, such a design strategy negatively impacts the overall speed performances. In particular, some considerations can be done in reference to the Xillybus bandwidth.

The FIFO configuration provided by Xillybus has a maximum bandwidth of about 200 MB/s for each transfer direction [17]. On the contrary, the Zynq PS high performance ports are able to access the DDR3 memory achieving a bandwidth of 1600 MB/s for a 64-bit transfer at 100 MHz clock rate [22].

In this section, we examine an alternative design, based on the direct use of Video Direct Memory Access (VDMA) IP cores [23]. Using this approach, much more architectures design knowledge and digital system debugging practice are required. The VDMA is a soft core, which provides high bandwidth access to external memory and video processing IP cores with AXI-Stream interface. The architecture designed in accordance with this strategy is illustrated in Figure 8. In this case the PS does not support an OS, thus the system is oriented to bare-metal application architectures. An OmniVision OV7670 CMOS Camera has been connected through an I2C interface and an appropriate frame capture control sub-system is required. The VDMA0 transfers captured frames to the DDR3 and, then, after the elaboration, from the DDR3 to the VGA display port. The VDMA1 transfers the video stream to the custom hardware accelerator that performs the specific video algorithm. After that, the VDMA1 writes back the filtered results into the DDR3 memory.

Using High Performance AXI ports to access the external memory allows the computational load of the processor to be significantly reduced. Furthermore, by using two different High Performance ports, parallel operations to/from the DDR3 can be performed, thus obtaining a further considerable performance improvement. In fact, a new captured frame can be stored, or a result frame can be displayed, while the VDMA1 transfers the pixel stream to/from the hardware accelerator.

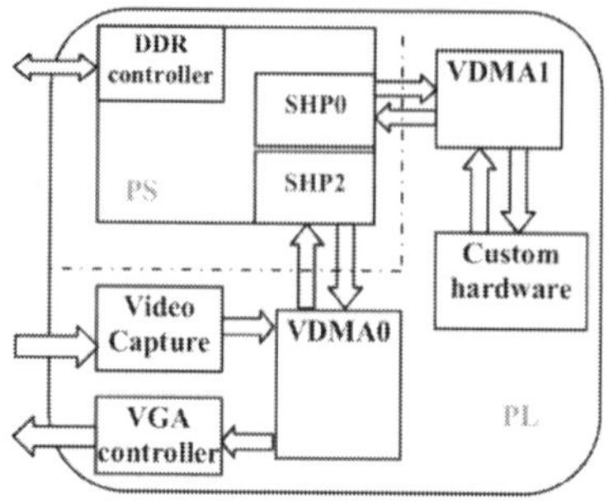

Figure 8. Architecture used within the ZedBoard to evaluate the VDMA-based platform.

Due to the overlap between the two phases above mentioned, this architecture reaches a processing rate much higher than the structure exploiting the Xillybus IP Cores. When the same Sobel filter accelerator is implemented within this structure, a total execution time of only ≈9.2 ms is achieved, thus leading to an overall performance ~13 times higher. This result has been obtained with a clock rate of 100MHz for the PL section, while the Video Capture IP core operates at 30 frames per second in VGA resolution.

VI. CONCLUSIONS

In the development of an embedded system based on heterogeneous SoCs, of course, the first important design step is the efficient HW/SW partitioning of the target application. After that, on the basis of the design environment, several other significant choices have to be done. When only high level description is desired, several precompiled supports could be of great help. As shown in this paper, an almost complete solution is offered by the Xillybus package that contains appropriate communication sub-modules and a light OS.

We designed a test architecture to evaluate the speed improvement attainable with such supports and measured a speed up of ≈4 times with respect to a pure software typical image processing elaboration. Such an approach allows very easy interface between the designed architecture and peripherals.

On the contrary, when the speed performance is the main concern, a direct and on-purpose design of the entire architecture is preferable. In such a case, a further x13 speed up has been observed, but at the expense of much more design effort and verification time.

ACKNOWLEDGMENT

Authors wish to thank Dr. Fabio Frustaci and Dr. Giovanni Staino for the helpful discussions during the present work.

REFERENCES

[1] W. Wolf, "The Future of Multiprocessor Systems-on-Chips" Proceedings of the 41st annual Design Automation Conference (DAC '04), pp. 681-685 , June 7-11 2004.

[2] B. Roux, M. Gautier, O. Sentieys, and S. Derrien, "Communication-Based Power Modelling for Heterogeneous Multiprocessor Architecture", IEEE 10th International Symposium on Embedded Multicore /Many-core Systems-on-Chip (MCSoC 2016), pp. 209-216, Sep 2016.

[3] J.A. Kalomiros and J. Lygouras, "Design and evaluation of a hardware/software FPGA-based system for fast image processing", Microprocessors and Microsystems, vol. 32, issue 2, March 2008.

[4] R. J. Petersen and B. L. Hutchings, "An assessment of the suitability of FPGA-based systems for use in digital signal processing". In: Moore W.; Luk W. (eds) Field-Programmable Logic and Applications. FPL 1995. Lecture Notes in Computer Science, vol. 975, pp. 293-302. Springer, Berlin, Heidelberg

[5] J. Teich, "Hardware/Software Codesign: The Past, the Present, and Predicting the Future", Proceedings of the IEEE, vol. 100, Issue: Special Centennial Issue, pp. 1411-1430, May 13 2012.

[6] A. Sangiovanni-Vicentelli and G. Martin, "Platform –based Design and Software Design Methodology for Embedded Systems", IEEE Design & Test of Computers, IEEE press, vol. 18, issue 6, pp. 23-33, Nov/Dec 2001, doi: 10.1109/54.970421.

[7] R. Ernst, "Codesign of Embedded Systems: status and trends", IEEE Design & Test of Computers, vol. 15, issue 2, pp. 45-54, Apr-Jun 1998, doi: 10.1109/54.679207.

[8] D. Andrews, D. Niehaus, and P. Ashenden, "Programming models for hybrid CPU/FPGA chips", Computer, IEEE press, vol. 37, issue 1, pp. 118-120, Jan. 2004, doi: 10.1109/MC.2004.1260732.

[9] G. Afonso, R.B. Atitallah, A. Loyer, J. Dekeyser, N. Belanger, and M. Rubio, "A prototyping environment for high performance reconfigurable computing" 6th International Workshop on Reconfigurable Communication-centric Systems-on-Chip (ReCoSoC), IEEE press, pp. 1-8, August 2011, doi: 10.1109/ReCoSoC.2011.5981497.

[10] Y. Li, X. Zhao, and T. Cheng, "Heterogeneous Computing Platofrom Based On CPU+FPGA and Working Modes", 12th International Conference on Computational Intelligence and Security (CIS), IEEE press pp. 670-672, December 2016, doi: 10.1109/CIS.2016.0161.

[11] P. Wehner, M. Ferger, D. Göhringer , and M. Hübner, "Rapid Prototyping of a Portable HW/SW Co-Design on he Virtual Zynq Platform using SystemC", IEEE 26th International SOC Conference (SOCC), IEEE press pp. 296-300, September 2013, doi: 10.1109/SOCC.2013.6749704.

[12] J. Anders, M. Mefenza, C. Bobda, F. Yonga, Z. Aklah, and K. Gunn, "A hardware/software prototyping system for driving assistance investigations" in Journal of Real-Time Image Processing , vol. 11, issue 3, pp. 559-569, March 2016.

[13] S.O. Ayat, M. Khalil-Hani, and R. Bakhteri, "OpenCL-based Hardware-Software Co-design Methodology for Image Processing Implementation on Heterogeneous FPGA Platform", 2015 IEEE International Conference on Control System, Computing and Engineering (ICCSCE), IEEE press pp. 36-41, November 2015, doi: 10.1109/ICCSCE.2015.7482154.

[14] M.A. Altuncu, T. Guven, Y. Becerikli, and S. Sahin, "Real-Time System Implementation for Image Processing with Hardware/Software Co-design on the Xilinx Zynq Platform", International Journal of Information and Electronics Engineering, vol. 5, no. 6, pp. 473-477, November 2015, doi: 10.7763/IJIEE.2015.V5.582.

[15] I. Stratakos, D. Reisis, G. Lentaris, K. Maragos, and D. Soudris, "A Co-Design Approach For Rapid Prototyping Of Image Processing on SoC FPGAs"Proceedings of the 20th Pan-Hellenic Conference on Informatics (PCI '16), November 2016, ISBN: 978-1-4503-4789-1, doi: 10.1145/3003733.3003797.

[16] Getting started with Xillinux for Zynq-7000 EPP v. 1.3 [Online]. Available from: http://xillybus.com/downloads/doc/xillybus_getting_started_zynq.pdf

[17] B.M. Kambalur, K. Kumar, and K.S. Athrey, "A Study of Implementing Custom Application on Zynq AP SoC using Xillybus IP Core", ITSI Transactions on Electrical and Electronics Engineering (ITSI-TEEE), vol.. 2 pp. 35-37 , issue 5-6, 2014.

[18] Getting started with the FPGA Demo Bundle for Xilinx v. 2.6 [Online]. Available from: http://xillybus.com/downloads/doc/xillybus_getting_started_xilinx.pdf

[19] Xillybus FPGA Designer's Guide v. 2.0 [Online]. Available from: http://xillybus.com/downloads/doc/xillybus_fpga_api.pdf

[20] N. Kanopoulos, N. Vasanthavada, R., and L. Baker, "Design of an Image Edge Detection Filter Using the Sobel Operator", IEEE Journal of Solid-State Circuits, vol. 23, issue 2, pp. 358-367, Apr 1988, doi: 10.1109/4.996.

[21] About OpenCV [Online]. Available from: http://opencv.org/about.html

[22] Zynq-7000 All Programmable SoC Technical Reference Manual, UG585 (v. 1.11) September 27, 2016 [Online]. Available from: https://www.xilinx.com/support/documentation/user_guides/ug585-Zynq-7000-TRM.pdf

[23] C. Kohn, "Partial Reconfiguration of a Hardware Accelerator on Zynq-7000 All Programmable SoC Devices" XAPP1159 Xilinx Jan. 21, 2013.

Table Reference-Based Acceleration of a Lithography Hotspot Detection Method Based on Approximate String Search

Shuma Tamagawa, Masato Inagi, Shinobu Nagayama, Shin'ichi Wakabayashi
email: shuma@lcs.info.hiroshima-cu.ac.jp, {inagi, s_naga, wakaba}@hiroshima-cu.ac.jp
Graduate School of Information Sciences, Hiroshima City University
3-4-1 Ozuka-higashi, Asaminami-ku, Hiroshima, 731-3194 Japan

Abstract—**In nanoscale large-scale integration (LSI) manufacturing, there exist hotspots on mask patterns, which cause failures of pattern transfer. Such hotspots are detected by optical simulation to remove them. However, it requires a long time. Thus, development of efficient hotspot detection methods is required. As one of the methods, an existing one based on approximate string search has been proposed. Although this method is expected to find hotspots more flexibly than commonly-used template matching, computation of edit distance matrices used for approximate string search still requires a long time. Thus, in this study, we accelerate the computation by using table-reference of precomputed values and simultaneous computation of multiple elements. Our experiments showed that our improved method achieved about 1/11 computation time compared to the original one.**

Keywords–lithography; hotspot; optical simulation; approximate string matching.

I. Introduction

In nanoscale large-scale integration (LSI) manufacturing, lithography process is one of the most important processes, in which mask patterns printed on photomasks are transferred to the wafer using exposure equipment. In the process, some patterns tend to be failed to be transferred because of optical diffraction. Such patterns are called *hotspots* [1].

Since the cost of manufacturing photomasks is quite high, it is better to remove hotspots from the mask patterns in advance. Thus, lithography engineers apply optical simulation to the mask patterns received from mask designers. If hotspots are found by the optical simulation, it is informed to the designers, and the patterns are revised. This is repeated until all the hotspots are removed. However, optical simulation is time-consuming. To reduce the number of times of optical simulation, mask designers need to detect and remove hotspots in advance. Therefore, some studies on efficient hotspot detection have been conducted [2]–[6].

[2] proposed a template-matching-based method, which directly matches mask patterns and hotspot patterns. A mask pattern and a hotspot pattern are shown in Figure 1, as examples. A hotspot pattern is a pattern which should be detected from a mask pattern. While this method has a high ability to detect known patterns, its ability to detect unknown patterns is low. [3] discussed some hotspot detection methods using some machine-learning methods, such as artificial neural network (ANN) and support vector machine (SVM). According to the nature of machine-learning-based methods, they can detect unknown patterns as hotspots. However, they cause a large number of false-positive detections. [4] proposed a hybrid method based on template matching and machine-learning. Though the hybrid approach improved the accuracy of detection, the number of false-positive detections is still large. In addition, it takes 10 to 100 times longer for detection. [5] adopted a fuzzy-matching model instead of ANN or SVM. They improved both of execution time of detection and the accuracy of detection. Although there exist aforementioned hotspot detection methods, some mask designers use template-matching to detect hotspot patterns since their execution time and accuracy do not meet the level required by the designers.

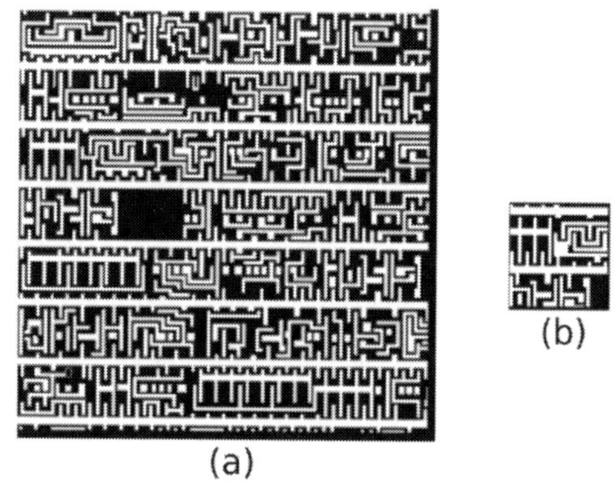

Figure 1. Circuit patterns: (a) mask pattern, (b) hotspot pattern

In [6], we proposed an approximate string matching-based hotspot detection method for flexible hotspot detection. Comparing to machine-learning-based methods, this method can detect hotspot candidates in a short time. Comparing to template-matching-based methods, this method can detect hotspot candidates more flexibly (*i.e.*, unknown patterns can be detected.) However, to calculate the value of each element in the edit distance matrix for approximate string matching, we need to refer to three elements in the matrix. Thus, comparing to template-matching-based methods, in which only one value is referred for the corresponding calculation, it takes a longer time for calculation (although it is just a constant coefficient factor).

Thus, in this paper, we improve the approximate string matching-based method [6] by using table-reference of pre-computed values and simultaneous calculation of multiple elements in the edit distance matrix. Each region of simultaneously handled elements is a $k \times k$ partial matrix of the edit distance matrix, where k is the user-defined constant which decides parallelism. In the proposed method, the calculation of a region for every possible input set is performed in advance, and the result is memorized in a reference-table. Then, the edit distance matrix is calculated by using the table. For efficient calculation, the values in a region is encoded to one word of memory to calculate the values of multiple elements with only one memory access. Experimental result showed the high effectiveness of the proposed method in execution time compared to the existing method [6].

The rest of this paper is organized as follows. First, in Section II, we explain about lithography, and we provide the definitions of the approximate string matching problem, the edit distance, the approximate string search problem, which is one of the variations of the approximate string matching problem, and on which our proposing method and [6] are based. Next, in Section III, the definition of the hotspot detection problem and the existing hotspot detection method [6] are shown. Then, in Section IV, we propose an improved method which uses table-reference. Section VI shows some experimental results, and finally conclusions are given in Section VII.

II. PRELIMINARIES

A. Lithography

Lithography is one of the processes of LSI manufacturing. In the process, a circuit pattern drawn on a photomask is transferred to the wafer using exposure equipment. A photomask is one of the masters to make a circuit on the wafer.

Figure 2 illustrates lithography process. In lithography process, a mask pattern drawn on a photomask is transferred onto the wafer via lenses, shedding light from above the photomask. While 193nm laser is commonly used in advanced lithography processes [7], the minimum pitch between wires is decreasing, and has reached 14nm. Therefore, some sub-patterns cannot be transferred correctly because of diffraction of light. Such a sub-pattern is called *a hotspot*. An example of a mask pattern is shown in Figure 3(a). The transferred image (by optical simulation) of Figure 3(a) is shown in Figure 3(b). In Figure 3(b), wires are connected at an unintended position, and some wires are too thin. Therefore, the pattern shown in Figure 3(a) is a hotspot pattern.

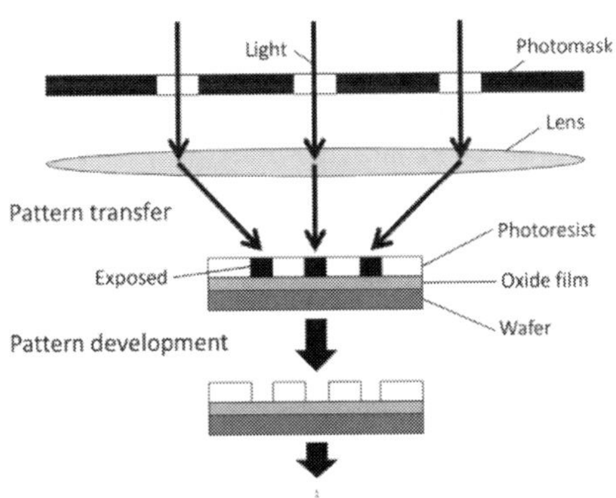

Figure 2. Principle of photolithography process

B. Approximate String Matching Problem

Approximate string matching problem [8] is one of the string matching problems, and is a problem to determine if two given strings are similar or not. In this study, the similarity between strings is measured by the edit distance explained in the next subsection. If the edit distance is less than or equal to a given threshold, we consider they are similar each other.

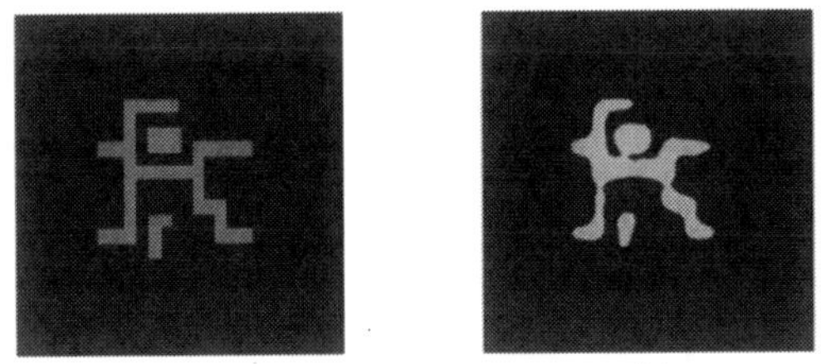

(a) (b)

Figure 3. Hotspot: (a) mask pattern, (b) its transferred image

C. Edit Distance

Let us consider a pair of characters $(a, b)(\neq (\epsilon, \epsilon))$, where ϵ is an *empty character*, which represents nonexistence of any character. The operation transforming character a in a string into b is called an *edit operation*, and is denoted by $a \rightarrow b$. For example, let us consider a string $A = gzh$. If an edit operation $g \rightarrow f$ is applied to the first character of A, we get $A' = fzh$ as the resultant string of the operation. If an edit operation $z \rightarrow \epsilon$ is applied to the second character of A, we get $A' = gh$. If an edit operation $\epsilon \rightarrow j$ is applied to the empty character between the second and third characters of A, we get $A' = gzjh$. Hereinafter, we call an operation $a \rightarrow b$ a *substitution* if $a \neq \epsilon$ and $b \neq \epsilon$. Likewise, we call an operation $a \rightarrow \epsilon$ a *deletion*, and call an operation $\epsilon \rightarrow b$ an *insertion*. Any string can be transformed into an arbitrary string by applying the edit operations. An edit operation has its cost denoted by $\gamma(a \rightarrow b)$. We assume the costs of edit operations satisfy the equation below.

$$\gamma(a \rightarrow a) = 0$$

$$\gamma(a \rightarrow b) + \gamma(b \rightarrow c) \geq \gamma(a \rightarrow c)$$

Suppose strings A and B on alphabets Σ are given. A sequence of edit operations to transform A into B is denoted as $O = o_1, o_2, \ldots, o_m$. The cost of O is defined as

$$\gamma(O) = \sum_{i=1}^{m} \gamma(o_i).$$

The minimum value among the costs of all the sequences each of which transforms A into B is defined as *the edit distance between A and B* [8].

D. Approximate String Search Problem

Approximate string search is to find substrings similar to a given pattern in a long input sequence. More precisely, approximate string search is to find all the substrings whose edit distance to the pattern P are the minimum among all the substrings (or less then the given threshold t), in the input sequence S.

We here explain a dynamic programming-based (DP-based) algorithm for approximate string search [8], [9]. Prepare an $(n + 1) \times (m + 1)$ two-dimensional array D, where D has $n + 1$ rows and $m + 1$ columns, n is the length of the pattern $P = a_1 a_2 \cdots a_n$, and m is the length of the input sequence $S = b_1 b_2 \cdots b_m$. An element $D(i, j)$ (at $(i+1)$-th row, $(j+1)$-th column) of D is defined by the following equations:

$$D(0,0) = 0, \quad D(0,j) = 0,$$

$$D(i,0) = D(i-1,0) + del(a_i),$$

$$\begin{aligned} D(i,j) \quad = \min\{ \quad & D(i-1,j) + del(a_i), \\ & D(i,j-1) + ins(b_j), \\ & D(i-1,j-1) + sub(a_i,b_j) \ \} \end{aligned}$$

where the functions ins, del, and sub denote the insertion, deletion, and substitution costs. Figure 4 illustrates the DP-based calculation of an edit distance matrix, and Figure 5 shows the resultant edit distance matrix. D is called *edit distance matrix*, and $D(n,j)(1 \leq j \leq m)$ gives the edit distance between the pattern P and a substring (whose terminal character is b_j) in the input sequence S. If the value is the minimum among all the $D(n,j)(j = 1,2,\ldots,m)$ (or less than the user-defined threshold t), we consider that the substring is similar to the pattern. The initial character of such a substring is found by tracing back the DP-based calculation on D. Figure 6 illustrates how to identify similar substrings. The details of the identification of similar substrings in our proposed method are explained in Section III.

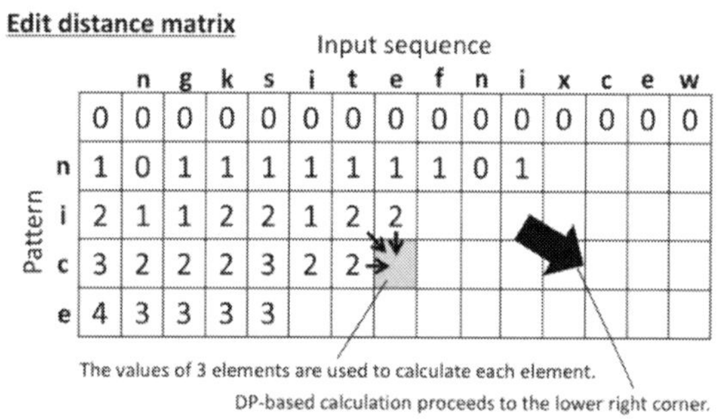

Figure 4. Calculation of edit distance matrix

Edit distance matrix — Input sequence (columns), Pattern (rows)

		n	g	k	s	i	t	e	f	n	i	x	c	e	w
	0	0	0	0	0	0	0	0	0	0	0	0	0	0	0
n	1	0	1	1	1	1	1	1	1	0	1	1	1	1	1
i	2	1	1	2	2	1	2	2	2	1	0	1	2	2	2
c	3	2	2	2	3	2	2	3	3	2	1	1	1	1	3
e	4	3	3	3	3	3	3	2	3	3	2	2	2	1	2

Figure 5. Edit distance matrix

III. Hotspot Detection Based on Approximate String Search

In this section, the existing hotspot detection method based on approximate string search [6], which we improve in this study, is explained. In this method, the mask pattern and a hotspot pattern, which are both two-dimensional data, are transformed into one-dimensional strings to apply approximate string search calculating array D by dynamic programming.

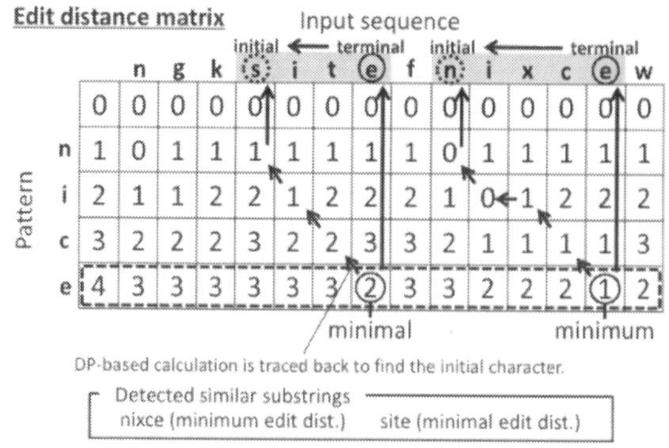

Figure 6. Identification of similar substrings

A. Transformation into One-dimensional Data

Mask patterns and hotspot patterns are image data. We transform them into two-dimensional array of characters, in which wire area is represented by 1 and empty area is represented by 0.

An example is shown in Figure 7. In the left image in it, the white areas represent wires (or other objects), and the black area represents an empty space.

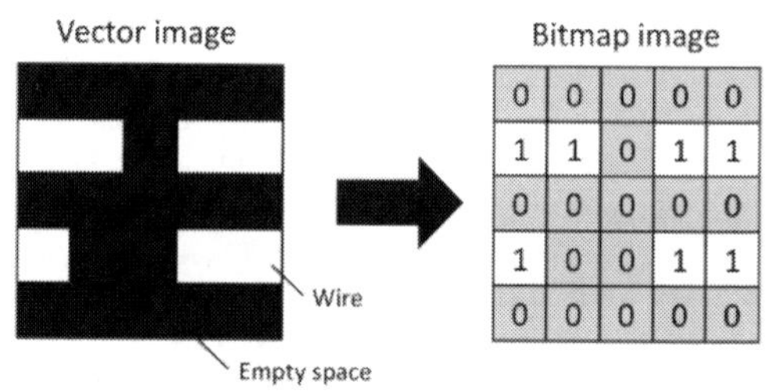

Figure 7. Image data and its corresponding array

We transform the two-dimensional arrays into one-dimensional data. First, the two-dimensional array of the mask pattern is divided into rows. Then, the tail of the first row and the head of the second row are connected. And, the tail of the second row is connected to the head of the third row. Likewise, all the rows are connected and the two-dimensional mask pattern is transformed into one-dimensional data (Figure 8).

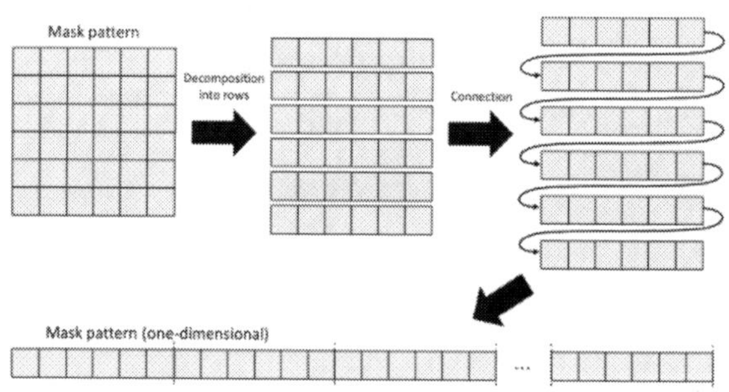

Figure 8. Transformation of mask pattern data

Next, the array of the hotspot pattern is divided into rows, like the transformation of the mask pattern. Then, for each row, don't-care characters are added so that the number of characters of the row becomes equal to that of a row of the mask pattern (Figure 9). A don't-care character is the special character which matches any character. By adding don't-care characters, mismatch of the positions of the head characters of the rows of the hotspot pattern is corrected. Note that such consecutive don't-care characters can be substituted by a special character, called a large-don't-care, to efficiently calculate the edit distance matrix [6]. Hereinafter, the hotspot pattern is processed just like the mask pattern.

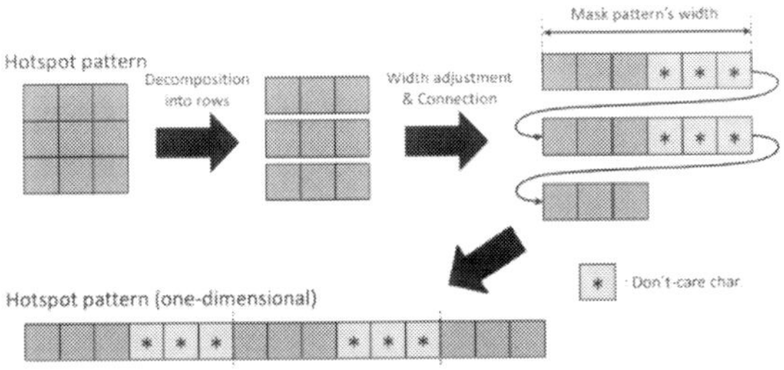

Figure 9. Transformation of hotspot pattern data

B. Dynamic Programming

In both of our proposed method and our previous one [6], since hotspot candidates are searched by using approximate string search, array D is calculated by using the dynamic programming shown in the previous section. Except the first row and column, the value of each element of the array D is calculated by using the value of its upper, left and upper-left elements. These calculations are done line by line from the top to the bottom.

C. Detection of Hotspot Candidates

After calculating array D, substrings similar to the hotspot pattern are detected as hotspot candidates. To detect hotspot candidates, we focus on the elements with the minimal values (less than a user-defined threshold) in the bottom row of D. Each of these elements is considered to correspond to the terminal character of a hotspot candidate. Since we assume the hotspot candidate has the length same as the hotspot pattern, the initial character can be identified from the terminal character. The assumption is based on the fact that a hotspot pattern and candidates similar to the pattern are originally two-dimensional images, and have the same size or almost the same size. Figure 10 illustrates an example of hotspot candidate detection of our methods. (In the example, patterns are described in regular strings for simplicity.)

IV. Proposed Method

In this section, we propose an improved hotspot detection method based on table-reference. Our proposed method is an extension of the existing method [6]. First, we explain the basis of table-reference-based edit distance calculation, some problems for implementation, and our solutions of the problems. Then, we explain our proposed method, by describing mask pattern encoding, hotspot pattern encoding, calculation of the encoded edit distance matrix, and detection of hotspot candidates.

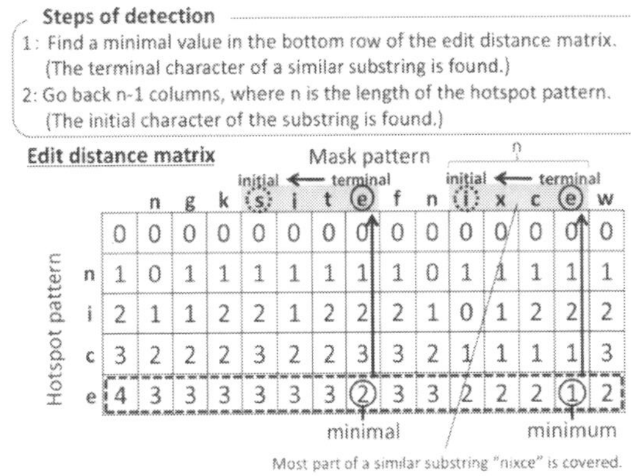

Figure 10. Detection of hotspot candidate

A. Table-reference

In our proposed method, calculation of the edit distance matrix is accelerated by using table-reference of precomputed values and simultaneous calculation of multiple elements in the matrix. Each region of simultaneously handled elements is a $k \times k$ partial matrix of the edit distance matrix, where k is the user-defined constant which decides parallelism. Figure 11 shows an example of 3×3 region. The number of inputs and outputs necessary for calculating each region is decided by k, as shown in Figure 12 (a) and (b). In addition, the values of the outputs are uniquely determined by the values of the inputs. Thus, a reference table for calculating a region can be developed. Hereinafter, a set of inputs for a table refers to an address (or index) of the table.

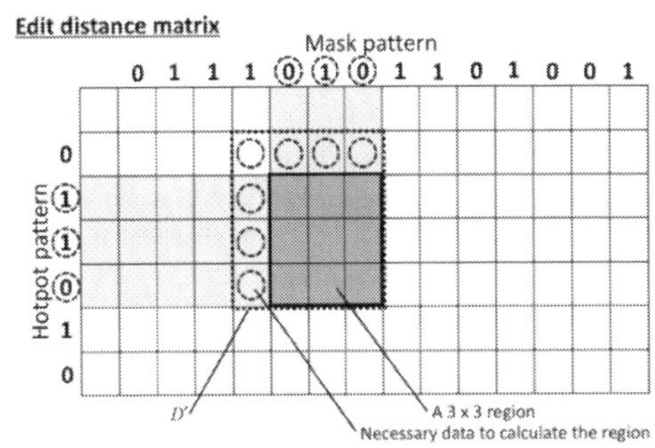

Figure 11. 3 x 3 region in edit distance matrix

A set of inputs for the table consists of the necessary values for DP-based calculation of the elements in a region. That is, it consists of the corresponding characters of the mask and hotspot patterns ($2k$ characters), the k elements to the left of the region, the k elements to the upper of the region, and the element to the upper-left of the region ($2k + 1$ elements in total). A set of outputs consists of the values of the elements in the region. Given a region, then we call the partial matrix of D which includes the region and the elements corresponding to the inputs of the region, D' (Figure 11). D' is equivalent to the region expanded one column and one row to the upper-left direction.

However, it is not practical to directly make a table of

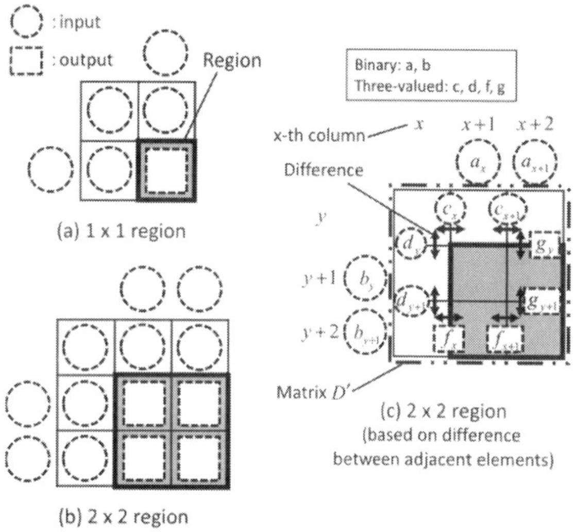

Figure 12. Input-output relation on the calculation of a region : (a) case of 1×1, (b) case of 2×2, (c) case of 2×2 using the difference between adjacent elements in the edit distance (with input-output names)

region calculation, because it requires a huge memory space. This is because the range of the value of each element is large, and thus the number of combinations of the input values of the table explodes. Thus, we focus on the fact that, by deciding the reference element (*e.g.*, the upper-left one) of D', the value of an element can be represented by the difference between the element and the reference one, and the value can be calculated by using only the differences between elements. In addition, we found the fact that the difference between the adjacent two elements is -1, 0 or 1 (when an edit cost is defined as 0 or 1). (The proof is omitted due to the limitation of space.) By adopting difference calculation considering the facts, we mitigate the virtual range of the value of each element, and thus the required memory space. Furthermore, only the values of the elements in the bottom row and the right-most column in D' are necessary for calculating the edit distance matrix D (the values of the other elements are not necessary), because only the bottom row of D is necessary for hotspot detection. Thus, the computational complexity of each region can be reduced to $O(k)$ from $O(k^2)$ by table-reference. Examples of sets of inputs/outputs of a table (the necessary values for calculating regions) are shown in Figure 12(c).

Moreover, a set of inputs/outputs can be encoded into one word when k is small. Thus, in that case, the edit distance matrix can be calculated in the encoded values, so that the computational complexity of each region is reduced to $O(1)$ from $O(k)$. Figure 13 illustrates encoded inputs and outputs.

Let (x, y) be the coordinate of the upper-left element of D' in the edit distance matrix D. Then, the inputs are

- $a_x, a_{x+1}, ..., a_{x+(k-1)}$: mask pattern characters corresponding to the region (input1)
- $b_y, b_{y+1}, ..., b_{y+(k-1)}$: hotspot pattern characters corresponding to the region (input2)
- $c_x, c_{x+1}, ..., c_{x+(k-1)}$: the differences between adjacent two elements in the upper-most row of D' (input3)
- $d_y, d_{y+1}, ..., d_{y+(k-1)}$: the differences between adjacent two elements in the left-most column of D' (input4),

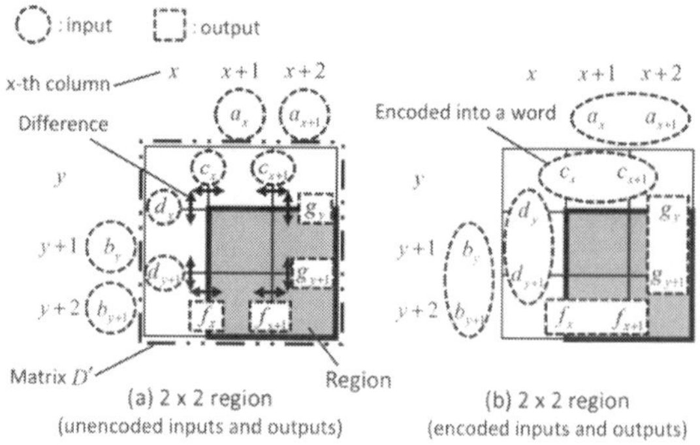

Figure 13. Encoding of inputs/outputs of region: (a) unencoded inputs/outputs of 2×2 region, (b) encoded inputs/outputs

and the outputs are

- $f_x, f_{x+1}, ..., f_{x+(k-1)}$: the differences between adjacent two elements in the bottom row of D' (output1)
- $g_y, g_{y+1}, ..., g_{y+(k-1)}$: the differences between adjacent two elements in the right-most column of D' (output2).

The inputs/outputs are encoded by the encoding functions

$$P(p_x, p_{x+1}, ..., p_{x+i}) = \sum_{i=0}^{k-1} p_{x+i} \times 2^{(k-1)-i} \quad (1)$$

$$Q(q_x, q_{x+1}, ..., q_{x+i}) = \sum_{i=0}^{k-1} q_{x+i} \times 3^{(k-1)-i} \quad (2)$$

to develop a table.

Hereinafter, we call the four inputs, input1, input2, input3, and input4, and the two outputs, output1 and output2. The ones composed of binary variables are encoded by using (1), and the ones composed of three-valued $(-1, 0, 1)$ variables are encoded by using (2). Therefore, the outputs can be memorized in two words of memory if $\log_2 3^k$ is less than or equal to the bit width of a word. In that case, $k \times k$-element calculation can be done accessing the memory only two times, so that the computational complexity of each region is $O(1)$. Note that the number of possible combinations of the inputs is $2^{2k} \times 3^{2k}$ and is an exponential function of k. In our experimental environment, we developed tables up to $k = 5$ (0.23GB).

B. Hotspot detection using table-reference

In this subsection, we explain our table-reference-based hotspot detection method. As mentioned in the previous subsection, a table is developed by calculating the output values of a region for each possible combination of input values before starting hotspot detection. Then, the table is used for efficient hotspot detection.

1) Pattern encoding: The mask and hotspot patterns in two-dimensional arrays are transformed into one-dimensional strings in the same way as [6]. Next, the mask and hotspot patterns are divided into k-character substrings and then each substring is encoded to use the reference table for calculating the edit distance matrix. Note that, in the hotspot pattern, since large don't-care characters cannot be calculated in the encoded form, large don't-care characters are not encoded, and thus they are not included in a k-character substrings. Each k-character substring is encoded by using (1). The terminal substring (of the mask pattern) whose length are less than k is left as an unencoded string. Likewise, in the hotspot pattern, large don't-care characters and the substrings whose length are less than k (including those resulting from the inserted large don't-care characters) are left as unencoded strings.

2) Calculation of edit distance matrix D: Using the encoded patterns, the calculation of the edit distance matrix D is performed by referencing the table. Let us explain the calculation using Figure 14. First, the values of the element of the first row and column are set according to the definition of the edit distance matrix. Next, the region whose upper-left element corresponding to the element $D(1,1)$ (region (1)) is calculated by table-reference. After calculating region (1), the region adjacent to the right of region (1) (region (2)) is calculated. Let region (5) be an example. The input3 of region (5) is from the output1 of region (3), and the input4 of region (5) is from the output2 of region (4). In this way, the encoded outputs of regions can be directly used as inputs to calculate other regions. After table-reference-based calculation, the values of the elements in the bottom row of the edit distance matrix D can be restored by using the value of the left-most element and the differences between adjacent two elements obtained by decoding the output1 of each bottom region.

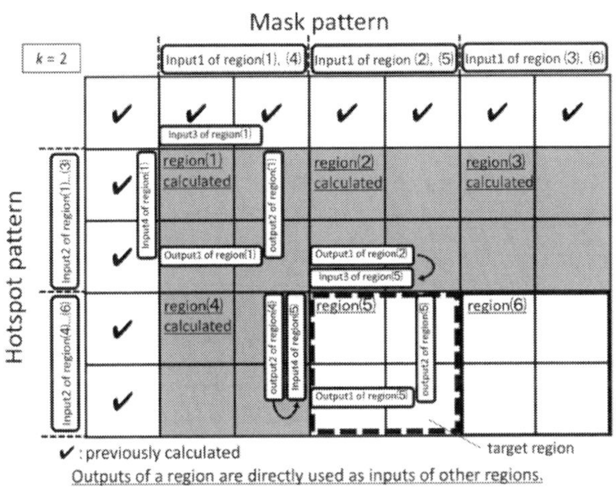

Figure 14. Calculation of edit distance matrix by table reference

We have explained the edit distance calculation ignoring unencoded substrings. Here, let us explain how to handle unencoded mask pattern substrings using Figure 15(a). First, the output2 of the region just before the unencoded mask pattern character is decoded to the differences between adjacent elements in the corresponding column. Next, the values of the elements are restored using the value of the upper-most element and the differences between elements. Then, the values of the elements corresponding to the unencoded substrings are calculated according to the DP-based definition in the same way as [6].

Next, let us explain how to handle unencoded hotspot pattern substrings using Figure 15(b). First, the output1s of the regions just above the unencoded hotspot pattern character are decoded to the differences between adjacent elements in the corresponding row. Next, the values of the elements are restored using the value of the left-most element and the differences between elements. Then, the values of the elements corresponding to the unencoded substrings are calculated according to the DP-based definition in the same way as [6]. Also the substrings before the large don't-care characters are handled in the same way. Since each row of hotspot pattern (in a two-dimensional hotspot pattern) means one large don't-care character, a hotspot pattern string contains multiple large don't-care characters. This calculation is performed for each large don't-care character.

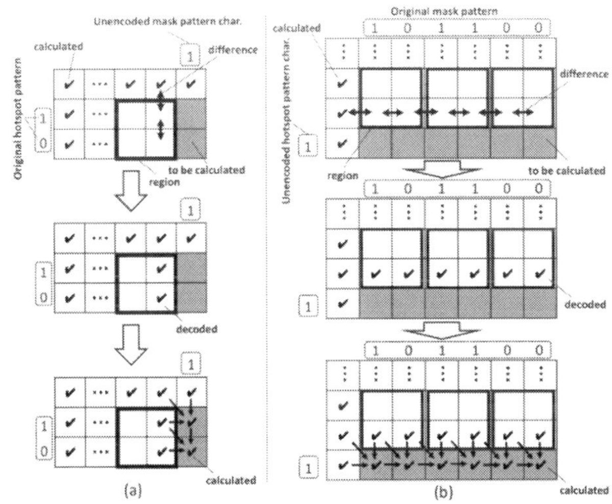

Figure 15. Calculation for unencoded character: (a) mask pattern character, (b) hotspot pattern character

Finally, if the hotspot pattern character corresponding to the bottom row is encoded, the values of the elements in the bottom row of the edit distance matrix D are restored to find hotspot candidates. If the hotspot pattern character is not encoded, the values of the elements in the bottom row of D are calculated according to the definition as mentioned in the previous paragraph.

3) Detection of similar patterns: After calculating the edit distance matrix D, patterns similar to the hotspot pattern are detected from the values of the bottom row of D. The elements with minimal values (less than the user-defined threshold) are identified in the same way as [6]. Each of them corresponds to the terminal character of a hotspot candidate. The initial character can be identified by the terminal character because the length of a hotspot candidate is the same as the given hotspot pattern.

V. EXPERIMENTAL RESULTS

We performed experiments to evaluate our method. In the experiments, we evaluated the execution time of template-matching, the existing method [6], and our proposed method for $k = 1, \ldots 5$, for the same mask pattern (1020×1020 pixels) and the same hotspot pattern (250×250 pixels), on a CentOS (release 6.3 (Final)) PC equipped with Intel Core i7-3770 CPU @ 3.4GHz and 7.6GB memory using gcc 4.4.7.

The experimental results are shown in Figure 16. Our proposed method achieved the better result compared to [6]

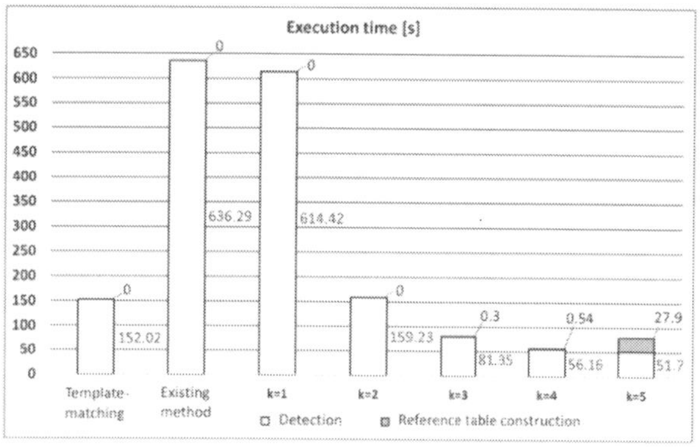

Figure 16. Calculation time

for each setting of k. When $k \geq 3$, our method outperformed template-matching. We confirmed that the calculation time of the edit distance matrix D was drastically reduced.

The calculation time of D is inversely proportional to k^2. Thus, it is expected that the decreasing rate of the calculation time decreases with increasing k. In addition, the time to make the reference table is proportional to the number of combinations of input values (*i.e.*, $2^{2k} \times 3^{2k}$). That is, the time is proportional to an exponential function of k. Therefore, from Figure 16, the sum of the time to make the reference table and the time to calculate D increases when $k \geq 5$. Thus, we conclude that $k = 4$ is best under the experimental environment. The execution time when $k = 4$ was about 1/11 compared to the existing method [6]. Note that once a reference table is made, it can be reused. In such a case, $k \geq 5$ are potentially effective.

VI. Conclusions

In this paper, we proposed and evaluated an efficient hotspot detection method. Experimental results showed that our proposed method found hotspot candidates much faster than the existing one [6] on which our method is based. Our future work includes further improvement of the execution time and improvement of the accuracy of hotspot detection.

References

[1] T. Higashi and Y. Onishi, "Trends in semiconductor lithography technologies and Toshiba's approach," TOSHIBA review, vol. 67, no. 4, pp. 2-6, 2012. (in Japanese)

[2] H. Yao et al., "Efficient range pattern matching algorithm for process-hotspot detection," IET Circuits Devices Syst., vol. 2, issue 1, pp. 2–15, 2008.

[3] D. Ding, A. J. Torres, F. G. Pikus, and D. Z. Pan, "High performance lithographic hotspot detection using hierarchically refined machine learning," in Proc. the 16th Asia and South Pacific Design Autom. Conf. (ASP-DAC), pp. 775–780, 2011.

[4] J. Wuu, Fedor G. Pikus, and M. Marek-Sadowska, "Efficient approach to early detection of lithographic hotspots using machine learning systems and pattern matching," in Proc. SPIE 7974, Design for Manufacturability through Design-Process Integration V, 79740U, pp. 1–8, April 04, 2011.

[5] W. Wen, J. Li, S. Lin, J. Chen, and S. Chang, "A fuzzy-matching model with grid reduction for lithography hotspot detection," IEEE Trans. CAD, vol. 33, no. 11, pp. 1671–1679, Nov. 2014.

[6] S. Tamagawa, R. Fujimoto, M. Inagi, S. Nagayama, and S. Wakabayashi, "A hotspot detection method based on approximate string search," in Proc. the 9th International Conference on Advances in Circuits, Electronics and Micro-electronics, pp. 6–12, 2016.

[7] H. Yaegashi, "Pattern fidelity control in multi-patterning towards 7nm node," in Proc. the IEEE 16th Int. Conf. on Nanotechnology (IEEE-NANO), pp. 452–455, Aug. 2016.

[8] R. A. Wagner and M. J. Fischer, "The string-to-string correction problem," Journal of the ACM., vol. 21, issue 1, pp. 168–173, Jan. 1974.

[9] Y. Utan, S. Wakabayashi, and S. Nagayama, "An FPGA-based text search engine for approximate regular expression matching," in Proc. the 2010 International Conference on Field-Programmable Technology, pp. 184–191, Dec. 2010.

[10] D. E. Knuth, J. H. Morris, Jr., and V. R. Pratt, "Fast pattern matching in strings," SIAM J. Comput., vol. 6, no. 2, pp. 323–350, 1977.

Energy-Efficient Real-Time Operating Systems: An Approach using Dynamic Frequency Scaling and Worst-Case Execution Time Aware Scheduling

Thomas Jerabek, Benjamin Aigner, Florian Gerstmayer, Jürgen Hausladen

University of Applied Sciences Technikum Wien
Vienna, Austria
Email: {thomas.jerabek, benjamin.aigner, florian.gerstmayer, juergen.hausladen}@technikum-wien.at

***Abstract*—Embedded systems are at the core of many new emerging technologies and applications, deeply integrated into our daily lives. Especially, the demand for battery-powered solutions in consumer-related applications is growing, to support different environments and fields of application. Therefore, energy efficiency measures for embedded systems become even more important. In this paper, a dynamic frequency scaling approach for embedded systems is presented to reduce the overall energy consumption while still meeting time constraints within a real-time operating system. Starting with a general discussion and mathematical derivation along with an elaboration of the state of the art, our concept and implementation is discussed. This includes primarily the developed Worst-Case Execution Time (WCET) aware Earliest Deadline First (EDF) scheduler which is used to dynamically scale the frequency at runtime. Moreover, a use case targeting a real-time smart home application is provided, which was used to evaluate and compare our implementation in regard to it's energy consumption. The respective results are elaborated alongside possible future work and improvements.**

Keywords*—*dynamic frequency scaling; worst-case execution time analysis; energy-efficient computing.

I. Introduction

Embedded systems are the key to many new technologies, deployed in numerous products and applications, such as smart homes or modern cars. Especially their interconnection and coupling with existing networks – in particular, the Internet – enables new services and functionalities such as sensor fusion, maintenance, firmware updates, or remote access/control.

However, numerous challenges such as safety and security concerns emerge, but also energy consumption needs to be targeted. The latter, is especially of relevance for battery powered devices deployed in constraint environments. By developing new storage technologies, or by further reducing power consumption, battery run- & lifetime can be stretched to reduce the number of recharge cycles or battery replacements. Although devices, e.g., ones used in smart homes, require only a fraction of energy, in sum, the recorded overall power consumption is not to be neglected. Power usage optimizations can thus have a significant impact, facilitating also the development of more maintenance friendly products.

Hence, while originally motivated for general purpose computers and servers, Dynamic Frequency and Voltage Scaling (DFVS) approaches find their way in the embedded systems domain. The idea is to reduce clock frequency and/or voltage, when no computational resources are required, to reduce the overall energy consumption. At the same time, responsiveness and other properties must still be ensured in case computation intensive tasks are raised.

In the context of embedded systems, this is especially of relevance for real time applications which have to deliver results in specified time frames, e.g., to guarantee deadlines. While some being hard ones that have to be met under any circumstances, e.g., X-by-wire systems, as life threatening incidents may be the result, others are soft that may be missed rarely without consequences. The system and its resources are designed to ensure that the deadline of each task is met even in worst-case scenarios. One such critical scenario can be compliance with the Worst-Case Execution Time (WCET), determined either by code instrumentation and runtime measurements or by static analysis. The latter can be done, e.g., by using numerous autonomous tools such as [1] for the respective embedded architecture. However, these worst-case scenarios will scarcely occur in the field.

Therefore, the Central Processing Unit (CPU) will frequently be underutilized, consuming power for doing nothing of purpose for tasks that have already been finished in time before being scheduled again. This circumstance leaves room for improvement, e.g., by applying Dynamic Frequency Scaling (DFS) approaches, to optimize each task according to its deadline. In particular, the CPU's clock frequency can be reduced to a minimum that is required by a task, but which still ensures that all deadlines are met. As a result, the time the CPU is idle and the overall energy consumption can be reduced. Another positive side-effect of reducing the power consumption is, that less heat is generated by the device which directly influences the mechanical design. This in turn can make the difference for the need of a passive or active cooling system, further reducing costs and mean time to failure. However, for this approach, schedulers are required which not only take the task's deadlines into consideration but also their WCET to set the clock frequency accordingly depending on the current workload to prevent deadline violations. In this context, also numerous requirements regarding the system's architecture and peripherals have to be anticipated. For instance, separate clock domains are necessary to prevent errors in clock sensitive communication channels, e.g., Universal Asynchronous Receiver Transmitter (UART), that are caused by frequency variations. In this paper, the challenges and opportunities of DFS in embedded systems are elaborated. Moreover, the concept and implementation of a Earliest Deadline First scheduler (EDF) is discussed which takes the derived WCETs from [1] into account in this scheduling algorithm. To ease the deployment in existing workflows, an autonomous approach is pursued to reduce entry barriers and enhance usability. The applicability and effectiveness of our approach is shown by a use case targeting a real time smart home application.

The remainder of this paper is structured as follows. In Section II, the theoretical background of this paper is elaborated. Besides the energy consumption model, this also includes the two major strategies in the context of DFS pursued, being race-to-halt and frequency variation. Afterwards, in Section III related work is discussed. Then, in Section IV the developed EDF scheduler is elaborated as well as the architectural prerequisites. Section V discusses the use case and identified problems in regard to DFS and embedded systems. Moreover, the effectiveness of our approach in regard to energy consumption reduction is shown. Finally, in Section VI this paper concludes and gives an outlook regarding future work.

II. Theoretical Background

For the concept and implementation, the effectiveness of energy saving approaches and scheduling algorithms has to be estimated and compared. Therefore, the following paragraphs elaborate the defined energy consumption model and its components which will be used and referenced in this paper. Moreover, possible approaches for energy consumption reduction are discussed.

A. Energy-Model

Generally speaking, power consumption of a CPU is a function of voltage (V), frequency (f), and capacitance (C), as in (1).

$$P = V^2 * C * f \tag{1}$$

In other words, depending on the platform's layout, e.g., wire lengths and peripherals, a certain capacitance is present. Hence, optimizations in regard to the printed circuit board design can be made to lower energy consumption. However, one can expect that this results only in marginal improvements. Another key element in this equation is voltage due to its square contribution. Lowering the supply and operating voltage of a device can therefore have a major impact on energy consumption. However, in the context of this paper, embedded devices deployed in a smart home environment are assumed, which already run on lower voltages. Considering that several peripherals also require a minimum supply voltage, further improvements in this field of application are considered marginal in contrast to advances in frequency scaling. Thus, the focus of this paper is primarily on this, last, contributor of the equation. Variations in frequency have a direct proportional impact on energy consumption. For instance, a reduction of frequency by a tenth, yields in an energy reduction of a tenth. In theory, lowering the frequency to zero in (1), results in a power consumption of zero. In reality, this is not feasible due to parasitical effects and leaks on devices, e.g., caused by peripherals and other components, a static power consumption is present. Hence, in (2), a more accurate equation is provided which takes this factor into consideration by adding a constant energy drain.

$$P = (V^2 * f * C) + P_{static} \tag{2}$$

Slight deviations due to different hardware instructions, e.g., more or less high bits that have to be applied on the instruction and data bus are not taken into consideration in our energy consumption model.

Based on (2), several power consumption levels can be derived, depending on the frequency used. Besides zero, the lower bound is derived from the platform dependent minimum frequency (f_{min}). This frequency depends on peripherals or system requirements, e.g., guaranteed response time. The corresponding equation can be seen in (3). The upper bound is, again dependent on the target platform and its maximum frequency f_{max}, shown in (4). In between these boundaries, several discrete frequencies f_{dsc} are applicable, cf. (5). A continuous frequency spectrum is not possible as neither a phase locked loop component does provide that functionality nor do certain peripherals support it, e.g., UART.

$$P_{min} = (V^2 * f_{min} * C) + P_{static} \tag{3}$$

$$P_{max} = (V^2 * f_{max} * C) + P_{static} \tag{4}$$

$$P_{dsc} = (V^2 * f_{dsc} * C) + P_{static} \tag{5}$$

B. Approaches

In regard to how energy consumption can be reduced, two major strategies [2] are prevalent, which are elaborated more in detail in the following paragraphs.

Race-to-Halt: In a race-to-halt strategy, calculations are performed with maximum frequency, so that the result is available as soon as possible. Afterwards, the CPU switches to the idle state which operates at the minimum frequency, until the respective deadline is reached. Hence, energy consumption consists of two parts. A certain amount of time t_1, using the maximum frequency and thus, considering (4), results in maximum power consumption, and the time t_2, while in idle state which has minimum power consumption according to (3). Equation (6) describes this coherence.

$$E_{avg} = t_1 * P_{max} + t_2 * P_{min} \tag{6}$$

Dynamic Frequency Scaling: In case of the dynamic frequency scaling [3] approach, the WCET and the deadline of a task are used as parameter to modify the operating system frequency of the processor. It is designed for systems that provide high peak performance when needed and in turn dynamically reduces the power consumption by decreasing the operating frequency of the CPU whenever possible. When a task is scheduled, the processor's highest frequency is multiplied with the rate calculated from the previous parameters, which results in the frequency of the processor. The lowered processor frequency in turn stretches the execution of the task that still meets the required deadlines. This principle can be seen in Figure 1. In contrast to (6), the sum of a certain amount

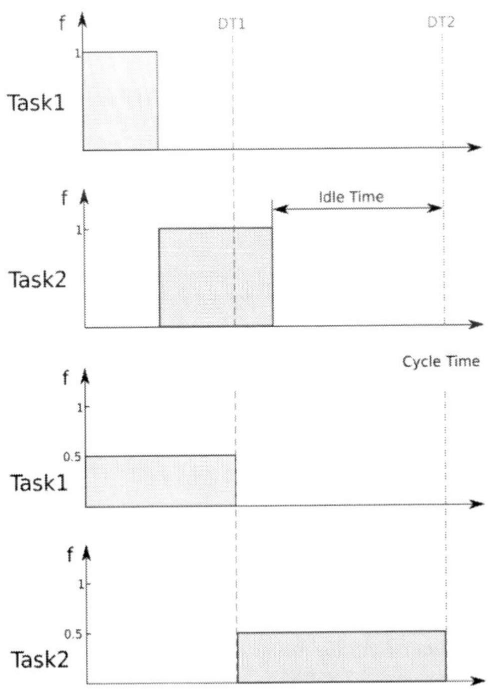

Figure 1. DFS - Concept.

of time t_1 and t_2, using the discrete frequency and thus, considering (5), results in reduced power consumption. Equation (7) describes this coherence.

$$E_{avg} = (t_1 + t_2) * P_{dsc} \tag{7}$$

III. RELATED WORK

In general, power-aware scheduling [4][5] is a significant key strategy for battery powered real-time embedded systems to reduce the power consumption and extend battery life time. Real-time embedded systems consist of a set of tasks that are scheduled in a specific order, leaving time slots in which the processor is underutilized but still draining the battery. Therefore, modern processors offer a range of sleep modes, to reduce power consumption. However, due to periodic task execution (often on an average of a few milliseconds), these are generally not applicable. In contrast, the time required to first enter and later on leaving the sleep mode is in the order of tens of milliseconds which can easily be in the order of a magnitude of a task's period. Hence, sleep modes are often not suitable for real-time embedded systems. However, reducing the frequency of the processor for the execution while still satisfying the given deadlines as done with DFS is a feasible solution, which leads to a remarkable reduction of the energy consumption.

A general overview on the energy-efficiency of DFS in resource constraint embedded devices, as well as desktop and server grade processors is conducted in [6]. Cho et al. [3] proposes a different approach where frequency and voltage is scaled down when processing external peripherals. The idea is to save energy during the time waiting for the results from the external peripheral. Shin et al. [7] developed a tool that converts existing programs into a low-energy version based upon the remaining WCET. The tool automatically retrieves the appropriate locations in the program where voltage scaling mechanisms can be inserted.

There exist different scheduling algorithms such as earliest deadline first that can be used in conjunction with DFS. An evaluation of several scheduling algorithms is provided in [8]. The authors conducted an exhaustive simulation in which they retrieved the most important parameters that affect the energy consumption. In [9], an optimized version of the EDF algorithm has been proposed, that further improves energy savings by about 28% to the original algorithm. [10] extended the DFS approach for the use with multicore processors.

IV. IMPLEMENTATION

The implementation of our DFS concept needs modifications in the Real-Time Operating System (RTOS) components (A) task management, (B) scheduling, (C) context switching, and (D) application tasks, as described subsequently.

A. Task Management

In real-time systems, it is common to split the application into tasks where each of them is responsible for a certain functionality. Each task has an application specific priority and stack size that needs to be configured by the developer. This information along with runtime parameters such as the current task state or associated event flags is maintained in a data structure called Task Control Block (TCB). Every task requires a TCB, which is only accessed by the real-time kernel and never by the application code due to consistency reasons. For our implementation, an extension of the TCB is necessary to preserve the task's (a) WCET and (b) deadline. These two parameters are provided as 32-bit unsigned integer and specified in microseconds. Thus, the maximum value for a WCET or deadline can be 71.58 minutes which is precise enough for most applications. The deadline is set to zero in case of an uncritical task where no deadline is given. The implemented scheduler needs to consider this as well as an unspecified WCET (equals zero) to avoid starvation. In addition, the task control block is extended by two parameters to define (c) the deadline type, and (d) the time when a task's deadline will be reached. Parameter (c) defines if a deadline occurs cyclic (e.g., every 10 ms) or depends on a certain event (e.g., 10 ms after falling edge on a designated input pin). Parameter (d) defines the absolute deadline as time value in order to create a reference point for the scheduler. In summary, these four arguments are added to the TCB for scheduling purposes.

B. Scheduling

The scheduler selects a process from the ready list to execute, which is determined by scheduling criteria. Our scheduling algorithm is based on an earliest deadline first approach with additional knowledge about the WCET as shown in Figure 2. The scheduler creates a temporary task control block for the Task To Schedule (TTS) and sets its deadline initially to zero. Afterwards, an iteration loop on the list of Ready Tasks (RT) evaluates the task with the earliest deadline. In the case of equal deadlines of two or more tasks, the algorithm chooses the task with the longest WCET. If there are no deadlines specified, a task selection is not possible with this algorithm, therefore, a priority based scheduling will be performed. At this point, the scheduling is completed and the RTOS continues with the dynamic frequency scaling algorithm followed by the context switch and the clock adjustment.

```
WCET_AWARE_EDF_Sched()
  DISABLE_INTERRUPTS()
  TCB TTS
  TTS.curDeadline = 0
  i = 0
  while i < MAX_TASKS
    if RT[i].curDeadline < TTS.curDeadline
      TTS = RT[i]
    else if RT[i].curDeadline == TTS.curDeadline
      if TTS.WCET < RT[i].WCET
        TTS = RT[i]
  i = i +1

  if TTScurDeadline == NONE
    TTS = PRIO_Sched()

  dfs_div = DFS(TTS)
  if(dfs_div < 1)
    dfs_div = 1
    error
  OS_TASK_SW()
  cpu_clk = Set_CPU_CLK(dfs_div)
  Adj_PB_CLK(cpu_clk)
  SysTickUpdate(cpu_clk/TickRate)

  ENABLE_INTERRUPTS()
  return
```

Figure 2. WCET-Aware EDF Scheduler.

C. Context Switching

The dynamic frequency scaling algorithm is executed right before the actual context switch, as shown in Figure 2. This algorithm (cf. Figure 3) starts with the maximum clock divider and evaluates if the frequency scaling does not violate any deadlines.

Since the ratio between execution time and processor frequency is considered linear, a temporary WCET for the task to schedule can be calculated by multiplying its WCET with the clock divider. An Administrative Overhead (AO) for context switch, scheduling etc. is added. If this DFS dependent WCET is below the task's deadline, the DFS divider is applicable. However, it is mandatory to consider that all subsequent tasks need to meet their deadlines too. By adding the WCET and AO of the task with the next larger deadline, one can verify its compliance. This step is repeated for all ready tasks. For this iteration (cf. Figure 3 Line 9-14), the algorithm assumes that the RT array is sorted by ascending deadlines, which is done at the very beginning of the function. Once a divider is applicable for the entire system, the algorithm returns this value. A divider of one means, the deadlines can only be reached without downscaling. An early detection of deadline violation in the RTOS is also done by returning a value of zero, which means that at least one deadline cannot be fulfilled even without reducing the CPU clock. This can be used to settle appropriate measures, e.g., implement a callback function to bring the system to a safe and secure state.

```
1  DFS(TTS)
2    dfs_flag = true
3    dfs_div = MAX_DFS_DIV
4    sort(RT,DEADLINE_ASC)
5    while dfs_div > 0
6      WCETtemp = dfs_div*TTS.WCET + AO
7      if WCETtemp < TTS.curDeadline
8        i = 0
9        dfs_flag = true
10       while  i < MAX_TASKS
11         WCETtemp = WCETtemp + RT[i].WCET + AO
12         if WCETtemp >= RT[i].curDeadline
13           DFS_Flag = false
14           break // config not possible!
15         i = i + 1
16
17       if dfs_flag == true // config works!
18         return dfs_div
19
20     dfs_div = dfs_div - 1
21   return dfs_div
```

Figure 3. Dynamic Frequency Scaling.

D. Deadline Handling by Application Tasks

Since an absolute value for each deadline is necessary to calculate the DFS divider, the function in Figure 4 needs to be implemented. It updates the task's deadline either on a periodic base where the deadline is added to the current value or event triggered where the deadline is set according to the current system time. To guarantee a proper functionality of the scheduler and DFS algorithm, this function is called after each task completion (e.g., task cycle done) by the application's tasks themselves. For event triggered use cases, it is mandatory to update the deadline at the occurrence of influencing events either by the task itself or another task. Therefore, the developer is responsible to trigger the deadline updates.

E. Deployment

The selected real-time operating system is Micrium uCOS-III because it enables the necessary kernel modifications and supports the chosen target hardware, the Infineon XMC4500-F100K1024 microcontroller. The microcontroller features an

```
updateDeadline(TCB Task)
  if Task.DeadlineType == PERIODIC
    tempDeadline = Task.curDeadline + Task.Deadline
  else // deadline event triggered
    tempDeadline = getSysTime_uS() + Task.Deadline
  Task.curDeadline = tempDeadline
  return
```

Figure 4. Deadline Handler.

ARM Cortex-M4 processor core and allows a system clock division up to 256 in single steps. Thus, one can adjust the system clock from 120 MHz down to 468.75 kHz, which is ideal to test the presented concept. In previous work, the OTAWA Stack and Worst-case execution time Analysis (OSWA) tool [1] was developed to evaluate a tasks WCET and is therefore used for the evaluation in Section V. This analysis tool is provided by our cloud-based Integrated Development Environment (cloud-IDE), as presented in [11].

V. EVALUATION

For the evaluation of our concept, a dedicated use case with a generic implementation of a gateway for smart home devices was used. The requirements for the use case are as follows:

- Bluetooth Low Energy (BLE) to ZigBee Gateway
- Soft-deadlines for usability reasons

According to [12], a device with human-machine interaction requires that the maximum response time is $\leq$ 100 ms to be experienced as reacting instantaneously by the operator. In order to provide a well-founded maximum execution time limit for the implementation of this use case, the following boundary conditions are defined:

- 60 ms reaction time, sensor from or to ZigBee gateway
- 13 ms reaction time, BLE gateway from or to actuator

The ZigBee latency is assumed and based on the work of Baviskar et al. in [13], where an average latency of 58 ms was measured. Moreover, an additional safety margin is added, resulting in an assumption of 60 ms latency from the ZigBee device to the gateway. A BLE network is usually fast regarding the time required for the connection establishment and subsequent data transfer. According to [14], BLE needs approximately 3 ms for these tasks. Concerning a relay-based actuator, an additional time overhead of 10 ms for the relay operation is required.

When using the maximum 100 ms reaction time (T_{maxRT}), the subtraction of the delay times for each hardware interface results in a maximum execution time limit of 27 ms for the defined task structure, as shown in Equation (8).

$$\begin{aligned} T_{tasklimit} &= T_{maxRT} - T_{ZigBee} - T_{BLE} \\ T_{tasklimit} &= 100ms - 60ms - 13ms = \mathbf{27ms} \end{aligned} \tag{8}$$

Each radio frequency interface (BLE and ZigBee) utilizes two different tasks, one for receive operations and one for transmit operations, as depicted in Figure 5. Data is shared via queues, which are used to transport data from the RF-controller to the bridge task and vice-versa. The bridge task is used to determine any operations that are required to share data between these two links. In addition, a processing task can be used to insert data, e.g., a gateway condition.

To eliminate influencing external factors on the DFS measurements, the BLE and ZigBee connections are replaced by a physical loopback via the corresponding UART RX/TX pins, as shown in Figure 5.

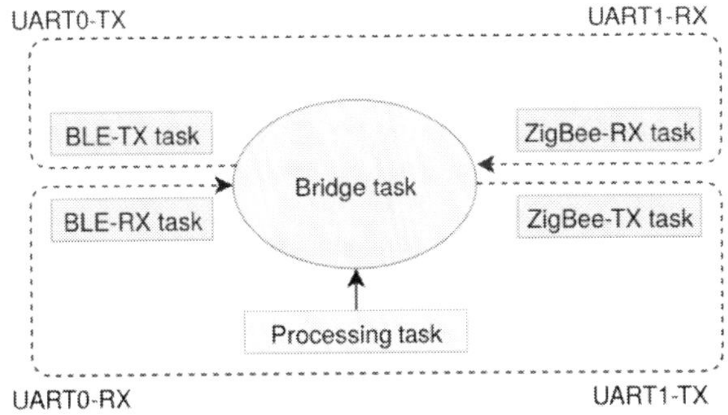

Figure 5. Task Structure with Loopback.

A. *Results*

According to Equation (8), the maximum execution time limit for receiving, processing and transmission is 27 ms. Thus, the deadlines of involved tasks are estimated in order to do not exceed this limit. In particular, the segmentation is as follows: 7.5 ms for the receive task, 12 ms for the bridge task, and another 7.5 ms for the transmit task. The deadlines and types are described in the application, as shown in Table I.

TABLE I. TASK PARAMETERS.

Task	Deadline type	Deadline	WCET
BLE RX	once	7.5 ms	1.21 ms
BLE TX	once	7.5 ms	1.26 ms
ZigBee RX	once	7.5 ms	1.16 ms
ZigBee TX	once	7.5 ms	1.20 ms
Bridge	once	12 ms	0.96 ms
Processing	periodic	1000 ms	1.13 ms

The tasks WCET already include an administrative overhead [1] and were estimated with the OSWA tool. The WCET analysis also considers internal RTOS functions that are relevant. However, no program flow information, e.g., loop bounds are available for RTOS internal sections. The evaluation of these is the most sophisticated part of the entire analysis because loop bounds cannot be directly derived from the RTOS source code, since they depend on application specific parameters. Once the WCET analysis is successfully accomplished for each task as can be seen in Table I, the results are imported into the application.

Depending on the deployed peripherals, it is not feasible to use any CPU frequency because it can prevent specific peripheral clock configurations that are necessary for external devices or certain tasks. In case that the peripheral clock is derived from the CPU clock, the DFS implementation is rather limited as the peripherals cannot operate at their appropriate frequency. Therefore, this use case only considers the maximum CPU frequency (120 MHz) and the half CPU frequency (60 MHz), since the peripheral clock can remain on the same 60 MHz independent of the selected frequency.

Table II shows the three evaluated configurations where the CPU clock is either set to 120 MHz, variable (DFS) or set to 60 MHz. The measurements show, that in our use case the power consumption can be reduced by 19.01% using the DFS implementation. This is very close to the case where the CPU clock is generally set to the lower frequency. However, there are situations where the RTOS switches the CPU frequency to 120 MHz to avoid deadline violations. Operating only on 60 MHz is no option as it would lead to deadline violations.

TABLE II. COMPARISON OF POWER CONSUMPTION.

CPU frequency	current	power consumption
120 MHz	151.5 mA	499.95 mW
variable (DFS)	122.7 mA	404.91 mW
60 MHz	121.5 mA	400.95 mW

Our DFS implementation closes the gap between power efficiency and performance for this application. Other use cases may leave even more space for optimization, while others cannot be optimized at all because the peripheral clock configuration would be too restrictive for DFS.

VI. CONCLUSION

In this paper, the implementation and evaluation of a WCET aware earliest deadline first scheduler for uCOS-III is presented. The principle of dynamic frequency scaling is applied therein to achieve a power consumption reduction for real-time embedded systems applications.

The proof-of-concept and benefits are shown in an exemplary use case, by reference of a smart home application that implements a ZigBee to BLE gateway requiring certain responsiveness. By the use of the implemented WCET aware scheduler, a power reduction of 19% was achieved while still meeting the given deadlines.

The process of deriving the WCET bounds was accomplished with the aid of our previously implemented and in [1] presented OSWA tool. Its integration in state-of-the-art IDEs provides the possibility to offer the herein presented DFS implementation with ease to numerous developers due to it's seamless integration in prevalent workflows. Therefore, a widespread field of possible applications is derived as a developer neither requires in-depth knowledge on DFS nor its implementation.

The contribution of the herein presented approach leads to the conclusion, that a major energy consumption reduction is achieved through the application of the DFS algorithm while preserving the full capabilities of the system. This is especially beneficial for low-power devices through:

- Reduced hardware costs by reducing battery capacity
- Dynamic adjustment of CPU utilization determined by deadline constraints
- Real-time and power constraints are met in different usage scenarios

Future work is geared towards the possible problem of deadline inversion, similar to the well known priority inversion problem. In particular, considering task 1 having a disproportional or no deadline, task 2 might have to wait for task 1 to complete, resulting in a miss of the deadline of task 2. This problem might be solved by the application of mechanisms, such as priority inheritance, e.g., by inheriting deadlines.

ACKNOWLEDGMENT

This work has been conducted in the context of the public funded R&D projects Toolbox for Rapid Design of Smart Homes & Assistive Technologies (ToRaDes) and Software Analysis Toolbox (SAT) managed by the Vienna City Council MA23.

REFERENCES

[1] T. Jerabek and M. Horauer, "Static worst-case execution time analysis tool development for embedded systems software," in *9th International Conference on Dependability (DEPEND)*, Jul. 24-28, 2016, pp. 7–14.

[2] L. Tan and Z. Chen, "Slow down or halt: Saving the optimal energy for scalable hpc systems," in *Proceedings of the 6th ACM/SPEC International Conference on Performance Engineering*, ser. ICPE '15. New York, NY, USA: ACM, 2015, pp. 241–244.

[3] K. M. Cho, C. H. Liang, J. Y. Huang, and C. S. Yang, "Design and implementation of a general purpose power-saving scheduling algorithm for embedded systems," in *2011 IEEE International Conference on Signal Processing, Communications and Computing (ICSPCC)*, Sept 2011, pp. 1–5.

[4] M. Bambagini, M. Marinoni, H. Aydin, and G. Buttazzo, "Energy-aware scheduling for real-time systems: A survey," in *ACM Trans. Embed. Comput. Syst.* ACM, 2016, pp. 7:1–7:34.

[5] K. Seth, A. Anantaraman, F. Mueller, and E. Rotenberg, "Fast: Frequency-aware static timing analysis," in *Proceedings of the 24th IEEE International Real-Time Systems Symposium (RTSS)*. IEEE Computer Society, 2003, pp. 40–51.

[6] E. Le Sueur and G. Heiser, "Slow down or sleep, that is the question," in *Proceedings of the 2011 USENIX Conference on USENIX Annual Technical Conference*. USENIX Association, 2011, pp. 1–6.

[7] D. Shin, J. Kim, and S. Lee, "Intra-task voltage scheduling for low-energy hard real-time applications," in *IEEE Design Test of Computers*, March 2001, pp. 20–30.

[8] P. Pillai and K. G. Shin, "Real-time dynamic voltage scaling for low-power embedded operating systems," in *Proceedings of the Eighteenth ACM Symposium on Operating Systems Principles*, 2001, pp. 89–102.

[9] H. El Ghor and E. Aggoune, "Energy efficient scheduler of aperiodic jobs for real-time embedded systems," in *International Journal of Automation and Computing*. Springer, 2016, pp. 1–11.

[10] J. L. March, S. Petit, J. Sahuquillo, H. Hassan, and J. Duato, "Dynamic wcet estimation for real-time multicore embedded systems supporting dvfs," in *2014 IEEE International Conference on High Performance Computing and Communications (HPCC)*, Aug 2014, pp. 27–33.

[11] J. Hausladen, B. Pohn, and M. Horauer, "A cloud-based approach to development of embedded systems software," in *2015 ASME/IEEE International Conference on Mechatronic and Embedded Systems and Applications*, Aug. 2-5, 2015., pp. 1–7.

[12] R. B. Miller, "Response time in man-computer conversational transactions," in *Proceedings of the December 9-11, 1968, Fall Joint Computer Conference, Part I*, ser. AFIPS '68 (Fall, part I). New York, NY, USA: ACM, 1968, pp. 267–277.

[13] J. Baviskar, A. Mulla, M. Upadhye, J. Desai, and A. Bhovad, "Performance analysis of zigbee based real time home automation system," in *2015 International Conference on Communication, Information Computing Technology (ICCICT)*, Jan 2015, pp. 1–6.

[14] A. J. Jara et al., "Evaluation of bluetooth low energy capabilities for tele-mobile monitoring in home-care," in *Journal of Universal Computer Science*, vol. 19, no. 9, 2013, pp. 1219–1241.

Low Power Charge Recycling D-FF

Karol Niewiadomski, Dietmar Tutsch
University of Wuppertal
Chair of Automation and Computer Science
Wuppertal, Germany
Email: {niewiadomski, tutsch}@uni-wuppertal.de

***Abstract*—The rising number of mobile applications leads to the necessity of powerful and energy-efficient designs. Field Programmable Gate Arrays (FPGAs) depict a suitable solution to this upcoming challenge. In the recent years, different FPGA designs have been released, covering the range from low-cost demands up to high-end applications in different industries. The downside of the increasing number of electronic functions in, e.g., vehicles, smartphones, etc., is limited resources of the built-in batteries. To overcome these limitations, appropriate power reduction measures have to be implemented at the circuit and architectural level. The correct function of each FPGA relies on data flip-flops (D-FFs) as basic data storage element. In this paper, a new D-FF cell design is introduced and implemented with focus on substantial power savings for low power applications and a higher resistance against differential power analysis (DPA), which is an inevitable step of side-channel attacks. This new D-FF design is compared to various, already existing implementations.**

Keywords*—*FPGA; D-FF; charge recycling; leakage-current reduction; differential power analysis.

I. Introduction

Mobile applications like notebooks, smartphones, tablets and wearables have changed the usage behavior over the last years. The access to information shall be available everywhere and completely independent from classic computers. This trend can be clearly seen in the current digitalization of vehicles, providing more and more features like driving assistance systems and interfaces for the connection of smartphones for displaying installed apps on the embedded infotainment system. A modern, upper-class vehicle contains more than 70 electronic control units (ECUs) to provide all features desired by consumers these days [1]. Such applications rely on the provision of sufficient processing power, which in turn requires adequate energy resources. Both, handheld computation units and vehicles have only limited battery capacities, therefore a necessity for power optimized integrated electronics is given.

One approach to overcome these challenges are FPGAs. These integrated circuits play a major role for the realization of adaptive and efficient systems, offering vast reconfiguration abilities [2] [3]. Reconfigurability goes back on arrays of memory cells like static random access memory (SRAM). In order to optimize an FPGA in terms of energy efficiency, these memory cells have to be extended with power reduction measures [4]. In addition to that, each FPGA works with flip-flops, which have an influence on the overall speed of the design since they are driven by the system clock. Furthermore, approximately 30% - 70% of the total power in a clocked design is dissipated by the clocking network, which is absolutely crucial for the operation of these circuits [5]. In consequence, by carefully re-designing these commonly used D-FFs, energy consumption can be decreased by applying static and dynamic power reduction measures. Power constraints are one of the most important challenges in modern circuit design. In addition, cyber security has become a frequently discussed topic in recent years, due to many incidents and a rising awareness for data protection. Side-channel attacks, which are based on differential power analysis, illustrate a possibility how to reveal confidential data without physical access to critical devices [6]. Thus, dedicated circuit modifications at circuit level shall be used for catching potential threats.

In this paper, we investigate selected D-FF cell designs on their low power characteristics, which can not be neglected in battery-powered systems. In Section II, we give an overview about related work and key aspects of dependencies between performance and power consumption. In Section III, we investigate a selection of existing D-FF designs on their assets and drawbacks and discuss the simulation results. In Section IV, we present our charge recycling (CR) D-FF and explain the implemented circuit improvement methods for static and dynamic power reduction. In Section V, we discuss simulation results of the D-FF and analyze the benefits of power reduction measures based on these simulations. In Section VI, all previous discussions are summarized and concluded.

II. Related Work

D-FFs are the working horse in different applications, like storage registers, counters, frequency dividers, etc. FPGAs resort on these circuits in each slice, which is a basic computational element, shown in Figure 1.

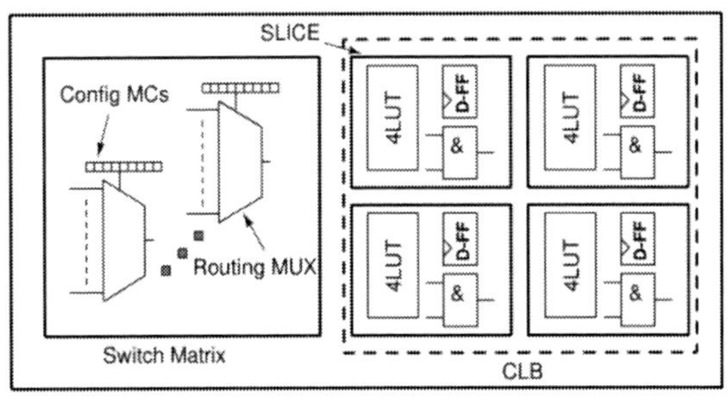

Fig. 1. Simplified SLICE structure of an FPGA

Each slice contains one D-FF for storage of computed values prior to forwarding them to the next configurable logic block (CLB). Since even a low-cost FPGA, e.g., Xilinx Spartan 3A, contains up to 8320 CLBs [7], one can see the strong impact on area and energy consumption of these clocked devices. The relation between consumed power and the supply voltage, load capacitance and system clock can be seen in (1):

$$P = \alpha C V^2 f_{Clk} \quad (1)$$

The activity factor α represents the cadence of write requests. A reduction of α can be achieved by special memory cell designs [8] or alternatively with auxiliary comparator circuitry. Another efficient approach is reducing the operating voltage. This can be achieved by techniques like dynamic voltage scaling (DVS), which was evaluated in various publications [9]. Power gating is certainly the strongest way to achieve a measurable reduction of energy consumption. However, this can be only applied, if there is no focus on data retention. A further possibility for raising the energy efficiency is lowering the clock frequency f_{Clk}. Circuitry, which is not timing critical can be clocked down to a minimum speed, which ensures a reliable operation of the system. If certain circuit parts can be completely stopped while retaining stored logic values, full clock gating can be a feasible solution to save power [10]. Both methods can be combined on a coarse-grain or fine-grain level.

These techniques are only an extract of a set consisting of different methods on how to handle the challenges of demanding functions. A majority of these solutions require additional circuitry to be added and implemented at a higher architectural level. Our approach goes one step further and is based on direct circuit level improvements to a D-FF by reasonable selection of a suitable D-FF cell design and substantial modifications of the internal cell circuitry to achieve better efficiency. The improvements achieved on that level are essential for important energy dissipation suppression and are an inevitable step for optimization to be combined with architectural amendments.

III. D-FF Cell designs

Different concepts have been introduced in the recent years. In general, we can distinguish between latches and flip-flops. Whilst latches are level-sensitive designs, flip-flops are egde-sensitive. Latches are transparent and therefore not suitable for timing-critical applications due to possible glitches in the signal path. For avoiding glitches and in consequence timing problems in complex designs, many flip-flop designs implicate the principle of cascading master-slave D-FFs. This standard design in shown in Figure 2.

Both, master and slave unit, consist of a feedback loop of inverters and transmission gates. Once Clk is set to *HIGH*, the input data provided by D is latched in the master circuit. At this point, the transmission gate connecting master and slave circuit, is in cut-off mode and therefore avoiding any glitches, e.g., direct throughput of D to Q. When Clk is set

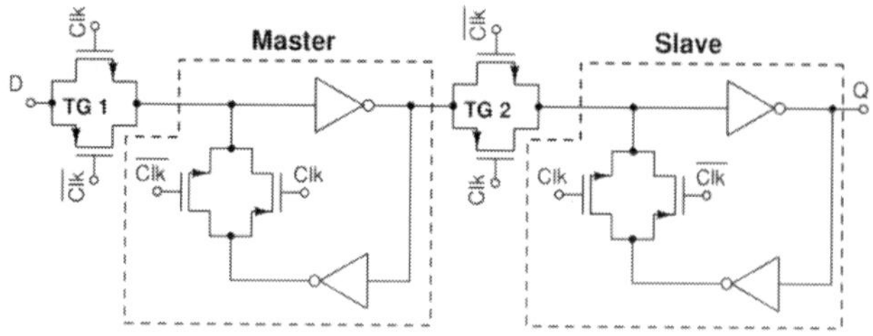

Fig. 2. Master-slave arrangement

to *LOW*, the stored data at the output of the master circuit is latched by the subsequent slave unit and provided at the output node Q. Any changes of D will not influence the logic value stored at Q due to the fact that both transistors of TG 1 are in cut-off mode. This legacy design was the starting point for numerous variations in the past. All simulations have been performed with Cadence tools and a $90nm$ technology provided by TSMC at an ambient temperature of 27°C. The clock frequency was set to $250MHz$.

1) SET D-FF: A simplified implementation is shown in Figure 3. Whilst the reference design of a D-FF uses 16 transistors in total, this design consists of 10 transistors only, leading to a higher chip density and reduced manufacturing costs [11].

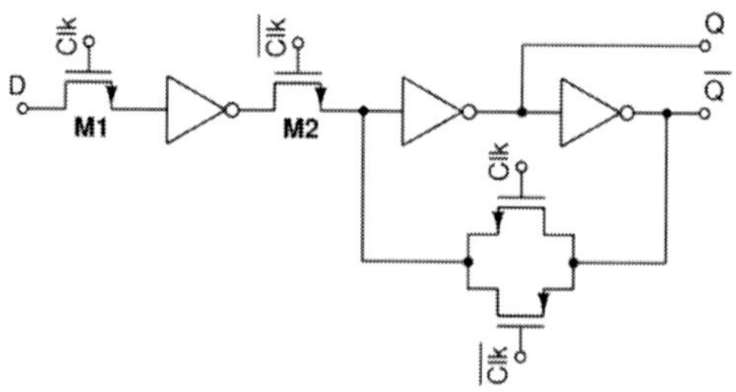

Fig. 3. Single Edge Triggerd D-FF

Instead of 4 TGs, this design works with 1 TG and achieves the same function by replacing the remaining TGs by nMOS transistors. This reduction of transistors comes along with cutting down the number of slower and larger pMOS transistors. Furthermore, this implementation provides the generation of both Q and $\overline{Q}$. The functionality of the SET D-FF is similar to the reference design: glitching is avoided by complementary control of both pass-transistors $M1$ and $M2$. Latching and generation of the output values is done in the feedback loop after the activation of $M2$. Analog to the previous standard design, this concept relies on the preparation of complementary Clk signals, which requires additional circuitry for signal generation.

2) Low-power D-FF: Another variation, which displays an attempt on how to optimize a D-FF with respect to power consumption, is shown in Figure 4. The key aspect of this design is to eliminate short-circuit power dissipation from the feedback path [12] due to the tri-state inverter. Although keeping the same number of transistor like in the reference design, considerable power savings can be achieved. This will be discussed in the last section of this paper.

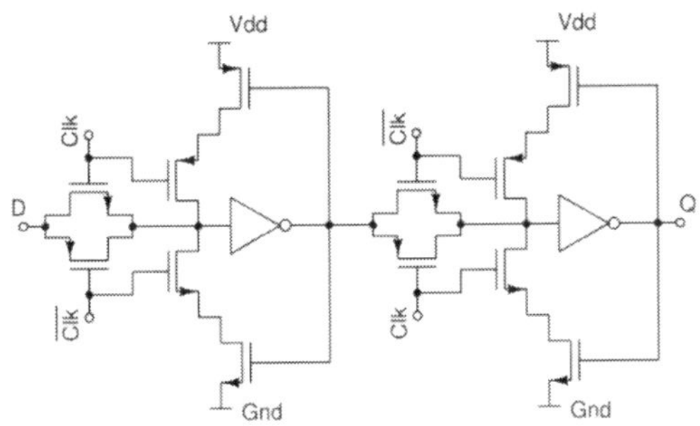

Fig. 4. Low-power modification of D-FF

3) PPI D-FF: In order to get a better performance of a conventional D-FF, the Push-Pull-Isolation (PPI) D-FF was presented in [12]. The main advantage of this implementation is the reduced clock-to-output delay from two gates in the reference design to one gate in the PPI D-FF, which is shown in Figure 5.

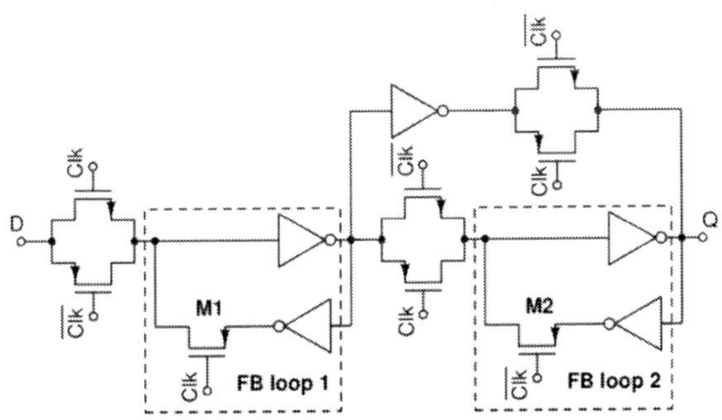

Fig. 5. Push-Pull-Isolation D-FF

The insertion of an inverter and a TG between the output nodes of master and slave latches provides a push-pull effect at the slave latch. In consequence, the input and output of the inverter in the slave unit will be driven to opposite logic values during operation. This design is approximately 31% faster than the reference D-FF, but has a power overhead of 22%. To counter the increased power consumption 2 pMOS transistors, $M1$ and $M2$, are added to the feedback loops in the master and slave latches. In direct comparison with the conventional D-FF, the PPI D-FF improves speed by 56% at an expense of 6% of additional power dissipation.

For all introduced cell designs in this paper, the average power consumption, the maximum and minimum power consumption during simulation time were traced and summarized in Table I. These results show that the reference D-FF dissipates the highest average power consumption by $1186nW$, due to lack of power savings measures. The maximum power dissipation confirms this result by revealing a higher consumption by the factor of approximately 4 in direct comparison with the optimized low-power D-FF. However, this result was expected and highlights the improvements of previously introduced designs.

TABLE I. SIMULATION RESULTS (PWR)

D-FF Type	*Average Power nW*	*Max. Power uW*	*Min. Power fW*
Reference	1186	233.3	51.47
SETD	280.3	26.21	22.39
Low-power	272.7	61.55	19.92
PPI	435.4	88.71	28.01

On the other hand, similar results are reflected by measuring the leakage current of each design, shown in Table II. The reference D-FF exhibits the highest average leakage current I_{leak} by $1262nA$, which is approximately fivefold higher than average I_{leak} of the low-power D-FF. Analog to the average leakage current, the maximum leakage current is also allocated to the reference design and points out that all power-optimized variations perform better in terms of energy efficiency.

TABLE II. SIMULATION RESULTS I_{Leak}

D-FF Type	*Avg. Current nA*	*Max. Current uW*	*Min. Current uW*
Reference	1262	336.3	346
SETD	265.7	48.94	50.41
Low-power	235.1	28.83	45.9
PPI	403.7	39.4	56.35

The respective simulation results are shown in Figure 6, which illustrates the input signal D, the clock signal Clk and the respective power dissipation output profiles for the presented input sequence with an alternating $0 \rightarrow 1 \rightarrow 0 \rightarrow 1$ sequence.

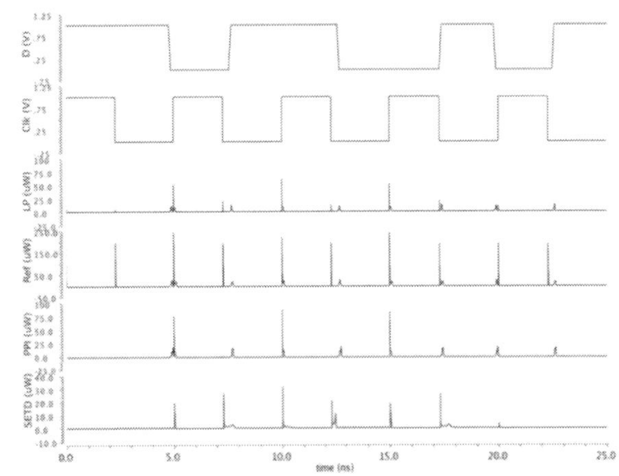

Fig. 6. Comparison Results

All designs exhibit strongly varying power consumption for each transition on the input nodes during the rising edge of the Clk signal, which comes along with an exploitable vulnerability for side-channel attacks. Glitches can be identified during the falling edge of Clk, which indicates weaknesses in the latching mechanism of master and slave latch, therefore revealing undesired transparency. None of the previously presented designs is optimized in terms of static leakage current suppression or energy recovery during runtime, which will be key aspects of our presented design in the next section.

IV. CR D-FF

Based on the analysis of drawbacks of existing D-FF designs, we present a new approach of a low-power, energy-efficient and glitch-free D-FF, which is suitable for security-relevant applications with limited energy resources. Referring to the standard design shown in Figure 2, our intention was to redesign a new flip-flop cell from scratch. Without any direct relation to the D-FFs presented in the previous section, we present our charge recycling (CR) D-FF, which is illustrated in Figure 7.

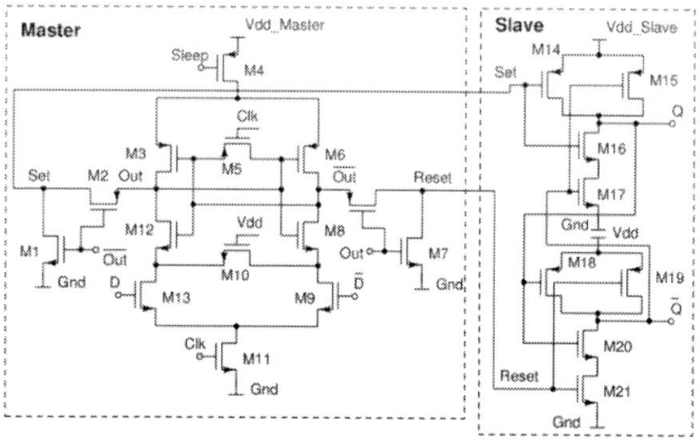

Fig. 7. CR D-FF

This design features a series of dedicated power savings mechanisms, which will be discussed in the following sections.

A. Charge recycling

Storing and processing logic values in flip-flops, registers, memories leads to charging and discharging of parasitic capacitances, which are an essential part of each integrated circuit. Since the CR D-FF features dynamic logic, periodic charge & discharge cycles are an integral part of the intended function and require special attention during the design. This design works with 2 alternating phases during runtime: precharge & evaluate, which are both triggered by the Clk signal. Whilst Clk turns to LOW, $M5$ is turned on and in consequence also switching on the pMOS transistors $M3$ & $M6$. Illustrating a critical point with respect to power savings within an integrated circuit, the precharge phase is the more deciding one. Due to the fact that these transistors are therefore in a conducting state, the capacitances at the output nodes Out & $\overline{Out}$ are shortened. Hence, not discharged electrons at one of the complementary output nodes are used for charging the previously discharged output node. This effect is used for equilibrating electron charges and thus relieving the battery due to the fact that less energy is needed. This is a strong method for achieving a better performance in terms of dissipation reduction during dynamic behavior.

After Clk applies a logic *HIGH* at the gate of $M4$, this transistor is turned off whereas $M11$ is turned on and subsequently starting the evaluation phase in terms of sensing the difference between the complementary inputs D & $\overline{D}$. One of the various benefits of sense amplifier based logic is that even a small Δ voltage between both input signals will be sensed and evaluated, providing a higher speed of the D-FF.

B. Dual Threshold CMOS

Leakage currents I_{leak} during standby contribute to a significant amount of total dissipation loss. By adding dedicated countermeasures, appreciable power savings can be achieved without investing much effort for realization. This can be done by the usage of transistors with a high threshold voltage V_{th}. Transistors with a high V_{th} require a proportional higher V_{GS} voltage at their gate nodes in order to be turned on, which implies a mitigation of leakage currents. This method can be combined be applying a negative V_{GS} for leading transistors into a deep turn-off status and therefore supporting suppression of leakage currents. This technique should be only applied carefully on circuit parts, which are not timing-critical since higher threshold voltages usually equal in slower signal transition. All transistors in our design are high V_{th} transistors for the sake of strongest suppression of I_{leak}.

C. Multi-oxide technology

Closely related to the previous section, static power dissipation can be further decreased by improving the tunneling-barrier for electrons. Undesired tunneling of electrons through the gate to bulk leads to current flows, which shall be eliminated. The relation between I_{leak} and the tunneling-barrier is shown in (2):

$$I_{leak} \propto A(\frac{V_{ox}}{T_{ox}})^2 \tag{2}$$

Increasing the tunneling-barrier can be realized by increasing the gate oxide thickness T_{ox}. A higher oxide thickness leads immediately to a reduction of the tunneling current density I_{leak}, following the goal to extend battery lifetime of mobile devices even in standby mode. The drawback of this technique is similar to the previous one: penalty of the circuit speed may occur if not applied carefully. Based on this reason, we decided to use high T_{ox} transistors for $M4$, $M5$ and $M11$. All of these transistors are not timing-critical, since $M4$ is used to activate a dedicated sleep mode and $M5$ for balancing the outputs. All of these functions are not slowing the circuit speed.

D. Clk- and power-gating

For further reduction of dynamic power dissipation, cutting off the Clk signal leads to transfer the circuit to a hold state, while maintaining the stored data inside the latches. Circuitry, which is not executing different operations over runtime, can be kept in a *WAIT* state, ready to continue calculation whenever the Clk signal is set to *HIGH* again. In the proposed design, $M5$ & $M11$ are used for stopping the D-FF from operating, but still keeping the correct data at the outputs of the cross-coupled inverters. Of course, additional circuitry driving and distributing the Clk signal over a whole design is an indispensable requirement. This can be provided by digital clock managers (DCMs), which are not covered by this paper.

In case that data storage is not necessary, gating of the supply voltage is an effective method how to save power in unused parts of a circuit. Power gating can be applied on different hierarchical levels. Our decision was to follow a fine-grain approach, leading to equipping the proposed D-FF with a power gating transistor $M4$. If the *SLEEP* signal turns from 0 to 1, $M4$ is off and therefore disconnecting the D-FF from V_{dd}. If this technique is applied in accordance with clock gating, total rail-to-rail-decoupling (V_{dd} & Gnd) can be realized.

E. Stacking

Transistor stacking is a further, strong technique for sub-threshold current reduction. Stacking transistors means to increase to source voltage V_S while keeping the gate voltage V_G at the same level. At a certain point of time, V_{GS} becomes negative, which leads the transistor into super cut-off mode and turns it deeply off. The more transistors are stacked in series, the better leakage current reduction will be. However, the most significant results can be achieved by adding a second transistor in series, because the effect of subthreshold current reduction becomes diminished with a rising number of transistors. Our proposed D-FF features stacking as a design principle, e.g., in the pull-down-networks of the slave latch, realized by $M16$ $M17$ and $M20$ & $M21$.

V. Simulation Results

The CR D-FF senses the inputs D & $\overline{D}$ at the positive edge of Clk and stores these data independently from any changes at the input nodes of this circuit. Due to all implemented circuit improvements, an average static leakage current of $173nA$ is achieved, which is sufficiently low to be accepted. During the negative edge of Clk, the CR D-FF turns into the precharge phase, where all internal and external nodes are charged. The characteristic curves in Figure 8 show one beneficial features of the CR D-FF over the other discussed designs. This can be seen in both output curves of Q & $\overline{Q}$.

Since this design features charge recycling, the output nodes and all internal nodes are precharged to $V_{dd} - V_{th}$ only, which is beneficial for the energy balance of this circuit. The reason for this is that precharge is finished by achieving an output voltage, which is one threshold voltage below V_{dd}. Thus, the less energy from the power supply is required for precharging the CR D-FF, the more suitable circuitry for low-power applications will be. Based on the reduced voltage range at the outputs of the master latch, it is possible to decrease permanently the supply voltage $V_{dd\ Slave}$. Hence, we choose a supply voltage of $800mV$ for the conventional slave circuit, which supports further power dissipation reduction. For a better comparison, we enhance Table I with relevant simluation results of the CR D-FF, shown in Table III.

The results in Table III show that the introduced CR D-FF outperforms most of the previously analyzed designs in terms of average power consumption. It achieves the second-best performance for average power consumption ($319.7nW$) and the best result for maximum power dissipation ($13.84uW$). The minimum power consumption of $27.59fW$ can be neglected, since the influence of these contributions is not significant for the overall performance of all discussed designs. Even though the conventional low-power flip-flop achieves a slightly lower average power consumption than the CR D-FF, the peak power dissipation is approximately quintuple higher and it offers no resistance features against DPA. Figure 9 shows a comparison of the average power consumption.

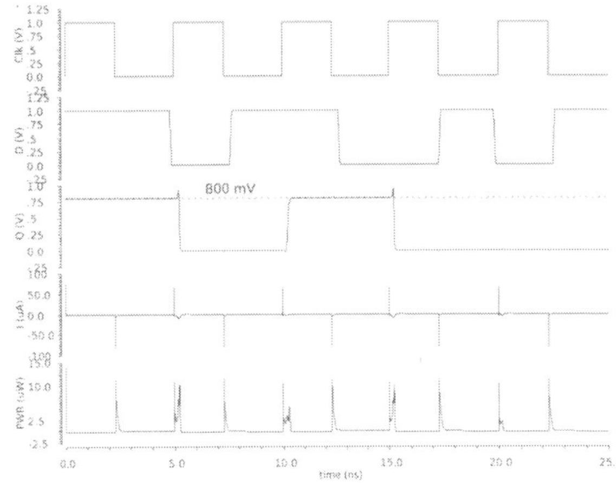

Fig. 8. Simulation Results CR D-FF

TABLE III. SIMULATION RESULTS (PWR)

D-FF Type	*Average PWR nW*	*Max. PWR uW*	*Min. PWR fW*
Reference	1186	233.3	51.47
SETD	374.1	32.01	22.39
Low-power	275.7	73.89	19.92
PPI	435.4	110.5	172.3
CR	**303.5**	**13.84**	**27.59**

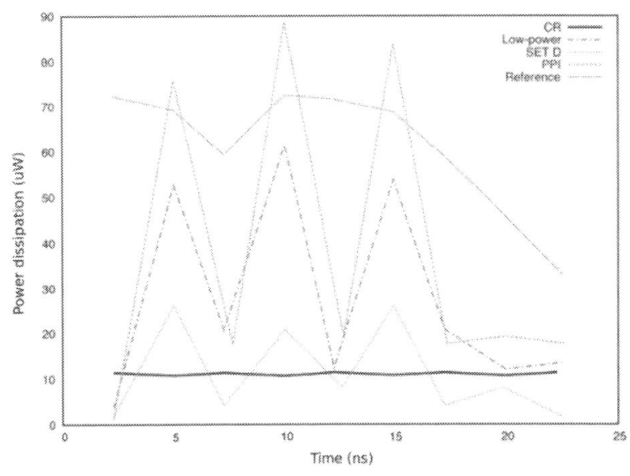

Fig. 9. Comparison of Average Power Dissipation

It can be clearly seen in Table III that the CR D-FF provides the most constant power consumption among all considered designs, therefore also providing the best opportunities to be chosen in security-sensitive applications. The smaller the differences in energy consumption between each data transition are, the more difficult a differential power analysis will be, which is always the starting point for a side-channel attack. Hence, the introduced CR D-FF provides both, remarkable low-power characteristics for mobile, embedded circuitry, which comes along with a necessity for robustness against intended attacks. However, benefits in superior energy efficiency and noticeable robustness against differential power analysis come at the cost of a higher number of transistors, shown in Table IV.

TABLE IV. TRANSISTOR COUNT AND POWER VARIATION

D-FF Type	*Reference*	*SETD*	*LP*	*PPI*	*CR*
No. of transistors	16	10	16	18	**21**
Max. PWR Δ (%)	18.78	94.7	94.03	98.62	**6.8**

This fact usually leads to a penalty in required area for manufacturing, which is certainly an aspect to be considered. A CR D-FF consists of 21 transistors and requires preparation of complementary input signals, which depend on additional wiring and therefore lead to extra area on the chip. On the other hand, this implementation provides also 2 complementary outputs with no delay between both signals and no necessity of additional circuitry for generation. Table IV also emphasizes the differences between the analyzed cells in switching behavior. Whilst the Δ of dissipated power of the CR D-FF never exceeds variations of 6.8% in maximum, the results of the alternative designs show much higher noticeable differences. Despite the fact that all designs have been analyzed without putting a stronger focus on speed and timing aspects, further measurements on the maximum operating frequency have been done. For this purpose, the elapsed time for each switching transition was measured and compared against each other. Figure 10 illustrates a direct comparison of the output Q of all considered circuits after being stimulated with an input signal D. Depending on the switching transition and the characteristics of the flip-flops, expected differences on the edge steepness can be identified.

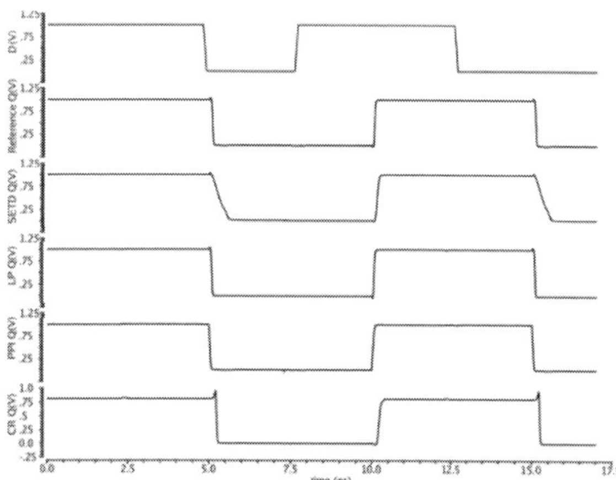

Fig. 10. Comparison of Switching Transitios Of All Designs

Based on these simulation results, the consumed time for a *HIGH* → *LOW* and a *LOW* → *HIGH* transition has been measured and summarized in Table V. The maximum achievable switching frequency f_{max} reveals the penalty in operating speed of the CR D-FF, due to the increased number of transistors. However, a maximum switching frequency of $\approx 6.4GHz$ is still a notable result.

TABLE V. TIMING COMPARISON

D-FF Type	*T High-Low ps*	*T Low-High ps*	*Max. freq. GHz*
Reference	42.5	58.3	9.9
SETD	422	101	1.9
Low-power	43.63	51.58	10
PPI	60.48	79.16	7.1
CR	**41**	**114**	**6.4**

VI. CONCLUSION

We analyzed a selected number of existing flip-flop designs upon their characteristics and suitability for usage in low-power applications. Beside that, we have investigated each design on its capabilities to be resistant against differential power analysis. Our goal was to design a D-FF, which provides both, a remarkable reduction of power consumption and robustness against side-channel attacks. Hence, we designed a charge recycling D-FF, which uses the not discharged electrons at one of the complementary output nodes to support the battery during the precharge phase. This benefit comes along with the fact that the outputs of the master latch are precharged to $V_{dd} - V_{th}$ only, providing the opportunity to power the slave latch with the same supply voltage ($\approx 800mV$). Furthermore, we applied additional power saving modifications and achieved remarkable improvements of power reduction and standby leakage suppression. Simulation results have shown that the CR D-FF offers the best overall performance with an average power consumption, which reduced the dissipated power by about $\approx 75\%$. Complementary generation of output signals with no requirement for delay correction is a further advantage of this circuit when compared to other designs, which do not feature parallel, complementary creation of D & $\overline{D}$. The variations of the measured power consumption do not exceed differences of $\approx 7\%$ and remain constant independent from the switching event, which is sufficient to withstand differential power analysis and which is not achieved by the alternative flip-flops. These benefits come at the cost of a higher number of required transistors and the layout after synthesis of a CR D-FF requires careful routing of all metal interconnections between these cells for keeping the parasitic capacitances as equal as possible.

ACKNOWLEDGMENT

The authors thank Pierre Mayr, from Ruhr University of Bochum, for his advice on verification strategies and procedures. We would like to give credit to Grant Martin, from Cadence Tensilica, for many interesting discussion about embedded devices and low-power technologies. We are grateful to Andreas Ullrich, from University of Wuppertal, for immediate PDK / tool support.

REFERENCES

[1] S. Fürst, "Challenges in the design of automotive software," in *Proceedings of the Conference on Design, Automation and Test in Europe*, ser. DATE '10. 3001 Leuven, Belgium, Belgium: European Design and Automation Association, 2010, pp. 256–258. [Online]. Available: http://dl.acm.org/citation.cfm?id=1870926.1870987

[2] M. Ullmann, M. Hübner, B. Grimm, and J. Becker, "An fpga run-time system for dynamical on-demand reconfiguration," in *Parallel and Distributed Processing Symposium, 2004. Proceedings. 18th International*. IEEE, 2004, p. 135.

[3] R. A. et al., "Towards a dynamically reconfigurable automotive control system architecture," in *Embedded System Design: Topics, Techniques and Trends*. Springer, 20017, pp. 71–84.

[4] K. Niewiadomski, C. Gremzow, and D. Tutsch, "4t loadless srams for low power fpga lut optimization," in *Proceedings of the 9th International Conference on Adaptive and Self-Adaptive Systems and Applications (ADAPTIVE 2017)*, February 2017, pp. 1–7.

[5] V. Stojanovic and V. G. Oklobdzija, "Comparative analysis of master-slave latches and flip-flops for high-performance and low-power systems," *IEEE Journal of Solid-State Circuits*, vol. 34, no. 4, pp. 536–548, Apr 1999.

[6] K. Tiri and I. Verbauwhede, "A vlsi design flow for secure side-channel attack resistant ics," in *Proceedings of the Conference on Design, Automation and Test in Europe - Volume 3*, ser. DATE '05. Washington, DC, USA: IEEE Computer Society, 2005, pp. 58–63. [Online]. Available: http://dx.doi.org/10.1109/DATE.2005.44

[7] *XA Spartan-3A Automotive FPGA Family Data Sheet*, Xilinx, 04 2011, rev. 2.0.

[8] R. E. Aly, M. I. Faisal, and M. A. Bayoumi, "Novel 7t sram cell for low power cache design," in *Proceedings 2005 IEEE International SOC Conference*, Sept 2005, pp. 171–174.

[9] J. M. Rabaey, A. Chandrakasan, and B. Nikolic, *Digital integrated circuits- A design perspective*, 2nd ed. Prentice Hall, 2004.

[10] C. Maxfield, *The Design Warrior's Guide to FPGAs: Devices, Tools and Flows*, 1st ed. Newton, MA, USA: Newnes, 2004.

[11] M. Sharma, A. Noor, S. C. Tiwari, and K. Singh, "An area and power efficient design of single edge triggered d-flip flop," in *2009 International Conference on Advances in Recent Technologies in Communication and Computing*, Oct 2009, pp. 478–481.

[12] U. Ko and P. T. Balsara, "High-performance energy-efficient d-flip-flop circuits," *IEEE Transactions on Very Large Scale Integration (VLSI) Systems*, vol. 8, no. 1, pp. 94–98, Feb 2000.

A Watt-Level 4G LTE CMOS Reconfigurable Power Amplifier with Efficiency Enhancement in Power Back-Off

Giap Luong, Jean-Marie Pham, Eric Kerhervé
IMS Bordeaux
Talence, France
E-mail : [quang-giap.luong; jean-marie.pham; eric.kerherve]@ims-bordeaux.fr

Pierre Medrel
XLIM Laboratory
Limoges, France
E-mail: pierre.medrel@xlim.fr

***Abstract*—This paper presents a reconfigurable two-stage power amplifier (PA) for use in 4G LTE unmanned aerial vehicles (UAVs) applications. The PA using the TSMC bulk 65-nm CMOS process exhibits a saturated output power of 29.8 dBm, a power gain of 35.6 dB, a maximum power added efficiency (PAE) of 27.2 % at 2.5 GHz and maintains PAE over 10 % in the output power's 8 dB back-off zone as required by LTE's power-to-average power ratio (PAPR) specifications. The proposed reconfigurable PA architecture, which includes four sub PA cells with the power cell switching (PCS) technique, allows the high level of efficiency in back-off of output power. The four sub-PA cells are composed of three differential cascode stages, supplied by 3.3 V and implemented with the segmented bias (SB) technique to maintain the high level of PAE, reduce the DC power consumption and reconfigure the output impedance.**

Keywords- CMOS; Power Amplifier; transformer; segmented bias; differential; neutralization technique.

I. Introduction

Since UAVs are highly mobile devices, they need transceivers that minimize space and power consumption whilst facilitating mobile applications requiring high bit rates over wide coverage areas. CMOS, as a powerful platform, has recently demonstrated a tremendous interest in industry with a fully integrated radio system-on-chip (SoC) solution for transceivers. CMOS power amplifiers designed for wireless communications standard, such as LTE, LTE-A and WiMAX, require good performances about output power, efficiency and linearity.

Modern high-data-rate communication systems, using spectrally efficient modern scheme like Orthogonal Frequency-Division Multiplexing (OFDM) with a high power-to-average- power ratio (PAPR), require RF power amplifiers about high linearity and high efficiency. The main challenge for LTE power amplifiers is hence to achieve the good trade-off between high linearity and high efficiency over wide power range. Furthermore, delivering watt-level output power is another challenge for CMOS RF power amplifiers because of low break-down voltage and high knee voltage of transistors. Several techniques hence have been investigated to overcome this limitation of CMOS namely stacked transistors [3].

To find the best linearity/efficiency trade-off while reducing thermal problems, the power cell switching (PCS) technique [1][2], which can be used to combine output power from sub-PA cells, provides a high level of efficiency and preserves a good linearity. To push upper back-off efficiency of PA, a combination of the PCS technique and the segmented bias (SB) [4][5] helps PA not only operate with higher efficiency in a wider range of output back-off power (OBO) but also deal with the problem of short battery life of mobile devices.

This paper proposes a reconfigurable multi-mode RF power amplifier to further enhance efficiency in back-off power zone. The proposed PA is composed of four differential cascode segmented-biased sub-PA cells to achieve high output power and high back-off efficiency, as shown in Figure 1. Implemented in the TSMC bulk 65-nm CMOS process, the PA achieves high efficiency to 8 dB of power back-off and also substantially scales down the thermal power consumption. Its operation modes are controlled by two bias voltages (Vbias1, Vbias2) of each sub-PA cell and two supply voltages (Vdd1, Vdd2).

This paper is organized as follows: Section II discusses the concept and design of the reconfigurable power amplifier. Section III presents the post-layout simulation results. These results include the continuous-wave (CW) simulation data, which meet linearity and output power requirements, with high efficiency for 4G LTE signals at 2.5 GHz. The paper will finish with a short conclusion in Section IV.

II. Circuit Design

A. Design of the proposed reconfigurable power amplifier

The 2.5 GHz CMOS reconfigurable multi-mode power amplifier is implemented and simulated using Keysight's Golden Gate in post-layout simulation.

In Figure 1, the architecture of the proposed reconfigurable multi-mode power amplifier is introduced. The four parallel sub-PA cells are designed in three-stage differential cascode topology with the segmented bias technique and the neutralization technique. The transformer TR1 achieves the impedance matching between the 100 Ohm RF input and the input impedance of driver. The transformer TR2 is a power splitter and can be used as an inter-stage impedance matching network. The transformer TR3 combines the power from the four sub-PA cells and matches the impedance from the four sub-PA cells to the 100 Ohm RF output.

By switching each sub-PA cell on/off and adjusting the bias point of each transistor in common source of sub-PA cells, this PA can be reconfigured to enhance back-off power efficiency.

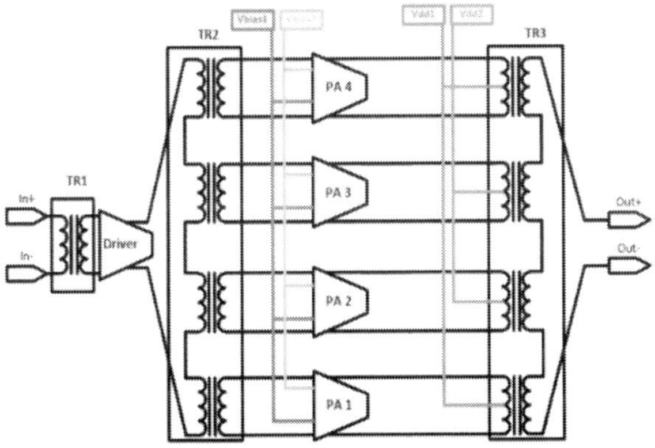

Figure 1. Architecture of the proposed reconfigurable multi-mode PA

B. Design of sub-PA cells

To stabilize each sub-PA cell, two neutralization capacitors C_9, C_{10} [6][7], which dramatically reduce the Miller effect capacitance of differential cascode, are carefully added for the sake of maintaining the circuit in the unconditionally stable region. Their chosen values are fixed at 1.23 pF.

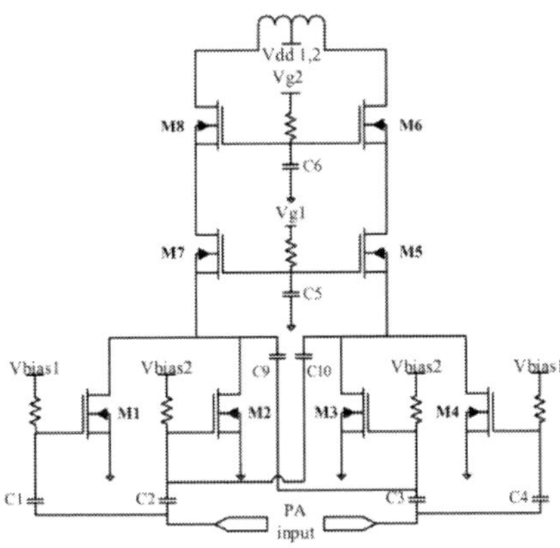

Figure 2. Sub PA cell with the segmented bias technique

In order to increase efficiency of the PA stage, a new topology based on individually biasing the common source stage is proposed in Figure 2. Stacked MOSFET differential cascode structure using deep N-well transistors consists of two common gate (CG) stages and one common source (CS) stage. The capacitors C_5, C_6 at the gates of each stacked transistor are chosen to balance drain source voltage swings of four transistors' CG stages. The external gate capacitance and the gate-to-source capacitance of each stacked transistor form a capacitive voltage divider to produce the proper in-phase voltage swing at the transistor's gate and drain [3]. Transistors M_5, M_6, M_7, M_8 are biased in class AB and sized with a width (W) and a length (L) of 60 µm and 60 nm, respectively.

In the CS stage, transistors $(M_1; M_2), (M_4; M_3)$ are biased separately in class AB with a size of W/3L (20 µm/60 nm) and class C with a size of 2W/3L (40 µm/60 nm) respectively. This method keeps the sub-PA cells in high power and high efficiency region due to the good performances of class AB amplifiers in low power region and of class C amplifiers in high power region. The segmented bias technique (SB) [4][5] allows to significantly scale down DC power consumption compared to class AB.

The estimated size of the sub PA cell's layout is 396.84 µm x 251.5 µm (Figure 10).

C. Design of Driver cell

The driver cell is designed with a differential cascode structure and biased in class AB with deep N-well transistors for the CG and CS stages (Figure 3). The supply voltage (Vdriver) is 2.4 V. This driver aims to increase a level of gain of the PA. The neutralization capacitors C_2, C_3 are also used to make this cell unconditionally stable. The size of the driver is 272 µm x 115.6 µm, as illustrated in Figure 10.

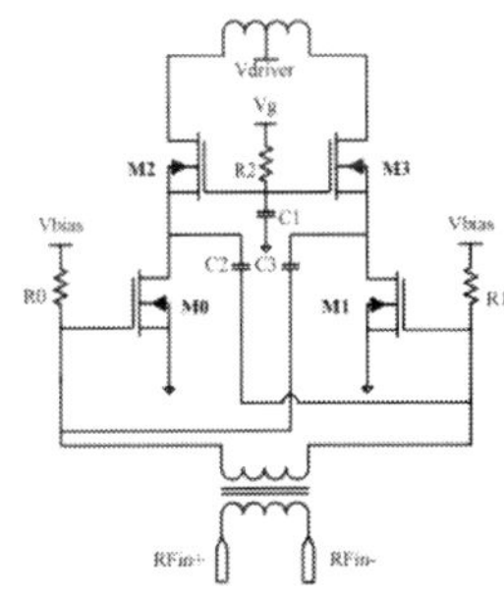

Figure 3. Driver's structure

D. Design of transformers

There are three stacked transformers (TR) [8][9] in the full design. The first one (TR1) in Figure 10 ensures the impedance matching between the driver's optimal impedance and the 100-Ohm input with the size of 252 µm x 674 µm. The second one (TR2) in Figure 10 converts the optimal output impedance of driver to the optimal input impedance of the four sub-PA cells with the size of 197.3 µm x 1706.1 µm. This transformer is also used as a splitter to distribute power homogenously to each sub-PA cell. The last one (TR3) in Figure 10 with the size of 209.3 µm x 1884 µm matches the optimal output impedance of the sub-PA cells to the 100 Ohm output. The transformer TR3 is carefully designed in order to be robust and reliable under high current levels from four sub-PA cells.

E. Reconfigurable states of PA

To fulfill the requirements of 4G LTE signals with high levels of efficiency, the PA can be switched into four possible states in Table. 1 to maintain efficiency over 10% in the 8 dB back-off power zone. The four states are defined by two bias voltages (Vbias1, Vbias2) of the common source transistors and two supply voltages: Vdd1 for the sub-PA cells (1, 4) and Vdd2 for the sub-PA cells (2, 3).

TABLE 1. CONTROLLED STATES TO RECONFIGURE THE PA

State	Vbias1	Vbias2	Vdd2	Vdd1	Number of active PAs
1A	0.6	0.6	3.3	3.3	4
1B	0.6	0.45	3.3	3.3	
1C	0.45	0.45	3.3	3.3	
2	0.6	0.45	0	3.3	2 (PA 1, PA 4)

Three states 1A, 1B and 1C are used in the high power (HP) region. In these states, four sub-PA cells are all active. More current will be delivered to the load, therefore output power can be increased. These states are determined by Vbias1 and Vbias2 to satisfy the demands of efficiency, output power or linearity. State 2 is used in the medium power (MP) region. In this state, the sub-PA cells 2 and 3 are turned off by having their supply source (Vdd2) off, whilst the sub-PA cells 1 and 4 controlled by Vdd1 are kept on. This configuration is outlined in Table 1.

III. POST-LAYOUT SIMULATION RESULTS

A. S-Parameters results

This PA achieves promising RF performances and performs such good input and output matchings (Figure 4 and Figure 5). The values of S_{11} and S_{22} at 2.5 GHz are all around -20 dB for the four states. The small-signal gains of the PA are 36 dB for state 1A and 30.6 dB for state 2 as shown in Figure 5. Stability of the circuit is illustrated in Figure 4 . The stability factor μ, whose values are over 6 for the four states, guarantees unconditional stability of the proposed PA.

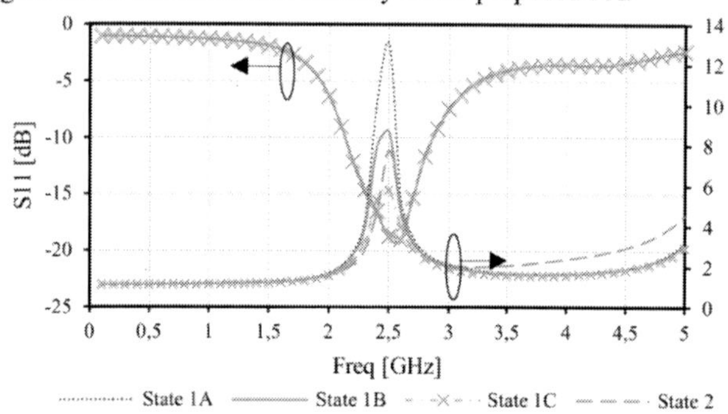

Figure 4. Input return loss $\mathbf{S_{11}}$ and the stability factor μ

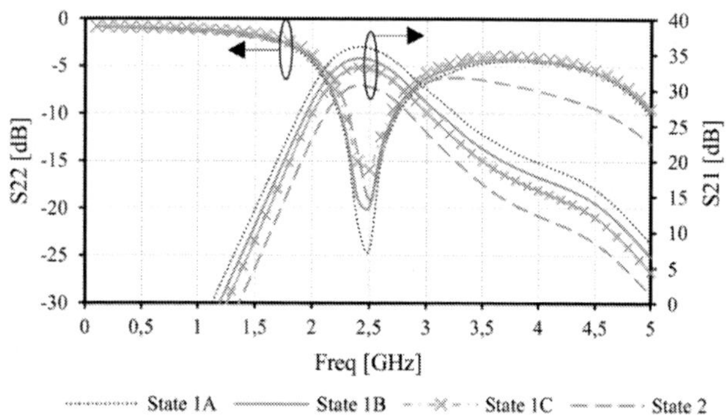

Figure 5. Small signal gain S_{21} and output return loss S_{22}

B. RF performances

The power added efficiency (PAE) is illustrated in Figure 6, the power gain and the output power with 2.5 GHz single-tone signals are shown in Figure 7. Both figures include the post-layout simulated data. Saturated output power P_{sat} of state 1A and state 2 are 29.8 dBm (high power) and 24.8 dBm (medium power), respectively. Maximum power gains of four stages are 35.6, 34.3, 32.8 and 30.1 dB, respectively. PAE at P_{sat} in state 1A is 27.2 % and PAE at 6dB of OBO in state 2 (Pout = 23.8 dBm) is 18 %, improved by 11%. State 2 improves significantly back-off efficiency at the MP region. To fulfill the requirement at 8dB of PAPR, this PA is reconfigured until 8 dB of OBO and reaches 11.8 % of PAE. With the SB technique, DC power consumption is reduced to 2.53 W for state 1B and 1.2 W for state 2 in Figure 8.

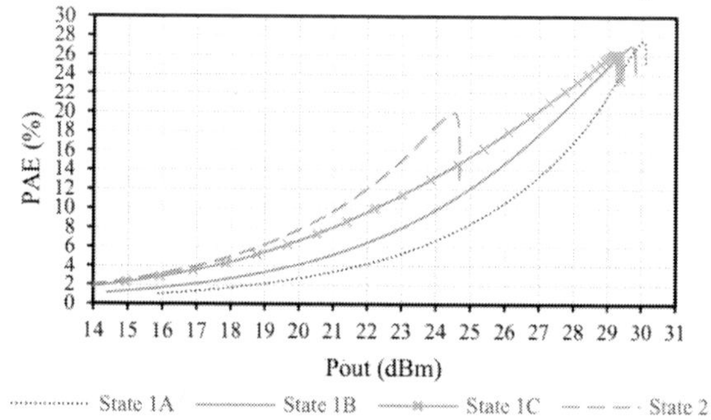

Figure 6. Simulated PAE versus output power

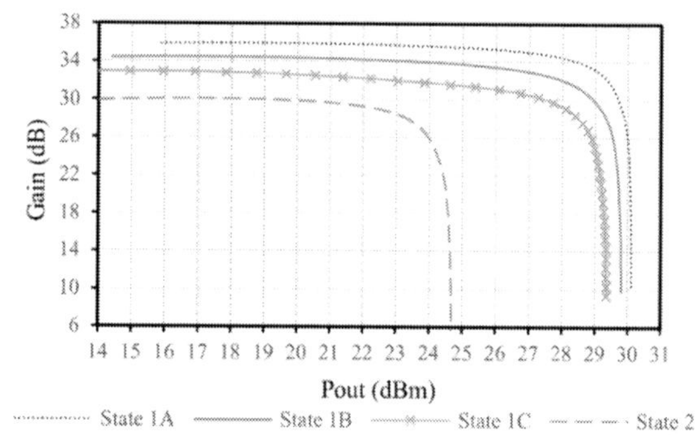

Figure 7. Simulated Gain versus output power

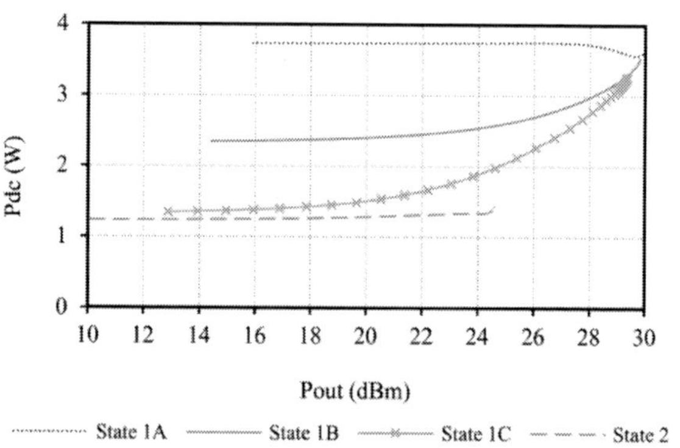

Figure 8. DC power consumption versus output power

TABLE 3. COMPARISON WITH RECENT 4G LTE MULTI-MODE CMOS PAs

Parameter		This work	[10]	[11]	[12]	[13]
Freq. [GHz]		2.5	1.95	0.7 – 1.0	1.7 - 2.0	1.9
Technology		65nm	130nm	180nm	180nm	40nm
PAPR [dB]		8	7	7	7.5	12
Size [mm^2]		2.98	4.48	2.52	1.56	2.94
Supply [V]		3.3	3.3	2	3.5	1.5
Psat [dBm]		29.8	29.3	> 13.6 (P_{-1dB})	26	28
Gain [dB]		35.6	29.3	19.6	15	22
PAE [%]	@Psat	27.2	31	25.5	31.6	34
	@OBO = 3dB	21	23.4	15.4	22.5	28.3
	@OBO = 6dB	19	20.5	-	18	25.5

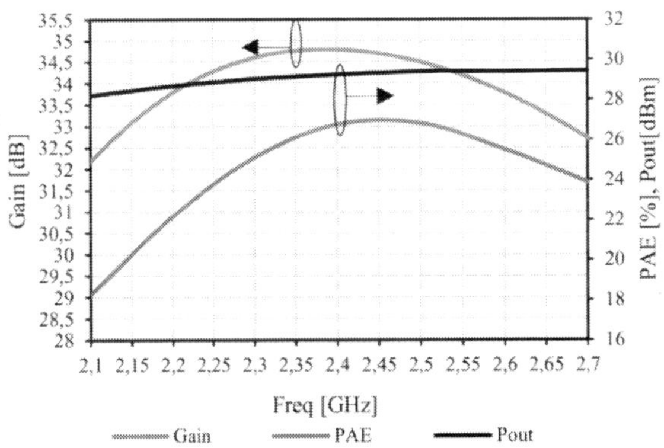

Figure 9. Simulated gain, PAE and output power versus frequency

The 3-dB bandwidth of this PA is 700 MHz from 2.05 GHz to 2.75 GHz, as illustrated in Figure 9.

Figure 10 is the layout of the 65-nm CMOS multi-mode reconfigurable PA. The estimated size of the entire circuit is 1.89 mm x 1.575 mm, including the pads. This layout is the version used for the incoming tape-out.

TABLE 2. CHOSEN STATE ACCORDING TO DESIRED PARAMETER

Desired parameter		State	Values
Max. Gain		1A	36 dB
Max. PAE			27.2%
Max. P_{sat}			29.8 dBm
High linearity P_{-1dB}			26 dBm
PAE in power back-off	High power (HP)	1C	↑ 6.8% @3dB OBO
	Medium power (MP)	2	↑ 8.2% @8dB OBO
Best trade-off	HP	1B	-
	MP	2	-

Table 2 compares this work with other state-of-the-art 4G LTE multi-mode CMOS PAs. This PA achieves a good trade-off between linearity and efficiency. Gain is significantly higher than previous CMOS integrated PAs.

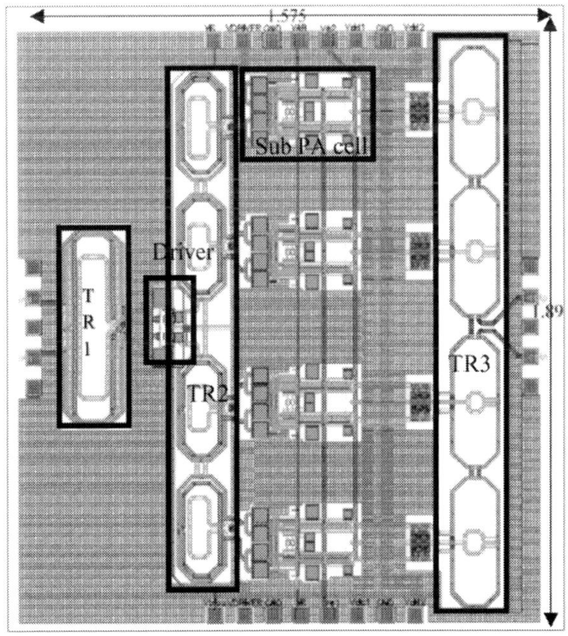

Figure 10. Layout of the reconfigurable power amplifier

Table 3 outlines the operation of this reconfigurable multi-mode PA. States of the PA are selected according to desired parameters. Therefore, the PA's efficiency is notably augmented in back-off power region. Furthermore, this PA is capable of being the best trade-off between efficiency and linearity in state 1B and state 2 for the high and medium power regions, respectively, as shown in this table.

IV. CONCLUSION

In this paper, a fully integrated 4G LTE reconfigurable CMOS PA is discussed and implemented. This PA achieves a maximum output power of +29.8 dBm and a maximum PAE of 27.2 % at 2.5 GHz. Using the segmented bias technique, this PA allows a PAE of over 10 % to be maintained in the output power's 8 dB back-off zone as required by LTE's PAPR specifications. The operation mode of the PA is controlled by two bias voltages of each sub-PA cell in order to trade-off between high linearity and high efficiency.

Moreover, for the purpose of preserving high back-off PAE, two sub PA cells can be turned off to keep the PAE over 14 % in back-off power zone of 5dB to 7dB.

ACKNOWLEDGMENT

This work is designed in TSMC 65-nm CMOS version CMN65LP with nine Cu metal levels and one Al metal level at the IMS Laboratory, in Bordeaux, France.

REFERENCES

[1] P. Haldi, D. Chowdhury, P. Reynaert, G. Liu, and A. M. Niknejad, "A 5.8 GHz 1 V Linear Power Amplifier Using a Novel On-Chip Transformer Power Combiner in Standard 90 nm CMOS," IEEE Journal of Solid-State Circuits, vol. 43, pp. 1054–1063, May 2008.

[2] P. M. Farahabadi and K. Moez, "A 60-GHz Dual-Mode Distributed Active Transformer Power Amplifier in 65-nm CMOS," IEEE Transactions on Very Large Scale Integration (VLSI) Systems, vol. 24, no. 5, pp. 1909–1916, May 2016..

[3] S. Pornpromlikit, J. Jeong, and C. Presti, "A Watt-level Stacked-FET Linear Power Amplifier in Silicon-on-Insulator CMOS," IEEE Transactioncs on Microwave Theory and Techniques, vol. 58, pp. 57–64, Jan. 2010.

[4] C. Lu, A.-V. H. Pham, and M. Shaw, "Linearization of CMOS Broadband Power Amplifiers Through Combined Multigated Transistors and Capacitance Compensation," IEEE Transactions On Microwave Theory And Techniques, vol. 55, pp. 2320–2328, Nov. 2007.

[5] E. Abiri, G. Najibi, and S. Najibi, "Improvement of CMOS RF Gain Amplifier Using Differential Circuit Transconductance Linearization," Second International Conference on Computer and Electrical Engineering, pp. 295–298, 2009.

[6] W. L. Chan and J. R. Long, "A 58–65 GHz Neutralized CMOS Power Amplifier With PAE Above 10% at 1-V Supply," IEEE Journal of Solid-State Circuits, vol. 45, pp. 554–564, Mar. 2010.

[7] S. Moghadami, J. Isaac, and S. Ardanah, "A 0.2–0.3 THz CMOS Amplifier With Tunable Neutralization Technique," IEEE Transactions On Terahertz Science And Technology, vol. 5, no. 6, pp. 1088–1093, Nov. 2015.

[8] A. Tuffery, N. Deltimple, B. Leite, P. Cathelin, V. Knopik, and E. Kerhervé, "A 27.5-dBm linear reconfigurable CMOS power amplifier for 3GPP LTE applications," in 2011 IEEE 9th International New Circuits and systems conference, Bordeaux, 2011, pp. 221–224..

[9] E. Kaymaksut, B. François, and P. Reynaert, "Analysis and Optimization of TransformerBased Power Combining for Back-Off Efficiency Enhancement," IEEE Transactions on Circuits and Systems I: Regular Paper, vol. 60, no. 4, pp. 825–835, Apr. 2013.

[10] Y. Lee, and S. Hong, "A Dual-Power-Mode Output Matching Network for Digitally Modulated CMOS Power Amplifier," IEEE Transactions On Microwave Theory And Techniques, vol. 61, no. 4, pp. 1570–1579, Apr. 2013.

[11] Y. Xiaobao, W. Meng, S. Ying, W. Zhihua, and C. Baoyong, "A PAPR-Aware Dual-Mode Subgigahertz CMOS Power Amplifier for Short-Range Wireless Communication," IEEE Transactions on Circuits and Systems II: Express Brief, vol. 63, no. 1, pp. 44–48, Jan. 2016.

[12] Y. Cho et al., "Transformer Based Dual-Power-Mode CMOS Power Amplifier for Handset Applications," presented at the European Microwave Integrated Circuits Conference. Rome, 2014, pp. 436–439.

[13] E. Kaymaksut and P. Reynaert, "Dual-Mode CMOS Doherty LTE Power Amplifier With Symmetric Hybrid Transformer," IEEE Journal of Solid-State Circuits, vol. 50, no. 9, pp. 1974–1987, Sep. 2015.

Virtualizing Reconfigurable Hardware to Provide Scalability in Cloud Architectures

Oliver Knodel, Paul R. Genssler and Rainer G. Spallek

Department of Computer Science
Technische Universität Dresden
Dresden, Germany
Email: {firstname.lastname}@tu-dresden.de

***Abstract*—Field Programmable Gate Arrays (FPGAs) provide a promising opportunity to improve performance, security and energy efficiency of computing architectures, which are essential in modern data centers. Especially the background acceleration of complex and computationally intensive tasks is an important field of application. The flexible use of reconfigurable devices within a cloud context requires abstraction from the actual hardware through virtualization to offer these resources to service providers. In this paper, we enhance our related Reconfigurable Common Computing Frame (RC2F) approach, which is inspired by system virtual machines, for the profound virtualization of reconfigurable hardware in cloud services. Using partial reconfiguration, our hardware and software framework virtualizes physical FPGAs to provide multiple independent user designs on a single device. Essential components are the management of the virtual user-defined accelerators (vFPGAs), as well as their migration between physical FPGAs to achieve higher system-wide utilization levels. We create homogenous partitions on top of an inhomogeneous FPGA fabric to offer an abstraction from physical location, size and access to the real hardware. We demonstrate the possibilities and the resource trade-off of our approach in a basic scenario. Moreover, we present future perspectives for the use of FPGAs in cloud-based environments.**

Keywords–Cloud Computing; Virtualization; Reconfigurable Hardware; Partial Reconfiguration.

I. MOTIVATION

Cloud computing is based on the idea of computing as a utility. The user gains access to a shared pool of computing resources or services that can rapidly be allocated and released "with minimal management effort or service provider interaction" [1]. An essential advantage, compared to traditional models in which the user has access to a fixed number of computing resources, is the elasticity within a cloud. Even in peak load situations, a sufficient amount of resources are available [2].

With the theoretically unlimited number of resources, their enormous energy consumption arises as a major problem for data centers housing clouds. One possibility to enhance computation performance by simultaneously lowering energy consumption is the use of heterogeneous systems, offloading computationally intensive applications to special hardware co-processors or dedicated accelerators. Especially reconfigurable hardware, such as Field Programmable Gate Arrays (FPGAs) provide an opportunity to improve computing performance [3], security [4] and energy efficiency [5].

A profound and flexible integration of FPGAs into scalable data center infrastructures which satisfy the cloud characteristics is a task of growing importance in the field of energy-efficient cloud computing. In order to achieve such an integration, the virtualization of FPGA resources is necessary. The provision of virtual FPGAs (vFPGAs) makes reconfigurable resources available to customers of the data center provider. Therefore, service providers will be called *users* throughout this paper. The users can accelerate specific services, reduce energy consumption and thereby service costs.

The virtualization of reconfigurable hardware devices is a recurring challenge. Decades ago, the virtualization of FPGA devices started due to the limitation of logical resources [6]. Nowadays, FPGAs have grown in size and full utilization of the devices cannot always be achieved in practice. One possibility to increase utilization is our virtualization approach which allows for flexible design sizes and multiple hardware designs on the same physical FPGA. One challenge of this approach are the unsteady load situations of elastic clouds, which process short- and long-running acceleration services.

In this paper, we introduce our virtualization concept for FPGAs, which is inspired by traditional virtual machines (VMs). One physical FPGA can consist of multiple vFPGAs belonging to different services with different runtimes. Each vFPGA can be configured using partial reconfiguration [7] and the internal configuration access port (ICAP). The vFPGAs are, therefore, flexible in their physical size and location. Moreover, they are fully homogenous among each other and thereby become a wholesome virtualized cloud component, which supports even an efficient migration of a whole vFPGA context. Especially the vertical scaleability of vFPGAs from small designs up to full physical FPGAs is gaining importance by providing efficient utilization of the reconfigurable resources in modern cloud architectures.

The paper is structured as follows. Section II introduces similar concepts and related research in the field of virtualization of reconfigurable hardware, cloud architectures and bitstream relocation. In Section III, we give an overview on our virtualization concept. Our prototype, which implements our concept with homogenous and in their size flexible vFPGAs, is presented in Section IV followed by device utilization, vFPGA size and performance results in Section V. Section VI concludes and gives an outlook.

II. RELATED WORK

The provisoning of reconfigurable hardware in data centers and cloud environments has gained more and more importance in the last years as shown by the overview from Kachris et al. [8]. Initially used mainly on the network infrastructure level, FPGAs are now also employed on the application level of data centers. Typical use cases in this field are background accelerations of specific functions with static hardware designs. The FPGAs' special feature to reconfigure hardware at runtime is still used rather rarely. Examples are the anonymization of user requests [9] and increasing security [4] by outsourcing critical parts to attack-safe hardware implementations. In most cases, the FPGAs are not directly useable or configurable by the user, because the devices are due to a missing provisioning or virtualization hidden deeply in the data center.

A comparable contribution with stronger focus on the transfer of applications into an FPGA grid for high performance computing is shown in [10]. The application focus on a single cloud service model with background acceleration of services using FPGAs. An approach which places multiple user designs on a single FPGA is introduced by Fahmy et al. [11], using tightly attached FPGAs to offload computationally intensive tasks. The FPGAs are partially reconfigurable and can hold up to four individual user designs. The approach was extended by Asiatici et al. in [12] with additional memory virtualization. A cloud integration model with network-attached FPGAs and multiple user designs on one FPGA is introduced by Weerasinghe et al. [13].

The term *virtualization* itself is used for a wide range of concepts. An example for abstractions on the hardware description level is VirtualRC [14], which uses a uniform hardware / software interface to realize communication on different FPGA platforms. BORPH [15] provides a similar approach, employing a homogeneous UNIX interface for hardware and software. The FPGA paravirtualization pvFPGA [16], which integrates FPGA device drivers into a paravirtualized Xen virtual machine, presents a more sophisticated concept. A framework for the integration of reconfigurable hardware into cloud architecture is developed by Chen et al. [17] and Byma et al. [18].

Approaches more closely related to the *context-save-and-restore* mechanism required by our migration concept can be found in the field of bitstream readback, manipulation and hardware preemption. In ReconOS [19], hardware task preemption is used to capture and restore the states of all flip-flops and block RAMs on a Virtex-6 to allow multitasking with hardware threads. In combination with homogenous bitstreams for different physical vFPGA positions, methods like relocation of designs as shown in [20], provide an opportunity for an efficient context migration of virtualized FPGAs.

III. FPGA Virtualization Approach

As the cloud itself is based on virtualization, the integration of FPGAs requires a profound virtualization of the reconfigurable devices in order to provide the vFPGAs as good as other resources in the cloud. Furthermore, it is necessary to abstract from the underlying physical hardware.

A. *Requirements for Virtual FPGAs in a Cloud Environemnt*

As discussed in Section II, the term *virtualization* is used for a wide range of concepts. The application areas of FPGAs in clouds require a direct use of the FPGA resources to be efficient. Thus, an abstraction from the physical FPGA infrastructure is only possible in size and location. Our approach is related to traditional system virtualization with VMs that corresponds to a Type-1 bare-metal virtualization with use of a hypervisor [21]. This kind of virtualization is designed for

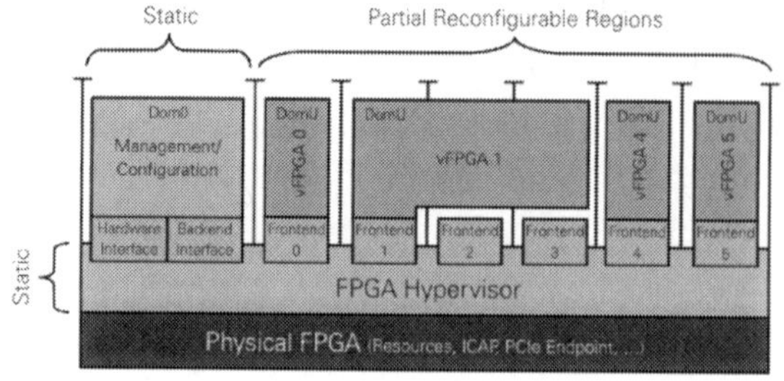

Figure 1. Paravirtualization concept used in RC2F to provide virtual FPGAs (vFPGAs) using partial reconfiguration. vFPGAs can be combined to group larger regions and thereby provide more resources.

the efficient utilization of the physical hardware with multiple users. Therefore, it is necessary to adapt the required FPGA resources closely to the requirements of the users' hardware design capsuled by vFPGAs. By this, an efficient utilization of the physical hardware with multiple concurrent vFPGAs on the same hardware can be achieved.

Furthermore, the vFPGA has to appear as a fully usable physical FPGA with separated interfaces and its own infrastructure management like clocking and resetting. For an efficient cloud architecture which requires elasticity [1], it is necessary to migrate vFPGAs with their complete context (registers and BlockRAM), which requires to enclose a complete state management of the vFPGA as described in [22]. An extraction of internal DSP registers is not supported in recent Xilinx FPGAs and must be considered in the design.

B. *FPGA Virtualization Approach*

We decided to virtualize the FPGA similar to a paravirtualized system VM executed by a hypervisor to provide access to the interfaces. Figure 1 shows an FPGA virtualization inspired by the paravirtualization introduced before. The virtualization is limited to the interfaces and the designs inside the reconfigurable regions, which constitute the actual vFPGAs as unprivileged Domain (DomU). Each vFPGA design is generated using the traditional design flow with predefined regions for dynamic partial reconfiguration [7] and static interfaces. The vFPGAs can have different sizes (Figure 1) and operate completely independent from each other. The infrastructure encapsulating the vFPGAs has to be located in the static region corresponding to a privileged domain (Dom0) or hypervisor.

The interface providing access to the vFPGAs is a so-called *frontend interface*, which is connected inside the hypervisor to the *backend interface* in the static FPGA region. There, all frontends are mapped to the static PCIe-Endpoint and the on-board memory controller inside the Dom0, which also manages the states of the vFPGAs.

IV. FPGA Prototype RC2F

Our prototype RC2F introduced in [23] provides multiple concurrent vFPGAs allocated by different users on a single physical FPGA. The main part of the FPGA frame(work) consists of a hypervisor managing configuration and user cores, as well as monitoring of status information. The controller's memory space is accessible from the host through an API. Input- and output-FIFOs are providing high throughput for streaming applications. The vFPGAs appear to the user as individual devices inside the System VM on the host.

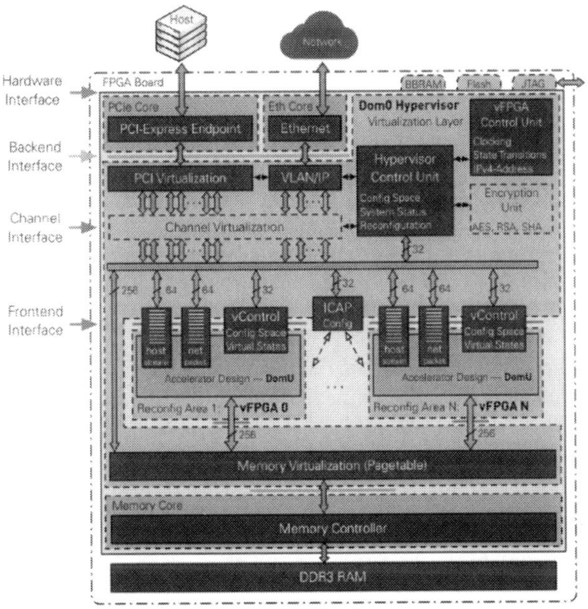

Figure 2. Virtualization frame RC2F with hypervisor, I/O components and partial reconfigurable areas housing the vFPGAs. The vFPGAs have access to the host using PCIe (FIFO interface and config space), to the Cloud network using Ethernet and the virtualized DDR3 memory.

A. *System Architecture*

The physical FPGAs are located inside a host system and are accessible via PCIe. On both hardware components (host and FPGA), there are hypervisors managing access, assignment and configuration of the (v)FPGAs. Based on our concept, we transform the FPGAs into vFPGAs with an additional state management and a static frontend interface as shown in Figure 1. Our architecture, designed to provide the vFPGAs, is shown in Figure 2. The hypervisors manage the on-chip communication between backend and frontend interfaces for PCIe (Our prototype uses a PCIe-Core from Xillybus for DMA access [24]), Ethernet and a DDR3 RAM. The RAM is virtualized using page tables, managed by the host hypervisor, which also manages the vFPGA states we introduced in [22]. The number of frontends and their locations are defined by the physical FPGA architecture as shown in Figure 6. The *Hypervisor Control Unit* manages the ICAP controller and the *vControl* units, which maintain and monitor the vFPGAs.

To exchange large amounts of data between the host (VM) and the vFPGAs a FIFO interface is used. To exchange state and control information the vFPGAs can be controlled by the user via a memory interface as shown in Figure 3. The memory is mainly intended for simple transfers and configuration tasks like resets, state management (pause, run, readback, migrate) and the selection of a vFPGA system clock. In addition to these static fields, there is also a user-describable memory region which can be used as virtual I/O. The communication using Ethernet is also provided but out of the scope of this paper.

B. *Configuration of the FPGA Hypervisor*

The tasks of the FPGA hypervisor are the management of its local vFPGAs and their encapsulation, the state management, as well as the reconfiguration using the ICAP. The interaction between host and FPGA hypervisor is based on the configuration memory shown in Figure 4, which includes

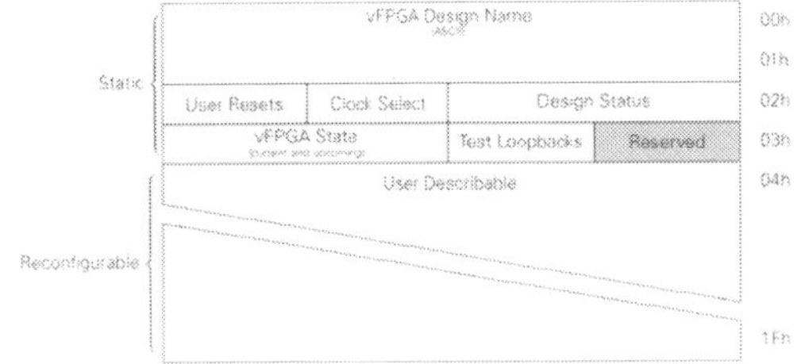

Figure 3. Register and memory interface for the management of vFPGAs accessible by the user VM (rc2f_cs).

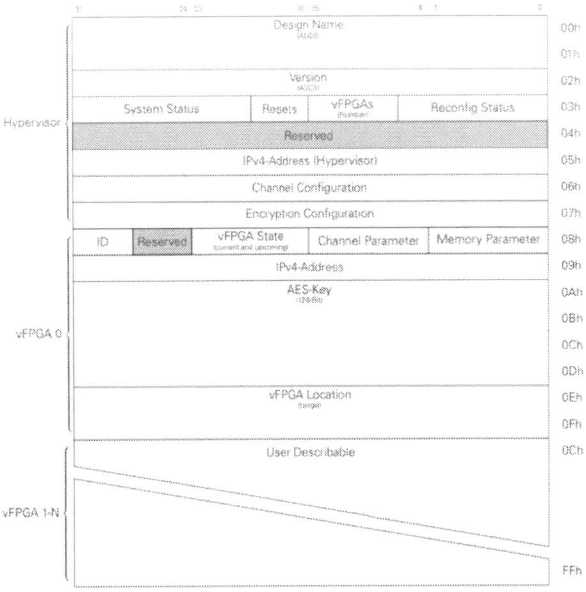

Figure 4. Register and memory interface for the management of the FPGA hypervisor accessible by the host hypervisor (rc2f_gcs).

configuration of the FPGA hypervisor (system status, reconfiguration data and status) and the administration of the vFPGAs. Other important vFPGA-related entries are an AES-key for encryption of the vFPGA-bitsteam and the allocated vFPGA region(s) for additional validation during reconfiguration. The information inside the FPGA hypervisor are only accessible and modifiable through the host hypervisor.

C. *The Role of the Host-Hypervisor*

Our virtualization concept on the host-system includes passing through the vFPGAs' FIFO channels and the configuration memories from the host-hypervisor to the user VMs (DomU) and the FPGA hypervisor memory to the management VM (Dom0). The overall system architecture on hypervisor level of host and FPGA is shown in Figure 5. The frontend FIFOs and the FPGA memories are mapped to device files inside the host hypervisor. There, our system forwards the user devices to the assigned VM using inter-domain communication based on vChan from Zhang et al. [25] in our Xen virtualized environment, similar to pvFPGA [16].

The management VM thereby accesses the FPGA hypervisor's configuration memory and the ICAP on the FPGA via a dedicated FIFO interface for the configuration stream (read and write). Thus, only the hypervisors can configure the vFPGA regions on the physical FPGA whereby a sufficient level of security can be guaranteed.

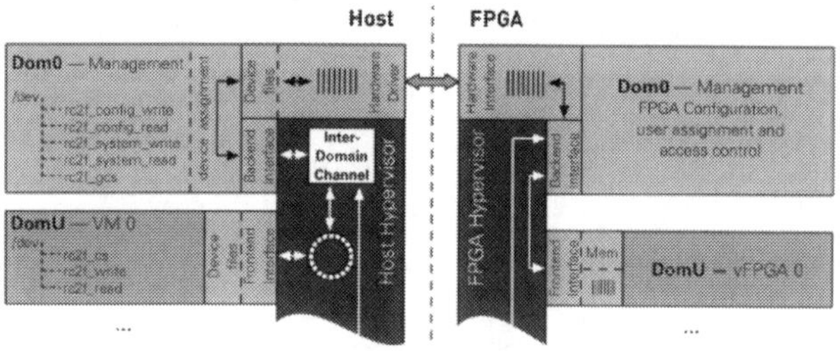

Figure 5. System architecture on the hypervisor level of the host system. FIFOs (rc2f_write, rc2f_read) and configuration memories (rc2f_cs) are displayed in the different host memories.

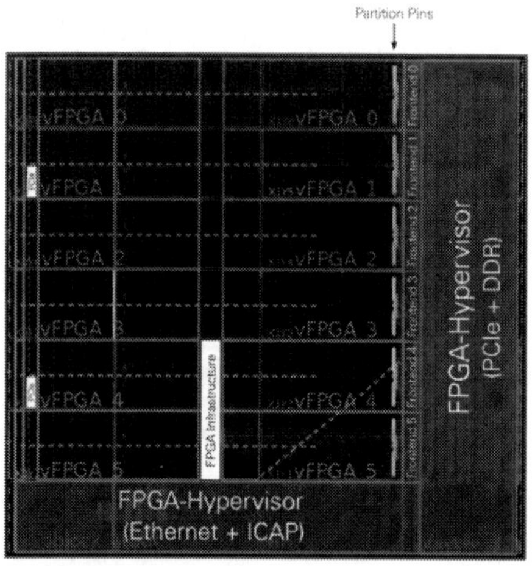

Figure 6. Layout of a Xilinx Virtex-7 XC7VX485T with six vFPGA regions configurable using dynamic partial reconfiguration. The regions and their number are determined by the height of the configuration frames, which consist of one complete column inside a clock region. Regions are homogenous to allow migration of vFPGAs.

D. Mapping vFPGAs onto physical FPGAs

In our example we use six frontends on a Xilinx Virtex-7. Depending on the resources required, the utilization of up to six different-sized vFPGAs is possible with the same static without reprogramming. If one of the vFPGAs covers more than one region, only one frontend connection is used as shown in Figure 1. Among the vFPGAs, the partition pins (PP) between the static and the reconfigurable regions are placed with identical column offset as shown in Figure 6. The regions forming the vFPGAs are not free from static routes as for example the region vFPGA 5 shows.

To reduce migration times, all components which hold the context of the current vFPGA design as registers, FIFOs or BlockRAM, are placed at the same positions inside each vFPGA. Therefore, it is necessary that all of these positions exist in each region. Hardmacros like PCIe-Endpoints or parts of the FPGA infrastructure interrupt the homogenous structures. Thus, we establish homogenous vFPGAs, which are identical among each other by excluding these areas in all vFPGAs as shown in Figure 6. The advantage of this approach is that only one mask file is necessary to extract the content of the different vFPGAs. Furthermore, it allows the provision of almost identical vFPGAs.

E. Extended Design flow

For our virtualization we extend the Xilinx Vivado design flow to generate vFPGA bitstreams from user-netlists for every possible vFPGA position. First, directly after synthesis the required region size (single, double, etc.) is chosen (see Table I for appropriate vFPGAs). Afterwards, the design is placed at a first vFPGA region. Before the routing step, the vFPGA region is expanded over the full width of the vFPGA for unlimited routing of the design inside the uninterrupted region. The placements of the same design for all the other vFPGA positions are created by setting the LOC (Location) and BEL (Basic Element Location) information accordingly to the initial placed design. Only the routing is carried out for the additional vFPGA designs to allow static routes inside the different vFPGAs, resulting in designs with identical register and BlockRAM positions for each vFPGA locations on the physical FPGA. After generation of the first bitstream, a mask for extracting the context bits is generated to allow an efficient migration in significantly less time compared to our first approach in [22]. This allows flexible placement of the vFPGA designs at various positions in a cloud system, as well as the migration between vFPGAs on the same or to other physical FPGAs. The bitstreams required for all possible vFPGA positions belonging to a single user design are stored as virtual reconfigurable accelerator images (vRAI).

F. Description of vFPGAs

The execution of a vRAI requires allocation of a vFPGA which fulfills all requirements. Therefore, it is necessary to describe the vFPGAs in a particular configuration file. Figure 7 gives an overview of such an configuration, which is evaluated by the resource management system to allocate the necessary resources. After allocation the host hypervisor chooses from the vRAI the appropriate bitstream and configures the device.

```
service = 'ba'                  #Background Acceleration Service
name = 'vfpga-kmeans'           #vFPGA/User Design Name
vm = ['vm1-pvm']                #VM-Instance Name
vfpga = 1                       #Number of vFPGA
size = [3]                      #vFPGA Size
memory = [2000]                 #DDR-Memory Size in MByte
vif = ['ip=10.0.0.43']          #vFPGA-IP
boot = ['running']              #Initial vFPGA-State
design = ['kmeans.vrai']#Initial Design
```

Figure 7. Configuration file for the allocation of a single vFPGA with network access and external memory of 2 GByte.

V. Implementation Results and Scenario

The resources required for the implementation described in the previous section are shown in the following with a real-world scenario based on our motivation from Section I.

A. Implementation

The resource consumption of our prototype introduced in Figure 2 is shown in Table I. Furthermore, the table introduces the size of homogenous vFPGA regions as outlined in Figure 6.

$$\vec{p} = \begin{pmatrix} SliceLUTs \\ SliceRegister \\ BlockRAM \\ DSP \\ \cdots \end{pmatrix} \tag{1}$$

is used in the following to describe the resources. The aggregated homogenous vFPGAs $\overrightarrow{\rho_{agg}}$ can be calculated using

$$\overrightarrow{\rho_{agg}} = \overrightarrow{\rho_{single}} \cdot n_{agg} - (n_{agg} - 1) \cdot \overrightarrow{\rho_{ppr}} \tag{2}$$

where $\overrightarrow{\rho_{single}}$ are the resources of a single vFPGA region, n_{agg} is the number of aggregated vFPGAs and $\overrightarrow{\rho_{ppr}}$ represents the partition pin region (PPR) necessary to exclude the unused frontend interfaces from the grouped vFPGAs. The open frontends are therefore treated as stubs and are securely sealed using a partial vFPGA bitstream. The cost of the provision of identical vFPGAs are in the case of our Virtex-7 XC7VX485T FPGA only 6.44% of slices registers/LUTs and 8.33% of the BlockRAM tiles compared to a compete, but inhomogeneous region. In our floor planning shown in Figure 6 there are no further DSPs affected. All regions except the largest one (Hexa), which has only one possible position, are homogenous.

The throughput between vFPGAs and host (PCIe Gen2 8x on a Xilinx VC707) with different numbers of concurrently active vFPGAs is shown in Figure 8. The throughput of a single design is limited by a user clock of 100 MHz and a 64-bit data interface. Starting from three vFPGAs, a limitation due to the concurrent users occurs. The throughput shown in Figure 8 is the minimal guaranteed throughput for each vFPGA.

The size of the vRAI packages and the number of possible locations on the physical device are shown in Table II. With 69.2 MByte, a quad vFPGA with bitstreams for three possible positions and a mask file for context migration is the largest vRAI package. Compared to our first approach, the information necessary for context migration is reduced by several orders of magnitude by using homogenous vFPGAs.

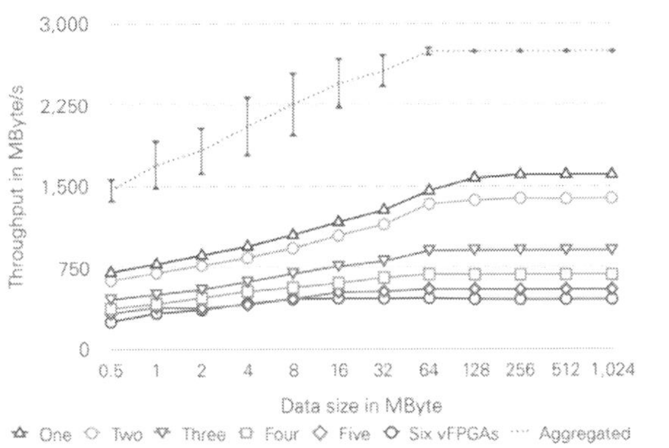

Figure 8. Throughput between host and FPGA with different numbers of concurrent vFPGAs. The diagram shows for each number of vFPGAs the average throughput of one representative vFPGA. The aggregated throughput is thereby the average throughput of all vFPGA compositions on the device.

B. *Scenario*

In the following, we show a scenario based on a typical real-world application for our virtualization approach. The goal is it to migrate vFPGA designs to achieve a high utilization as shown in Figure 9(c). In a system with jobs arriving and being finished at different points in time, situations as shown in Figure 9(a) can occur. The fragmentation of the physical FPGA restricts only one small vFPGA and one aggregated double sized vFPGA. By migrating the design from user 3 from vFPGA 5 to vFPGA 0 as shown in Figure 9(b), an area for a group of three vFPGAs (triple) becomes available and makes higher utilization of the physical device possible.

VI. Conclusion and Outlook

This paper presented a comprehensive virtualization concept for reconfigurable hardware and its integration into a cloud environment. Our definition of the term *virtualization*

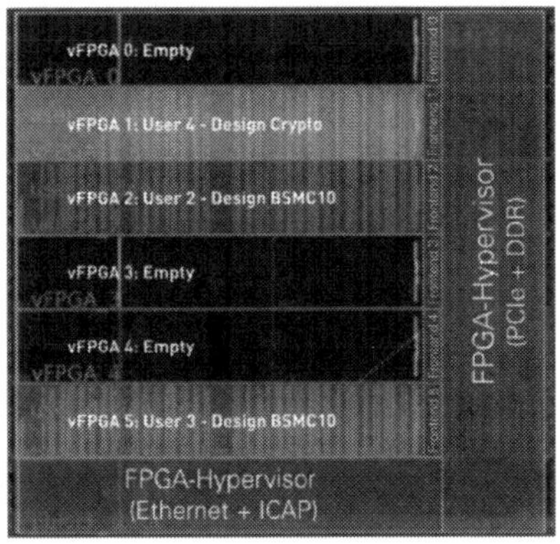

(a) Fragmentation of the physical FPGA caused by dynamic de- and allocation.

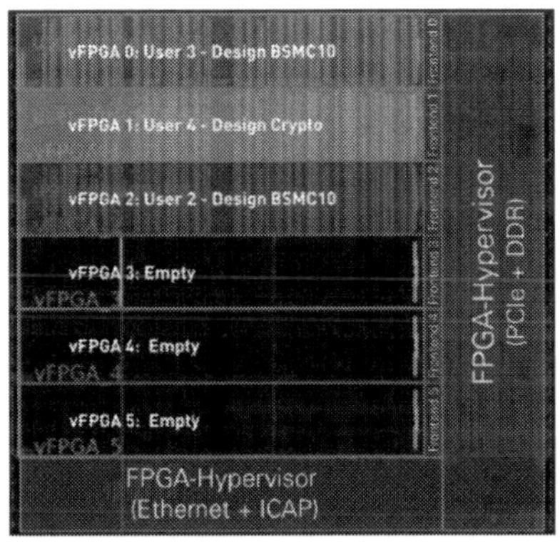

(b) Defragmentation providing aggregated vFPGA regions for larger designs.

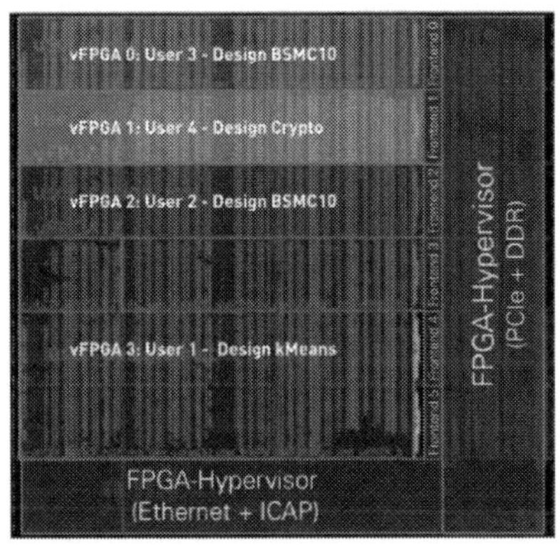

(c) Utilization of the free region with a design using three aggregated vFPGAs (Triple).

Figure 9. Szenario with different users and designs on a Xilinx Virtex-7 XC7VX485T with six (vertically) scaleable vFPGAs.

is inspired by traditional VMs whose functionalities are transferred to reconfigurable hardware. We develop a paravirtualized infrastructure on a physical FPGA device with multiple vFPGAs. The concept is integrated into a framework, which allows for interaction with the vFPGAs similar to traditional VMs. We create homogenous regions for the vFPGAs on the physical FPGA to optimize the process of vFPGA migration between different physical FPGAs. Implementation details are described, the necessary resources and the virtualization overhead are presented.

TABLE I. NUMBER OF AVAILABLE RESOURCES INSIDE THE STATIC AND THE AGGREGATED VFPGA REGIONS AND UTILIZATION OF STATIC CONTAINING INFRASTRUCTURE AND HYPERVISOR. THE PARTITION PIN REGION (PPR) IS NECESSARY TO EXCLUDE AND ISOLATE UNUSED PARTITION PINS (PP).

Ressource	Static region	Utilization of static region					PPR	Into aggregated vFPGA regions					
		HF[a]	P[b]	E[c]	M[d]	Total		Single	Dual	Triple	Quad	Quint	Hexa[e]
Slice LUTs	94,824	26%	3%	2%	11%	**42%**	1,200	30,800	60,400	90,000	120,800	151,600	188,400
Slice Register	189,648	11%	2%	1%	4%	**18%**	2,400	61,600	120,800	180,000	241,600	303,200	376,800
Block RAM Tile	369	23%	2%	2%	3%	**30%**	0	100	200	300	400	500	600
DSPs	726	–	–	–	–	–	20	340	660	980	1,320	1,660	1,940

[a]**HF**: Hypervisor and Frontends [b]**P**: PCIe-Endpoint [c]**E**: Ethernet [d]**M**: DDR3 Memory [e]Largest region without considering homogeneity

TABLE II. SIZE OF A SINGLE BITSTREAM FOR A VFPGA REGION, NUMBER OF POSSIBLE POSITIONS INSIDE THE FPGA AND SIZE OF THE VRAIS.

	Single	Dual	Triple	Quad	Quint	Hexa
Bitstream (MByte)	4.8	9.0	13.0	17.3	21.3	25.3
Locations	6	5	4	3	2	1
vRAI (MByte)	33.6	54.0	65.0	69.2	63.9	50.6

One significant result of this paper is that the provision of homogenous FPGA resources is possible with state-of-the-art FPGAs. We think that such approaches are necessary for establishing FPGAs in modern data centers housing clouds. Certainly, when cloud providers like Amazon expand their cloud architectures with high-end FPGAs, such as Xilinx Virtex-7 UltraScale devices [26] it is necessary to utilize the hardware efficiently with multiple designs in a scaleable frame inside one physical FPGA. Such kind of flexible approach allows for adaption the individual resources to the users' requirements.

REFERENCES

[1] P. Mell and T. Grance, "The NIST definition of cloud computing, Revised", *Computer Security Division, Information Technology Laboratory, NIST Gaithersburg*, 2011.

[2] M. Armbrust, A. Fox, R. Griffith, *et al.*, "A view of cloud computing", *Communications of the ACM*, vol. 53, pp. 50–58, 2010.

[3] T. El-Ghazawi, E. El-Araby, M. Huang, *et al.*, "The promise of high-performance reconfigurable computing", *IEEE Computer*, vol. 41, no. 2, pp. 69–76, 2008.

[4] J.-A. Mondol, "Cloud security solutions using FPGA", in *PacRim, Pacific Rim Conf. on*, IEEE, 2011, pp. 747–752.

[5] A. Putnam, A. M. Caulfield, E. S. Chung, *et al.*, "A reconfigurable fabric for accelerating large-scale datacenter services", in *Computer Architecture (ISCA), 41st Int'l Symp. on*, 2014.

[6] W. Fornaciari and V. Piuri, "Virtual FPGAs: Some steps behind the physical barriers", in *Parallel and Distributed Processing*, Springer, 1998, pp. 7–12.

[7] Xilinx Inc., *Vivado Design Suite User Guide – Partial Reconfiguration*, UG909 (v2017.1), April 5, 2017.

[8] C. Kachris and D. Soudris, "A survey on reconfigurable accelerators for cloud computing", in *Field Programmable Logic and Applications (FPL), 26th Int'l Conf. on*, 2016.

[9] K. Eguro and R. Venkatesan, "FPGAs for trusted cloud computing", in *Field Programmable Logic and Applications (FPL), 22nd Int'l Conf. on*, IEEE, 2012, pp. 63–70.

[10] J. Dondo Gazzano, F. Sanchez Molina, F. Rincon, and J. C. López, "Integrating reconfigurable hardware-based grid for high performance computing", *The Scientific World Journal*, 2015.

[11] S. A. Fahmy, K. Vipin, and S. Shreejith, "Virtualized FPGA accelerators for efficient cloud computing", in *Cloud Computing Technology (CloudCom), Int'l Conf. on*, IEEE, 2015.

[12] M. Asiatici, N. George, K. Vipin, S. A. Fahmy, and P. Ienne, "Designing a virtual runtime for FPGA accelerators in the cloud", in *Field Programmable Logic and Applications, Int'l Conf. on*, 2016.

[13] J. Weerasinghe, F. Abel, C. Hagleitner, and A. Herkersdorf, "Enabling FPGAs in Hyperscale Data Centers", in *Cloud and Big Data Computing (CBDCom), Int'l Conf. on*, IEEE, 2015.

[14] R. Kirchgessner, G. Stitt, A. George, and H. Lam, "VirtualRC: a virtual FPGA platform for applications and tools portability", in *FPGAs, Proc. of the ACM/SIGDA Int'l Symp. on*, 2012.

[15] H. K.-H. So and R. Brodersen, "A unified hardware/software runtime environment for FPGA-based reconfigurable computers using BORPH", *ACM Transactions on Embedded Computing Systems (TECS)*, vol. 7, no. 2, p. 14, 2008.

[16] W. Wang, M. Bolic, and J. Parri, "pvFPGA: Accessing an FPGA-based hardware accelerator in a paravirtualized environment.", *Hardware/Software Codesign and System Synthesis (CODES+ISSS), 2013 Int'l Conf. on*, pp. 1–9, 2013.

[17] F. Chen, Y. Shan, Y. Zhang, *et al.*, "Enabling FPGAs in the cloud", in *Computing Frontiers, Proc. of the 11th ACM Conf. on*, ACM, 2014, p. 3.

[18] S. Byma, J. G. Steffan, H. Bannazadeh, A. L. Garcia, and P. Chow, "FPGAs in the Cloud: Booting Virtualized Hardware Accelerators with OpenStack", in *Field-Programmable Custom Computing Machines (FCCM), 22nd Annual Int'l Symp. on*, IEEE, 2014, pp. 109–116.

[19] M. Happe, A. Traber, and A. Keller, "Preemptive Hardware Multitasking in ReconOS", in *Applied Reconfigurable Computing*, Springer, 2015, pp. 79–90.

[20] J. Rettkowski, K. Friesen, and D. Göhringer, "RePaBit: Automated generation of relocatable partial bitstreams for Xilinx Zynq FPGAs", in *ReConFigurable Computing and FPGAs (ReConFig), 2016 International Conference on*, IEEE, 2016, pp. 1–8.

[21] J. E. Smith and R. Nair, "The architecture of virtual machines", *Computer*, vol. 38, no. 5, pp. 32–38, 2005.

[22] O. Knodel, P. Genßler, and R. Spallek, "Migration of long-running tasks between reconfigurable resources using virtualization", in *ACM SIGARCH Computer Architecture News Volume 44, HEART 2016*, ACM, 2016.

[23] O. Knodel and R. G. Spallek, "Computing framework for dynamic integration of reconfigurable resources in a cloud", in *2015 Euromicro Conference on Digital System Design, DSD 2015*, IEEE, 2015, pp. 337–344.

[24] Xillybus Ltd., Haifa, Israel, *An FPGA IP core for easy DMA over PCIe*, Website, Online: http://xillybus.com, 2017.

[25] X. Zhang, S. McIntosh, P. Rohatgi, and J. L. Griffin, "Xensocket: A high-throughput interdomain transport for virtual machines", in *Middleware 2007*, Springer, 2007, pp. 184–203.

[26] Amazon Inc., *Amazon EC2 F1 Instances – Run Custom FPGAs in the AWS Cloud*, Website, Online: https://aws.amazon.com/ec2/instance-types/f1/, 2017.

Local Alignment Search in Genetic Sequences on a Low-Cost FPGA

Timm Bostelmann, Thomas Fabian Starke and Sergei Sawitzki

FH Wedel (University of Applied Sciences)
Wedel, Germany
Email: bos@fh-wedel.de, starke.thomas@yahoo.de, saw@fh-wedel.de

Abstract—**The search for local alignments in genetic sequences is a common challenge in the field of bioinformatics. The problem is to find similar subsequences in genetic sequences of different lengths. Usually, the search is done in a genome database that contains hundreds of millions of sequences and rising. Due to the large amount of data, the speed is of a high concern. The search for a local alignment between a query-sequence and a database-sequence is usually done with the Basic Local Alignment Search Tool (BLAST) algorithm. In this work, an implementation of an accelerator for the BLAST algorithm on a low-cost Field-Programmable Gate Array (FPGA) is presented. The data is processed in a tree-like hardware architecture. The advantages and disadvantages of the presented approach are shown and discussed. Finally, an outlook is given on the pending issues of the current implementation. The main contribution of this paper is the focus on an implementation with support of low-cost hardware.**

Keywords*–*FPGA; BLAST; DNA; local alignment

I. Introduction

In the field of bioinformatics, the comparison of genetic sequences is as challenging as it is important. Usually, a query-sequence is compared with a set of sequences that are stored in a genome-database. The goal is to find partial or complete similarities. This is for example useful if an unknown virus is analyzed because properties of the unknown virus can be derived from similarities to known entities.

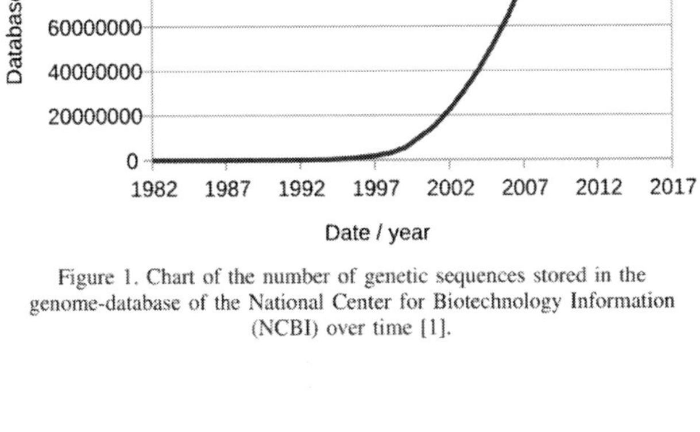

Figure 1. Chart of the number of genetic sequences stored in the genome-database of the National Center for Biotechnology Information (NCBI) over time [1].

Over the last decades, the size and number of genetic sequences stored in genome-databases has risen considerably, as shown in Figure 1. Further growth of the databases is to be expected, due to the shrinking costs of genome sequencing (see Figure 2). As a result, a fast and efficient implementation of the search-algorithms is mandatory.

The preferred method for the comparison of genetic sequences of different lengths is the local alignment search. Where the global alignment search is well suited to find similarities in sequences of equal or similar length, the local alignment search is utilized to find similar subsequences in genetic sequences of different lengths. However, this process conveys an extremely high computational effort. An established approach is the BLAST algorithm which has been introduced by Altschul et al. [3].

There have been several works on the acceleration of the local alignment search with high-performance FPGAs [4]–[6]. Usually, the proposed accelerators utilize clusters of several high-performance FPGAs. There are even industrial BLAST-accelerators based on such hardware available, like [7]. However, in this work an implementation on a low-cost FPGA development and education board is presented and analyzed. It is based on a tree-like data-flow [8] architecture.

The rest of this work is structured as follows. In Section II, the principles of the BLAST algorithm are introduced. Based on this introduction, in Section III, an implementation of the BLAST algorithm on a low-cost FPGA board is described. In Section IV, the results of this implementation are presented. Furthermore, the advantages and disadvantages compared to an implementation in software are discussed. Finally in Section V, this work is summarized and a prospect to further optimization is given.

II. Background

The BLAST algorithm is used for the search of similarities (i.e., local alignments) between a query-sequence and the sequences of a genome-database. It generates a list of positions or regions that are similar between the query-sequence and the database-sequence. Additionally, the significance of every hit is generated as a measure of the similarity.

The BLAST algorithm can be divided into five steps which are described in the following. It has to be remarked that the first four steps have to be executed for all entries in the genome-database and are therefore especially time-sensitive.

Step 1: Creation of the hit-matrix

For the search of a query-sequence w in a database-sequence u with a scoring-function $\sigma(\alpha \rightarrow \beta)$ both sequences are segmented into overlapping words of the length $q \in \mathbb{N}$.

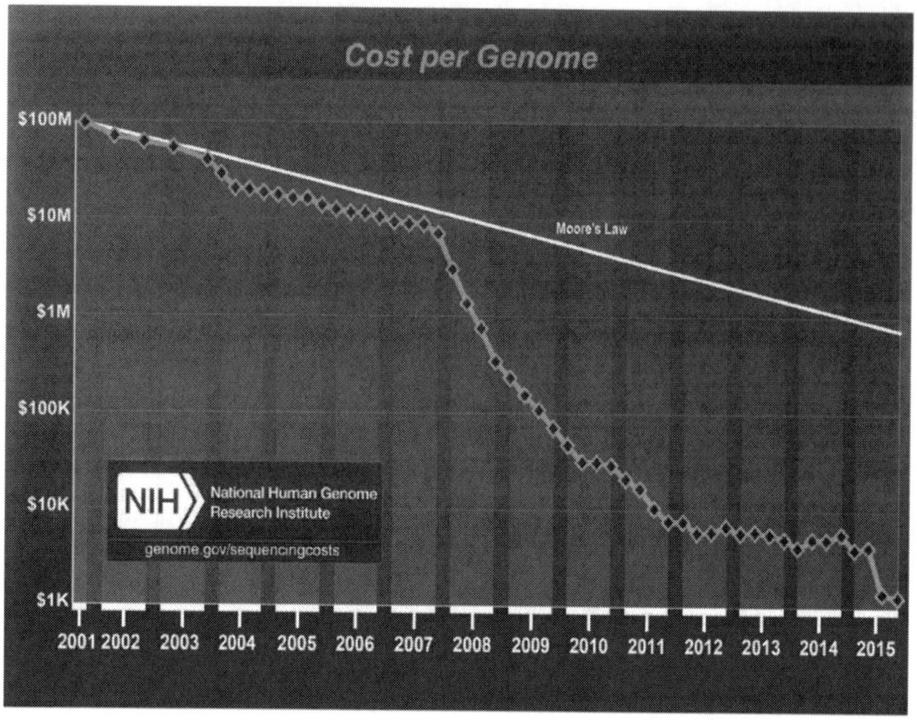

Figure 2. Chart of the cost per sequenced genome over time [2].

The following example is assuming a word length of $q = 3$:

$$\text{AVKTCSGA} \Rightarrow \{\text{AVK, VKT, KTC, TCS, CSG, SGA}\} \quad (1)$$

The resulting set of words is called w-mers. The generated words are called q-words. The scoring-function σ is used to determine the degree of similarity between a symbol of the query-sequence and a symbol of the database-sequence. Depending on the sequence-type usually either the Block Substitution Matrix (BLOSUM) or the Point Accepted Mutation (PAM) matrix is used to determine the degree of similarity. Deletions and insertions are handled as follows:

$$\sigma(\text{“-”} \rightarrow \beta) = \sigma(\alpha \rightarrow \text{“-”}) = -\infty \quad (2)$$

Assuming i and j are the indexes in the query- and the database-sequence, a pair (i, j) is a hit, if for a threshold k the following inequation is true:

$$i \in \{0 \ldots |u| - q + 1\} \quad (3)$$

$$j \in \{0 \ldots |w| - q + 1\} \quad (4)$$

$$score_{\sigma}(\underbrace{u[i \ldots i + q - 1]}_{\text{q-word in u}}, \underbrace{w[j \ldots j + q - 1]}_{\text{q-word in w}}) \geq k \quad (5)$$

Every q-word of the query-sequence is compared with every q-word of the database-sequence by the scoring-function σ. The results are stored in a hit-matrix, as shown in Figure 3.

Step 2: Extraction of relevant hits

To optimize the following steps three and four, the relevant hits in the hit-matrix are identified. Therefore, all hits that are located adjacently on a common diagonal are grouped like shown in Figure 4. Usually, a hit-length d is specified as the minimal length of the diagonals. The gray hits in Figure 4 are not grouped and will therefore be sorted out.

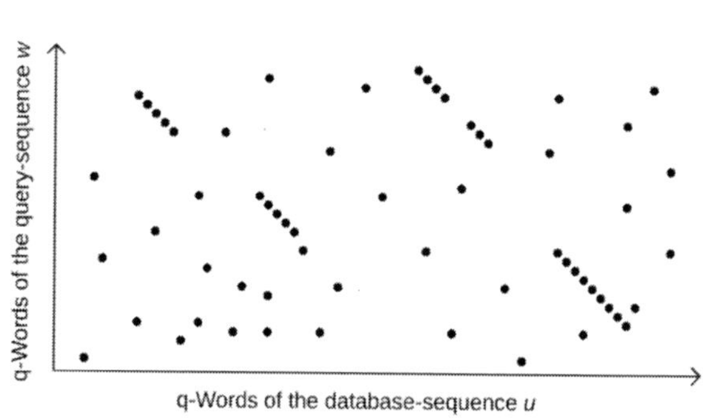

Figure 3. An exemplary hit-matrix generated by the first step of the BLAST algorithm.

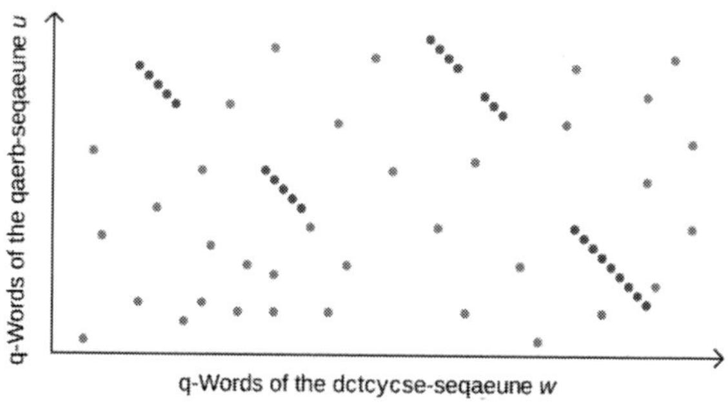

Figure 4. An exemplary hit-matrix after the extraction of relevant hits by the second step of the BLAST algorithm.

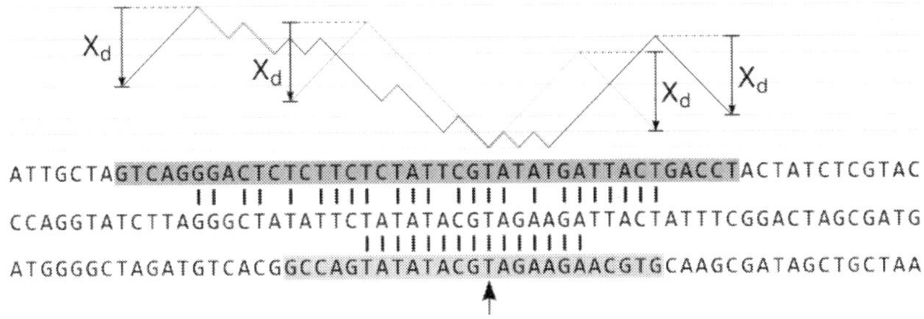

Figure 5. An example of a gapped extension for two different sequence pairs.

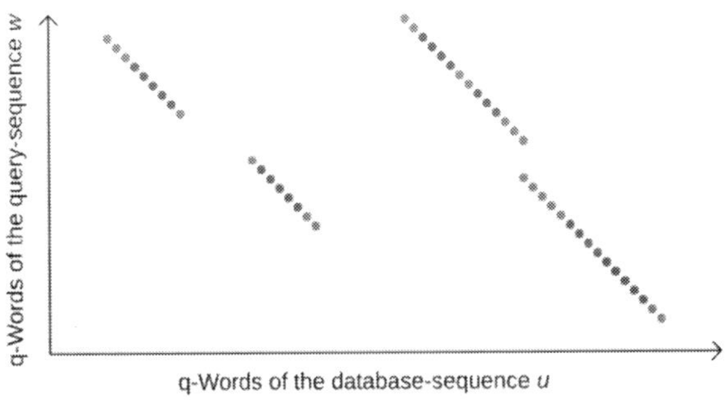

Figure 6. An exemplary hit-matrix after the ungapped extension by the third step of the BLAST algorithm.

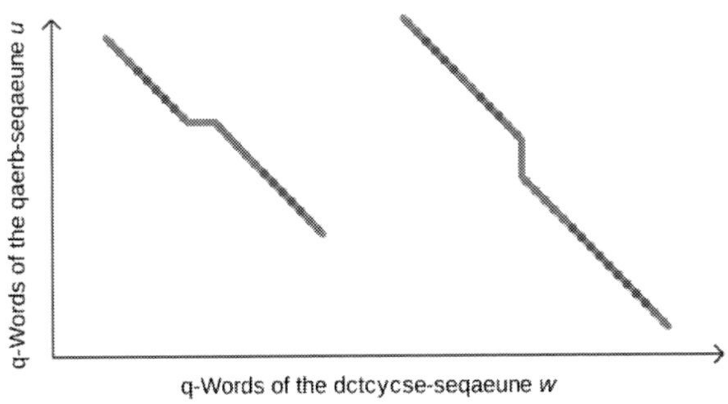

Figure 7. An exemplary hit-matrix after the gapped extension by the fourth step of the BLAST algorithm.

Step 3: Ungapped extension

If a pair of hits is aligned on the same diagonal and its distance is lower then the maximum distance δ, a point (i, j) between the hits is extended in both directions on the common diagonal. The sensitivity of the extension is determined by the drop-off parameter $X_d \geq 0$. For a leftward extension, the sequences $u[1 \ldots i-1]$ and $w[1 \ldots j-1]$ are compared. For a rightward extension, the sequences $u[i \ldots |u|]$ and $w[j \ldots |w|]$ are compared. The scores of those comparisons are summed up and the maximum X_{max} is stored. If this value is lower than the drop-off parameter $(X_{max} - X_d)$, the extension is stopped. The sequences generated by this stage are called maximum-scoring segment pair. An exemplary result is shown in Figure 6.

Step 4: Gapped extension

In this step, regions of high similarity with acceptable gaps between two sequences are determined. This is for example

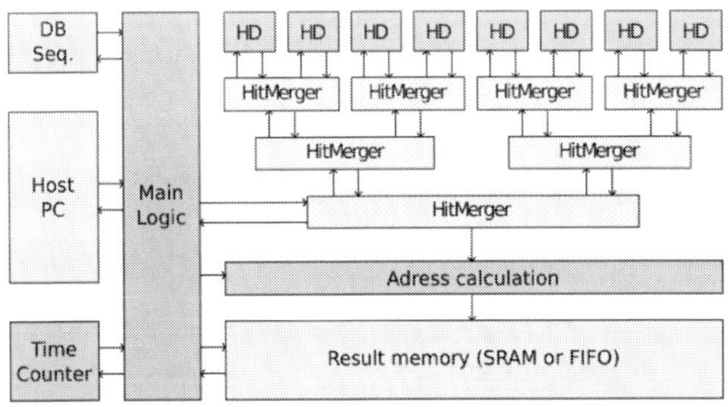

Figure 8. Global structure of the tree-like architecture for the acceleration of the BLAST algorithm on a FPGA.

useful to skip insertions or deletions in a sequence, which can be for example caused by mutations. In the hit-matrix, the result is a shift of the diagonal (see Figure 7).

After identifying a region of high similarity, a point (i, j) between two hits is chosen as a starting point. Then, this point is expanded towards the two selected hits. The symbols of the two sequences are compared and the result is summed up, where a match corresponds to +1 and a mismatch corresponds to −1. The extension is stopped when the sum falls below $X_{max} - X_d$. In Figure 5, this process is shown for two different sequence pairs.

Step 5: Output generation

In this step, the local alignments between the query- and the database-sequence are sorted by relevance and stored in a list.

III. Implementation

In this section, an implementation of the first two steps of the BLAST algorithm on a FPGA is described. These steps have been chosen because in sum they convey the majority of the computational effort, as has been shown by Cameron et al. [9]. The implementation is based on a tree-like architecture for the parallel extraction and combination of local alignments between a query- and a database-sequence (see Figure 8).

Due to restrictions of the current implementation, the scoring-function σ is realized as equality-function:

$$\sigma(\alpha \rightarrow \beta) = \begin{cases} \mathit{True},\ \mathit{Hit} & \text{for } \alpha = \beta \\ \mathit{False},\ \mathit{noHit} & \text{for } \alpha \neq \beta \end{cases} \tag{6}$$

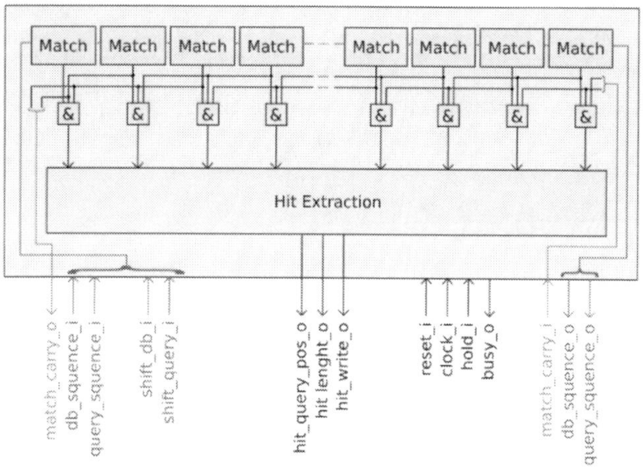

Figure 9. Structure of a hit-detector.

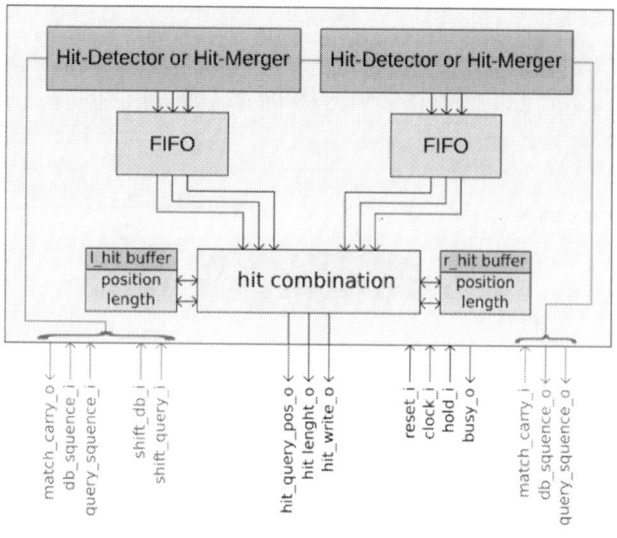

Figure 10. Structure of a hit-merger.

The maximal size of a sequence-element is five bit because a protein can have only up to 21 different amino acids. An empty or uninitialized element is described by the vector "00000".

The *Time Counter* (see Figure 8) is used for benchmark purposes only. The database-sequence is stored in the *DB Seq.* memory. The query-sequence is stored directly in the leaves of the tree-like structure. The rest of the blocks is described in the following subsections.

A. Hit-detector

The hit-detectors (*HD* in Figure 8) are the leafs of the tree. As shown in Figure 9, a hit-detector consists of a chain of n hit-matchers and a hit-extractor. The hit-matchers are basically arranged as two parallel shift registers – one for the query-sequence and one for the database-sequence – that can be shifted independently. Furthermore, they contain the logic for the scoring-function σ. The q-words introduced above are generated by AND gates of the width q.

First, the query sequence is loaded to the hit-matches. Then, the hit-extraction is started by shifting the database-sequence into the hit-matchers. The hit-extractor stores the positions and lengths of all hits that occur while shifting in the database-sequence.

B. Hit-merger

The hit-mergers (as depicted in Figure 10) are the nodes of the tree. They are used to merge overlapping hits of the previous stage in a binary tree. The previous stage can either be the hit-detectors of the first level or other hit-mergers.

The incoming hits are buffered in two FIFOs, one for the left child and one for the right child. If an entry of the left FIFO contains a right-aligned hit, the hit is stored in the left buffer. If an entry of the right FIFO contains a left-aligned hit, the hit is stored in the right buffer. If the hit combination unit detects an overlapping hit (between FIFO and FIFO or FIFO and buffer), the hits are merged and sent to the next level of hit-mergers or the result memory. Hits that can not be merged (i.e., do not overlap) are sent directly to the next level.

The length of the FIFOs depends on the hit-detector width w, the width of the q-words q and the current level in the tree th as follows:

$$f = \frac{w}{q+1} \cdot 2^{(th-1)} \tag{7}$$

The word-width of the FIFOs depends on the hit-detector width w, the current level in the tree th and the maximum query-length l_{max} as follows:

$$width = \mathrm{ld}(w) + \mathrm{ld}(th-1) + \mathrm{ld}(l_{max}) \tag{8}$$

IV. Results

In this section, the FPGA based implementation presented above is compared to an implementation in software and the impact of different parameters (i.e., query length, q-word size and hit-detector width) is evaluated. The FPGA based implementation is executed on an "Altera DE2 Development and Education board" with a clock of 50 MHz. The board contains a "Cyclone II 2C35" FPGA with 33 216 logic elements and 483 840 total RAM bits. The software implementation is executed on a Personal Computer (PC) with an Intel Core i5 Central Processing Unit (CPU) at 2.80 GHz and 8 GB Random Access Memory (RAM).

Variation of the query length: Table I shows a comparison of the computation times between PC and FPGA under variation of the query length. For all query-sequences, the same database-sequence with a length of 1 813 bases is used. The computation time of the software implementation is proportional to the query length. In contrast, the computation time of the FPGA implementation is rising much slower in relation to the query length. This is because the hits are combined in a binary tree, resulting in logarithmic characteristics.

TABLE I. Comparison of the computation times between PC and FPGA under variation of the query length.

Query length	Hits	PC / ms	FPGA / ms	FPGA / clock cycles
8	149	12.855	1.201	60093
32	786	55.155	1.219	60974
64	1598	94.331	1.246	62304
128	3050	195.607	1.296	64791
256	6263	316.306	1.406	70310
512	12081	640.919	1.611	80594
1024	23871	1241.095	2.006	100326

Variation of the q-word size: Table II shows a comparison of the computation times between PC and FPGA under variation of the q-word size. For all calculations, the same database-sequence and query-sequence are used. They have a length of 1 813 bases and 32 bases. Both, the PC implementation and the FPGA implementation show only little variance of computation time in respect to the q-word size.

TABLE II. COMPARISON OF THE COMPUTATION TIMES BETWEEN PC AND FPGA UNDER VARIATION OF THE Q-WORD SIZE.

q-Word size	Hits	PC / ms	FPGA / ms	FPGA / clock cycles
1	10844	47.630	1.288	64419
2	2866	47.009	1.230	61517
3	786	40.605	1.219	60974
4	199	52.516	1.217	60899
5	51	36.553	1.217	60888

Variation of the hit-detector width: Table III shows a comparison of the computation times between PC and FPGA under variation of the hit-detector width. For all calculations, the same database-sequence and query-sequence are used. They have a length of 1 813 bases and 127 bases. The hit-detector width has a high impact on the computation time of the FPGA implementation. This is because the results are processed sequentially in the hit-matchers. A lower hit-detector width results in more levels of hit-mergers and therefore a more parallel calculation. However, the global amount of necessary FIFO-memory is increased by lowering the hit-detector width. This is limiting the possible degree of parallelization, especially for large query-sequences.

TABLE III. COMPARISON OF THE COMPUTATION TIMES BETWEEN PC AND FPGA UNDER VARIATION OF THE HIT-DETECTOR WIDTH.

Hit-detector width	Hits	PC / ms	FPGA / ms	FPGA / clock cycles
4	3029	152.202	0.233	11897
8	3029	152.142	0.392	19630
16	3029	152.136	0.681	34086
32	3029	152.132	1.286	64295
64	3029	152.148	2.523	126160

V. CONCLUSION AND FUTURE WORK

It has been shown that the first two stages of the BLAST algorithm can be implemented efficiently in a parallel tree-like structure, even on a low-cost FPGA. However, for large nucleotide sequences the hit-detector width is limited to a lower bound, due to the available amount of fast on-chip memory. Of course, the hit-detector width can be increased to support larger sequences, but the result is an increased computation time.

In future work, the steps three and four of the BLAST algorithm could be implemented and evaluated according to the first two steps, to enable a complete calculation on the FPGA and thereby remove the overhead for communication. Additionally, the current implementation is not fully utilizing the available hardware, because the analysis of the next database-query is started only after the previous analysis is complete. It should be possible to decrease the computation time by starting the next analysis as soon as the FIFOs of the next level of hit-mergers are empty. However, a complex control logic would be necessary to prevent collisions and to attribute the results. Finally, an implementation of a more advanced scoring-function like the BLOSUM or PAM matrix would increase the quality of the results.

REFERENCES

[1] National Center for Biotechnology Information (NCBI), "GenBank and WGS statistics," http://www.ncbi.nlm.nih.gov/genbank/statistics/, accessed: 30. July 2017.

[2] National Human Genome Research Institute (NHGRI), "The cost of sequencing a human genome," https://www.genome.gov/sequencingcosts/, accessed: 30. July 2017.

[3] S. F. Altschul, W. Gish, W. Miller, E. W. Myers, and D. J. Lipman, "Basic local alignment search tool," Journal of Molecular Biology, vol. 215, no. 3, 1990, pp. 403–410.

[4] M. Gokhale et al., "Building and using a highly parallel programmable logic array," IEEE Computer, vol. 24, no. 1, Jan. 1991, pp. 81–89.

[5] M. R. Mahmoodi, H. Nikaein, and Z. Fahimi, "A parallel architecture for high speed BLAST using FPGA," in 2014 22nd Iranian Conference on Electrical Engineering (ICEE), May 2014, pp. 57–61.

[6] M. Yoshimi, C. Wu, and T. Yoshinaga, "Accelerating BLAST computation on an FPGA-enhanced PC cluster," in 2016 Fourth International Symposium on Computing and Networking (CANDAR), Nov 2016, pp. 67–76.

[7] "Accelerated BLAST performance with Tera-BLAST™: a comparison of FPGA versus GPU and CPU BLAST implementations," TimeLogic biocomputing solutions, Tech. Rep., 2013.

[8] P. Evripidou and C. Kyriacou, "Data-flow vs control-flow for extreme level computing," in 2013 Data-Flow Execution Models for Extreme Scale Computing, Sept 2013, pp. 9–13.

[9] M. Cameron, H. E. Williams, and A. Cannane, "Improved gapped alignment in BLAST," IEEE/ACM Transactions on Computational Biology and Bioinformatics, vol. 1, no. 3, July 2004, pp. 116–129.

A Synthesizable VHDL Export for the Custom Architecture Design Tool CustArD

Thomas Fabian Starke, Timm Bostelmann, Helga Karafiat and Sergei Sawitzki

FH Wedel (University of Applied Sciences)
Wedel, Germany
Email: starke.thomas@yahoo.de, {bos,kar,saw}@fh-wedel.de

Abstract—**The research of reconfigurable architectures usually goes hand in hand with a high amount of non-recurring work for Electronic Design Automation (EDA) tool development or adaption. Therefore, in previous work, a heterogeneous architecture template for application domain specific reconfigurable logic was proposed. The goal of this template is to allow the optimization of a reconfigurable architecture towards a specific application domain and to reduce the effort for tool generation in architecture research. In this work, a method to export the described architecture for synthesis is presented. It can be used for a silicon or Field-Programmable Gate Array (FPGA) overlay implementation and thereby extends the usability of the existing design flow. In the future, this work could even be used do derive a detailed timing-model for the designed architectures.**

Keywords–FPGA; architecture design; VHDL; CustArD

I. Introduction

Highly flexible FPGAs [1] address the demands of fast product lifecycles perfectly, where the non-recurring engineering costs and the slow development process of Application Specific Integrated Circuits (ASICs) are prohibitive. However, the main disadvantage of such flexible, reconfigurable logic structures lies in the vast amount of configuration and communication overhead and hampers their use for high volume or high performance applications. The overhead is caused by the configuration memory of the logic blocks and the routing resources, as well as by the routing network itself. As shown by Kuon et al. in [2] – compared to a standard cell implementation – this overhead increases the area of the chip by a factor of 40 and the power consumption by a factor of 12. Additionally the delay times are increased because the switch- and connection-boxes used for the flexible routing are much slower than fixed connections, resulting in a 3.2 times slower design. A very detailed analysis of the gap between FPGAs and ASICs is presented by the same authors in [3]. It is also shown, that the overhead can be reduced significantly if the right special function blocks (e.g., multipliers or memory) are included in the FPGA design. The main problem herein is, that the demand for special function blocks varies considerably with the application. Obviously, a high amount of unused special function blocks has a direct negative impact on the area efficiency. Moreover, the clock frequency can also be reduced because of longer signal paths between the actually utilized resources. Simply put, flexibility can be traded for efficiency (in a smaller set of applications) and the other way around (see also [4]).

In fact, modern FPGAs are equipped with coarse-grained logic to make them more competitive. Furthermore, many specialized reconfigurable architectures have been proposed by the scientific community over the last decades. For example, a datapath oriented FPGA architecture – implementing parallel routing – has been introduced by Leijten-Nowak et al. in [5]. It reduces the necessary amount of configuration memory by sharing configuration memory bits between routing resources as proposed by Cherepacha et al. in [6]. Furthermore, a highly hierarchical, heterogeneous architecture (*Tree-Based Heterogeneous FPGA Architecture*) was introduced and evaluated by Farooq et al. in [7]. Both techniques are shown to be beneficial for arithmetic intensive applications like Digital Signal Processing (DSP). At the same time, especially the usage of memory sharing reduces the flexibility of the architecture.

Unfortunately, architecture research often demands the development or at least an adaption of a complete toolchain. This makes the exploration of new architectures very time-consuming and complicates the comparison of architectures that have been developed using different tools. As in the papers quoted above, academic toolchains are usually customized towards a rather fixed architecture. They only allow to configure the proposed architecture to some extent, but not to modify its global structure. To some degree the *Verilog-to-Routing (VTR) Project for FPGAs* which has been introduced by Rose et al. in [8] is an exception in this regard. The VTR project offers a very flexible and sophisticated academic development toolchain for FPGAs. It allows a detailed description of a hypothetical architecture, including timing information. Even an export for synthesis has been proposed by Kim et al. in [9]. The architecture description language grants a very flexible definition of Configurable Logic Blocks (CLB). The CLBs can contain for example fracturable lookup-tables, custom routing resources like bus-multiplexers, custom logic and hierarchical clusters [10]. However, the general structure of the architecture – an island-style grid of logic blocks – is still fixed. Special function blocks and different CLBs have to be placed column-wise in the grid, meaning a column can only contain one type of logic. Considering this, even though VTR is great for EDA and island-style FPGA architecture research, its architecture description language is not fully suited for a wide and rapid exploration of the architecture design space as it is envisioned by the authors of this work.

Therefore, a heterogeneous architecture template for application domain specific reconfigurable logic was proposed in [11] by Bostelmann and Sawitzki. A class of reconfigurable architectures – a meta-architecture – which can be flexibly optimized towards a specific application domain was introduced. It supports hierarchical, heterogeneous structures, as well as parallel datapath connections. In addition, a concept for a corresponding design flow has been proposed in [12]. It allows a directed exploration of application domain specific architectural optimizations. By the derivation of specialized architectures from a very flexible meta-architecture the design flow allows to:

1) Rapidly optimize an architecture towards a specific application domain
2) Improve the comparability between different derived architecture instances
3) Reduce the effort for tool generation

In this work, based on the previous publications mentioned above, an extension for the export of the described architecture to a Hardware Description Language (HDL) is introduced. It can be used for a silicon or FPGA overlay [13] implementation of the designed architecture. The current implementation supports an export as synthesizable Very high speed integrated circuit HDL (VHDL) code with direct support of the Intel FPGA Quartus tools.

The rest of this work is organized as follows. In Section II, the concepts of the meta-architecture and the corresponding design flow that have been proposed in previous work are summarized. In Section III, the implementation of the HDL export is described. In Section IV, exemplary results of the HDL export are presented. Finally, in Section V, this work is summarized and an outlook to further work is given.

II. Background

This section is split into two parts. First the degrees of freedom and the global structure of the meta-architecture used in this work are described and then the concept of the extended design flow is depicted.

A. Meta-Architecture Description

The reconfigurable architecture is described on function block level. A basic set of configurable function blocks is provided, but can also be extended by the user. The basic set consists of the following function blocks:

LUT	lookup-table
REG	register or single flipflop
MUX	multiplexer
MEM	memory
IO	input and output buffer
SB	switchbox (bi- or unidirectional)
CB	connectionbox (bi- or unidirectional)
IP	fixed IP core from a library
GRID	grid of blocks or grids

The global structure of the architecture is based on two types of grid. The first one is a 'repeating grid' which repeats one block (or an other grid) $n \times m$ times. The second one is a 'custom grid' which can contain a custom compilation of blocks (or other grids like shown in Figure 1). By supporting recursive grids the design of highly hierarchical, tree-based architectures without a huge top-level grid is encouraged. Of course, the description of flat island-style architectures is possible as well, by simply using a top-level 'repeating grid'.

B. Design Flow

The design flow for the meta-architecture described above is shown in Figure 2 as proposed in [11]. The user creates an architecture in a graphical architecture design tool called Custom Architecture Design Tool (CustArD) or derives it from a template. The design tool was first presented by Sternberg et al. in [14]. CustArD exports an internal Architecture Description File (ADF), as well as an HDL description of the architecture. This feature is the major topic of this work. The user can then select a set of reference or benchmark applications, which are synthesized and mapped to the architecture based on the ADF. After this step, an analysis tool provides the user with an early evaluation of the block utilization. This is especially interesting if the impact of special function blocks for a given set of applications is explored. It allows for example a directed optimization of the provided resources towards a specific application domain. After a complete toolchain iteration the analysis tool provides a detailed evaluation including benchmark results and the utilization of routing resources. This can be used to explore new routing techniques or again to optimize the architecture towards a specific application domain, for example by adapting the width of parallel datapath routing elements.

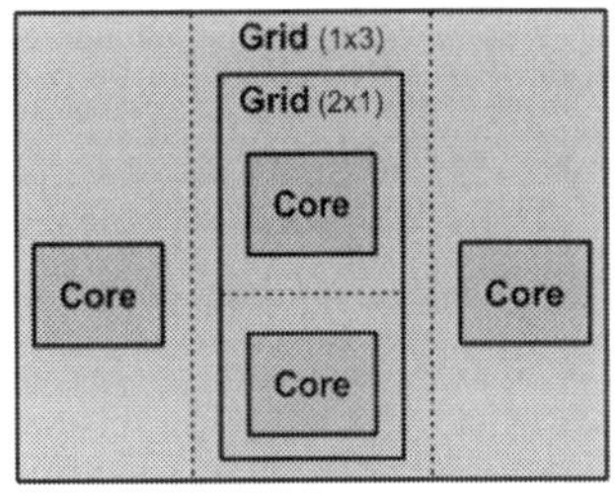

(a) Flat view of the recursive grid structure

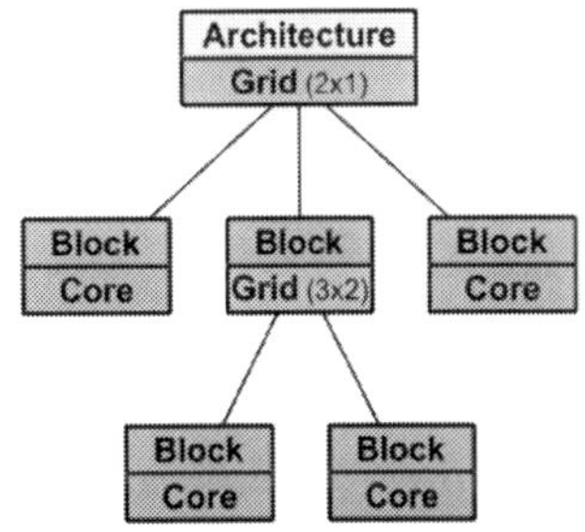

(b) Tree view of the recursive grid structure

Figure 1. An exemplary recursive grid structre, consisting of two grids and four cores

III. Implementation

The VHDL export plugin maps the CustArD representation of an architecture into a VHDL representation. This is achieved by mapping each CustArD architecture component to its corresponding VHDL representation.

A. VHDL Primitives

The architecture in CustArD consists of primitives whose complexity can vary from a simple logic gate to a complex Intellectual Property (IP) core. For the VHDL export the following primitives are used: logic gate (AND, NAND, NOR, NOT, OR, XNOR, XOR), multiplexer, flipflop, Lookup Table (LUT), selector, wire, Static Random-Access Memory (SRAM), Connection-Box (CB) and Switch-Box (SB). Further primitives can be added through storage of their VHDL

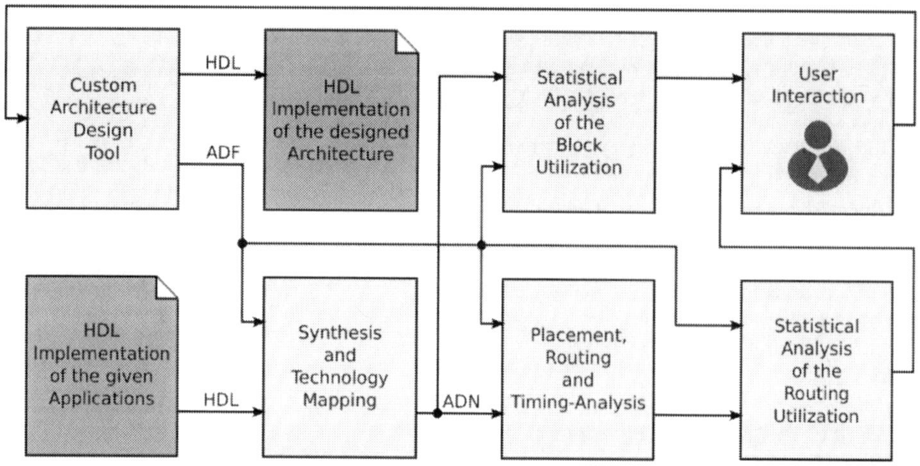

Figure 2. A Flowchart of the described design flow for heterogeneous reconfigurable architectures

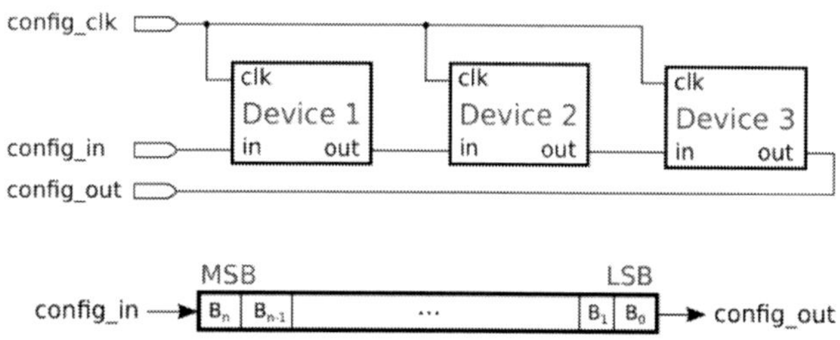

Figure 3. Schematic of the global organization of the configuration memory

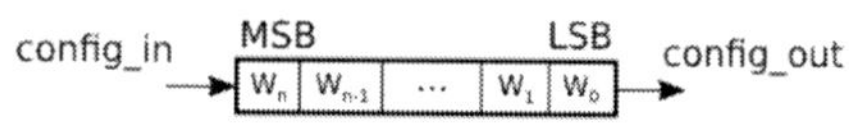

Figure 4. Organization of the configuration memory for a LUT

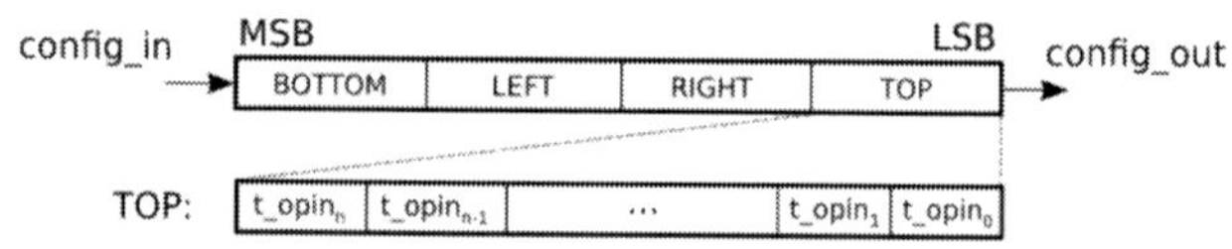

Figure 5. Organization of the configuration memory for a switchbox

representations in the export plugin.

Global Signals: Currently only fully synchronous designs are supported. As a result the signals *clk* and *reset* that are needed by some VHDL primitives like a flipflop are handled globally. In the VHDL export, they are marked with the prefix *global_* in all primitives that make use of them.

Configuration Signals: To use the exported architecture for an application some components like LUT or switchboxes have to be configured. This is done through a JTAG-like configuration mechanism with a shift register. All components that need configuration are serially connected as shown in Figure 3 and store the configuration information internally. The length of the configuration register depends on the information that is needed for each component. The signals used for configuration are marked with the prefix *config_* in the corresponding VHDL primitives.

Wire: A wire connects an input signal directly to an output signal. It is the most simple primitive in CustArD. Its export could have been implemented with a special treatment which would have reduced the complexity of the VHDL code. However, a special treatment would lead to a higher implementation complexity and less consistency. Therefore, even this trivial component is exported as a VHDL primitive.

Lookup Table: A LUT stores precomputed information that is available at runtime. The data is stored in the LUT during the configuration. Therefore the VHDL primitive of a LUT contains a configuration register (see Figure 4). It consists of $n = 2^{asw}$ words, where as *asw* stands for address signal width. The size W of a word corresponds to the output signal width *osw* of the LUT. As a result, the overall size of the configuration register has $W \cdot 2^{asw}$ bits.

SRAM: The SRAM is like a LUT, except that the information can be stored and changed at runtime. It is assumed that the input vector width *isw* is equal to the output vector width *osw* and that the number of words stored in the SRAM is 2^{asw}, where *asw* stands for address signal width. The resulting size of the SRAM is $2^{asw} \cdot isw$ bits.

Selector: The selector is similar to a multiplexer except that the output signal is chosen during configuration time instead of runtime. Therefore this component needs a configuration register of size $\mathrm{ld}(isw)$ bits.

Switchbox: The standard switchbox in CustArD uses bidirectional pins. In order to minimize the hardware complexity, an advanced switchbox has been implemented which has fixed input and output pins on each side. The internal connection structure was implemented as a disjoint switchbox. As a simplification, it is additionally defined that the amount of the vertical input and output pins must be the same as the amount of the horizontal ones. The configuration register (see Figure 5) defines in which way the input pins and output pins are connected, according to the contraints of a unidirectional disjoint switchbox.

Connectionbox: The connectionbox is a special form of a switch box and is used for configurable connections between logic elements and horizontal or vertical connecting structures. In order to provide maximum connectivity, any input pin can be assigned to any output pin of the connection box. Figure 6

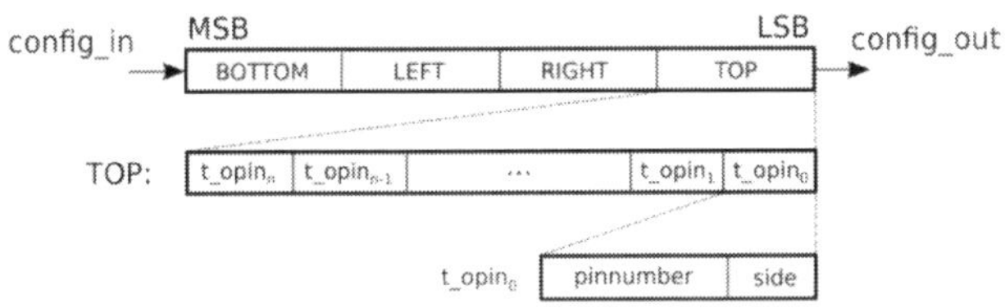

Figure 6. Organization of the configuration memory for a connectionbox

shows the structure of the configuration register within the connectionbox.

B. VHDL-Export-Plugin

The HDL-export traverses the architecture tree and calls the corresponding processing routine for every node, which then passes the calculated information towards the root. The utilzed routines are described below.

Core: The core object represents a leaf of the architecture tree. It is directly translated into a VHDL primitive. Therefore, the entity declaration of a VHDL file is read and the signal names, as well as the generic identifiers are mapped to the identifiers used in CustArD. The generic mapping declaration is designed from the configuration values deposited in CustArD. It is stored in VHDL objects. All related CustArD signals are stored in a dictionary like $\{Pingroup : [(Pinnumber, [(Terminal\_1, Terminal\_2, Net)^*])^*]\}$, where *Terminal_1* corresponds to the source and *Terminal_2* to the sink.

IO-cores which are the in- and output of the architecture, are processed differently. For them no VHDL primitives are created, but the signals of the IO-cores are integrated into a global list that is only processed at the root element of the tree.

Grid: A grid represents a node of the architecture tree and is translated into a VHDL file. For all elements of the grid the following steps are processed.

1) A VHDL file is created for each of the subtrees through a call of the block method.
2) The instantiation of the VHDL file is created and inserted into the grid VHDL file object including the creation and storage of the port and generic map declaration.
3) The signals of the instance are entered into the grid VHDL file as local signals.
4) If there are configuration signals within the port of the instantiated VHDL object, the configuration bus is extended by this object and the configuration action signals within the grid are adjusted.

All detected signals from the VHDL instances are assigned by a matching algorithm. All signals that couldn't be matched, lead to different parts of the architecture tree and are therefore passed up to the next instance.

Block: A block is a container class within the CustArD architecture tree and, in addition to a grid or a core element, contains further meta information, such as a unique block ID and a referenced flag. The processing method of a block, first creates the associated VHDL file object from the grid or core element. If this is not a primitive object, the associated VHDL file is generated from the VHDL file object. The determined signals of the subtrees are used as inputs or outputs of this VHDL entity and are specified in the port declaration. Blocks can also be used several times within the architecture tree. This is indicated by the reference flag within the block. If this is the case, the obtained information about the interface of these subtrees is stored in a global block cache. If such a block is recompiled, the translation can be interrupted directly at this level and replaced by the cached content, which significantly reduces the translation effort and the number of resulting VHDL files.

Architecture: The architecture element represents the root of the architecture tree. Similar to the block, it can contain a core or a grid element. The processing of this node is similar to that of the block, but all internal signals must be mapped at this level so that only the IO-core signals, as well as the $config\_$ and $global\_$ signals are included.

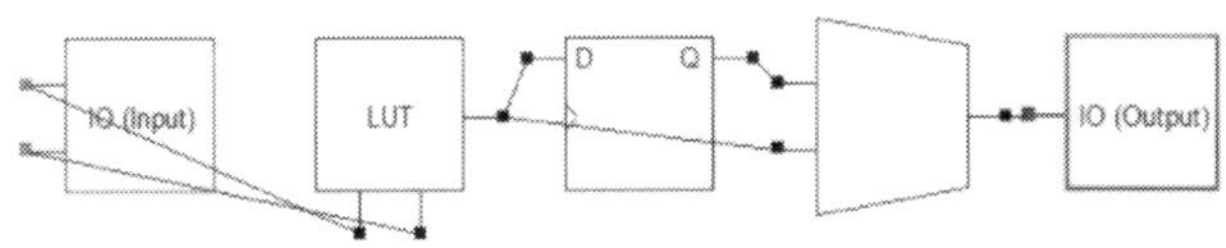

Figure 7. Imlementation of a simple CLB in CustArD

TABLE I. EXPORT TIME FOR AN ARCHITECTURE CONSISTING OF TWO PRIMITIVES IN A 5 X 5 GRID

Number of connections	time / s	used memory / MB
0	0.63	<1.5
320	0.68	<1.5

IV. RESULTS

In this section, the runtime and memory usage of the VHDL export plugin are discussed, depending on the number of connections, number of used primitives and the architecture tree depth. Figure 7 shows a simple CLB architecture designed in CustArD which consists of one 1 x 5 grid and five different primitives. The result of the VHDL export plugin consists of three VHDL primitives and one VHDL file representing the grid of the CLB architecture. Figure 8 shows a Register Transfer Level (RTL) plot of the export in Intel FPGA Quartus.

Table I shows the export time for an architecture consisting of two primitives in a 5 x 5 grid, with and without wiring. It shows that the number of connections has only little influence on the runtime of the export plugin. Table II shows the export time for an architecture consisting of ten different primitives in a architecture tree with a depth of four. The runtime of the export plugin depends on the number of primitives and the maximum depth of the architecture tree. This is manageable even for larger structures, since they usually consist of referenced blocks or grids that are used multiple times but are exported only once.

TABLE II. EXPORT TIME FOR AN ARCHITECTURE CONSISTING OF TEN DIFFERENT PRIMITIVES IN A ARCHITECTURE TREE WITH THE DEPTH OF FOUR

Number of connections	time / s	used memory / MB
0	0.50	<1.0
10	0.50	<1.0
30	0.65	<1.0

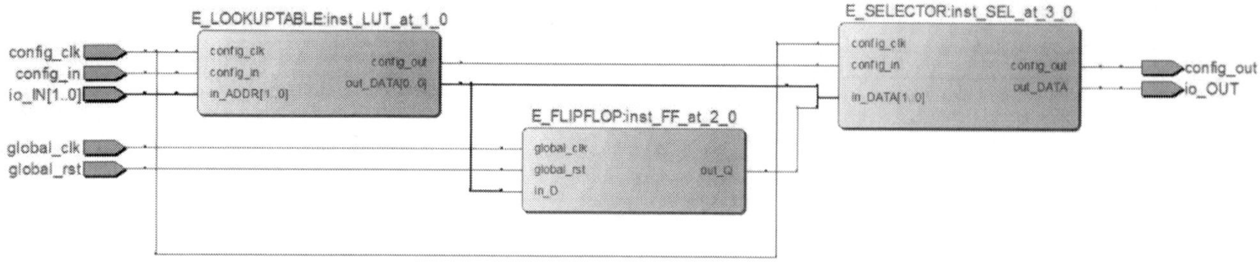

Figure 8. Intel FPGA Quartus RTL view of the exported CLB shown in Figure 7

V. Conclusion and Future Work

In this work, an extension for the custom architecture design tool CustArD was presented. It was shown how a reconfigurable architecture that has been optimized towards a specific application domain can be exported to a synthesizable VHDL format. The results for a simple LUT design were presented. Furthermore, it was shown that the export is reasonably fast for small designs. The automatic generation of project files for the Intel FPGA Quartus tools allow a seamless utilization of the results.

In future work, an export to the Verilog HDL language is planned to establish consistency between the input and output file formats. Since the internal data-structures and concepts are HDL-independent, this should not be very complicated. Furthermore, larger architectures should be benchmarked to show the real-world applicability of this approach. Finally, the usability of this export tool could be increased even further by the creation of more building blocks (e.g., configurable DSP blocks).

References

[1] W. Carter et al., "A user programmable reconfigurable logic array," in IEEE Custom Integrated Circuits Conference (CICC), 1986, pp. 233–235.

[2] I. Kuon and J. Rose, "Measuring the gap between FPGAs and ASICs," IEEE Transactions on Computer-Aided Design of Integrated Circuits and Systems, vol. 26, no. 2, Feb 2007, pp. 203–215.

[3] I. Kuon and J. Rose, Quantifying and Exploring the Gap Between FPGAs and ASICs, 1st ed. Springer Publishing Company, Incorporated, 2009.

[4] H. Parvez, Z. Marrakchi, and H. Mehrez, "ASIF: Application specific inflexible FPGA," in Field-Programmable Technology (FPT), Dec 2009, pp. 112–119.

[5] K. Leijten-Nowak and J. L. van Meerbergen, "An FPGA architecture with enhanced datapath functionality," in ACM/SIGDA International Symposium on Field-Programmable Gate Arrays (FPGA), 2003, pp. 195–204.

[6] D. Cherepacha and D. Lewis, "DP-FPGA: An FPGA architecture optimized for datapaths," VLSI Design, vol. 4, no. 4, 1996, pp. 329–343.

[7] U. Farooq, Z. Marrakchi, and H. Mehrez, Tree-Based Heterogeneous FPGA Architectures: Application Specific Exploration and Optimization. Springer, 2012.

[8] J. Rose et al., "The VTR project: Architecture and CAD for FPGAs from Verilog to routing," in ACM/SIGDA International Symposium on Field-Programmable Gate Arrays (FPGA), 2012, pp. 77–86.

[9] J. H. Kim and J. H. Anderson, "Synthesizable FPGA fabrics targetable by the Verilog-to-Routing (VTR) CAD flow," in 2015 25th International Conference on Field Programmable Logic and Applications (FPL), Sept 2015, pp. 1–8.

[10] J. Luu, J. H. Anderson, and J. Rose, "Architecture description and packing for logic blocks with hierarchy, modes and complex interconnect," in ACM/SIGDA International Symposium on Field-Programmable Gate Arrays (FPGA), 2011, pp. 227–236.

[11] T. Bostelmann and S. Sawitzki, "A heterogeneous architecture template for application domain specific reconfigurable logic," in 2015 Austrian Workshop on Microelectronics (Austrochip), Sept 2015, pp. 9–14.

[12] T. Bostelmann and S. Sawitzki, "Towards a guided design flow for heterogeneous reconfigurable architectures," in 2015 25th International Conference on Field Programmable Logic and Applications (FPL), Sept 2015, pp. 1–2.

[13] A. Brant and G. Lemieux, "ZUMA: An open FPGA overlay architecture," in Field-Programmable Custom Computing Machines (FCCM), April 2012, pp. 93–96.

[14] H. Sternberg, T. Bostelmann, and S. Sawitzki, "CustArD - a custom architecture design tool," presented at the Technical Demonstrations Session of the International Conference on Reconfigurable Computing and FPGAs (ReConFig), Dec 2014, p. 2.

Custom Hardware Integration into DBT-based Processor Simulation

Steffen Köhler and Rainer G. Spallek
Institute of Computer Engineering
Technische Universität Dresden
01062 Dresden, Germany
Email: steffen.koehler, rainer.spallek@tu-dresden.de

Abstract—**High performance simulation of processor architectures at instruction set / behavioral level often utilizes Dynamic Binary Translation (DBT) techniques to achieve an efficient mapping to the simulation host. While the behavior of most standard processor operations can be directly translated into host processor instructions due to their similarities, the behavior of complex application specific instructions or peripheral components are less suitable for host processor execution. In this paper we discuss the migration of application specific behavioral processor model partitions to field programmable accelerator hardware to achieve an overall co-simulation speedup. For an in-depth evaluation, the integration of an off-the-shelf Field Programmamble Gate Array (FPGA) into our DBT-based processor simulation framework RUBICS (Retargetable Universal Binary Instruction Conversion Simulator) was considered. RUBICS is a flexible behavioral modelling and simulation platform framework for embedded processor architectures and complete Systems-on-a-Chip (SoC). In a case study, we show the behavior model migration of an application specific peripheral co-processor into a synthesizable hardware description mapped to the FPGA accelerator. Only minor changes are required to the original ARMv7 processor model description given in RUBICS's dedicated Architecture Description Language (ADL). An overall simulation speedup between 300% and 540% has been achieved by migrating the main calculation partition of a numeric transform peripheral to the FPGA accelerator. Challenges of the communication-driven model partitioning as well as the achievable simulation speedup are discussed.**

Index Terms—**Processor Simulation; Dynamic Binary Translation; FPGA Accelerator.**

I. Introduction

The behavioral simulation of embedded processor cores is essential for a successful design of System-on-a-Chip (SoC) architectures. Beside the processor core behavior, a detailed analysis of interaction and communication between processor core and peripheral/dedicated components plays an important role in the SoC test/verification process.

The current complexity of hardware- and software-components requires an analysis of the SoC as a whole at an early stage of the design process. Contrary to performance-oriented approaches that focus on peripherally observable behavior (emulation), the behavioral simulation additionally has to provide a short modeling turn-around cycle as well as the demanded observability of the relevant model state. To achieve this, a behavioral processor simulator should provide rapid modeling capabilities at a high abstraction level (instruction set, instruction behavior, IO behavior), visibility of internal flow (registers, data path), as well as a high simulation speed. As an increased state visibility introduces additional modelling, execution and data recording effort, the simulation model has to be carefully adapted to the particular observation requirements. This can be achieved e.g. by injecting selective debug operations into the behavioral model specification.

Beside the early design stage requirements the simulation environment could also be used to reconstruct the execution profile of embedded software modules. Through architecture model instrumentation, a detailed control- and data-flow trace may be obtained for an in-depth software analysis.

The most essential part of the processor simulation is a model description that provides information for equivalent mapping the target instruction flow to the simulation host. The quality of the translation process and the resulting fitness to the host processor architecture determines the achievable simulation performance. Common methods used for high speed behavior level processor simulation utilize binary translation techniques [1]. The trade-off between translation effort amortization and available performance can be effectively improved by applying just-in-time (JIT) compilation, where target instruction sequences are dynamically mapped to the host processor at runtime. Common approaches of JIT-based simulators and emulators use widely available runtime environments, such as Java Virtual Machine (JVM) [2], Common Language Runtime (CLR) [3] or PyPy [4] as well as dedicated compilers like Tiny Code Generator (TCG) [5]. As a matter of fact, the translation quality essentially depends on the degree of similarity of both target and host processor architectures. This problem especially involves the mapping of dedicated custom target instruction set extensions or peripheral models. It can be overcome by supplying a more flexible mapping platform on the simulation host, thus allowing a higher degree of adaption as a result of the translation. A promising platform extension approach is the integration of FPGA hardware in conjunction with a partitioning of the simulation model.

In this work, we focus on static translation of the FPGA partition, although it might also be possible to benefit from just-in-time utilization of the FPGA.

Among different available simulation environments, we have chosen the RUBICS [6] platform framework, which utilizes the open ECMA International Common Language Runtime (CLR) [7] standard platform. Advanced retargetability and modeling capabilities are provided through a dedicated architecture description language (ADL), whereas extensibility is granted by the underlying CLR language support (C#, VB, etc.). External component libraries (DLL) facilitate the integration of complex peripheral model descriptions as well as FPGA-

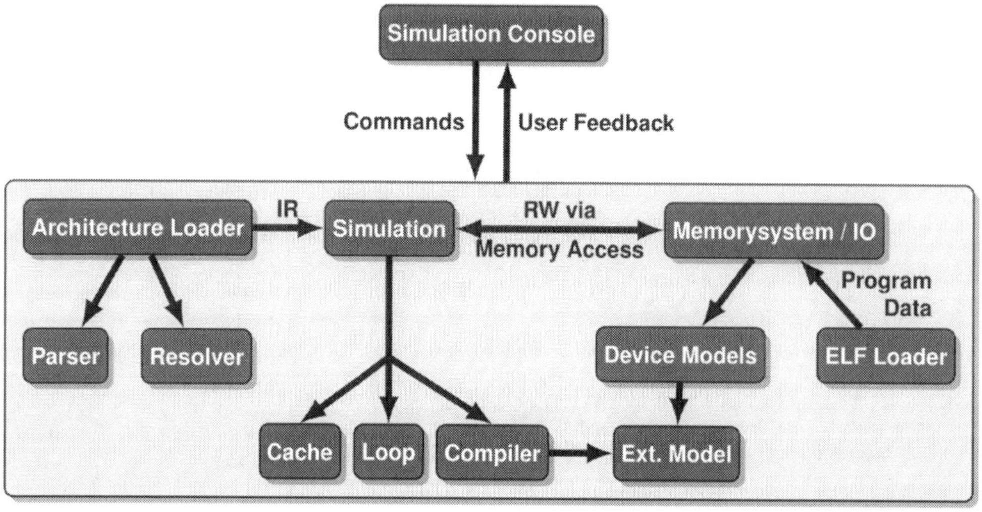

Figure 1. RUBICS Platform Framework

based model partitions into the ADL description without any changes to the simulation core.
In this paper, sections II and III introduce the RUBICS simulation platform and the provided processor architecture description methodology. Section IV outlines the binary translation based simulation process. A detailed description of custom hardware mapping to an FPGA accelerator and its performance evaluation is given in sections V and VI respectively. Finally, a summarized discussion and generalization of the achieved results is given in section VII.

II. Simulation Platform

The chosen simulation platform framework RUBICS provides the underlying infrastructure for high-performance processor simulation. It allows both structural and behavioral architecture description in a dedicated architecture description language (ADL) and supports embedding external core or peripheral models. Enhanced test and debug capabilities enable versatile control/observation of the simulation process. The framework is composed around a core component, that can be dynamically extended by loading simulation model or support libraries at runtime. Any Common Language Runtime (CLR) [7] compatible module can be made available to the RUBICS platform framework. Beside the behavioral model description in a supported language the CLR, it also grants direct access to the native system resources of the simulation host. This significantly simplifies both the integration of custom hardware models into the core model as well as extending the simulation host by additional FPGA-hardware. The CLR furthermore implements a dynamic execution interface to host processor which complies to the Common Intermediate Language (CIL) bytecode specification. The versatile bytecode interface is not only used for CLR module representation, but is also target by the dynamic binary translation process. Figure 1 gives an overview of the basic structure of the RUBICS framework.

The integration of FPGA hardware into the simulation host and its application as processor simulation accelerator is generally supported by the RUBICS platform framework in two different variations.

- Loose coupling by a bus interface for peripheral or co-processor models
- Tight coupling by a plugin interface for direct access from the ADL behavioral model

Although both possibilities could have been considered for further investigations, we focus on the bus interface integration for partitioning reasons. The plugin access would require advanced low latency communication properties, which the available interface of the chosen FPGA hardware platform unfortunately could not offer.

III. Architecture Model

The main concept of a retargetetable processor simulator by mean of combining a generic infrastructure with a dedicated architecture description language (ADL) was already suggested in [2]. Contrary to a programming language or hardware description language, an ADL model can be specified using a common structural template. The remaining description work only requires the specification of unique structure and behavior, such as processor state, instruction set, and instruction behavior. The architecture description is composed of different sections:

- `import` References to CLR library models,
- `bus` Bus-oriented loosely coupled devices
- `plugins` Tightly coupled plugins,
- `context`, Context state variables,
- `decoder`, Instruction decoder description,
- `behavior`, Instruction behavior description,
- `interrupts`, Interrupt description.

```
bus mem {
    unit = 8;
    endian = LITTLE;
    access {
        byte = 1;
        short = 2;
        word = 4;
    }
    devices {
        ram mem {
            base = 0;
            size = 0x40000000;
        }
        fpga fpga_dev {
            base = 0x40000000;
            size = 0x10000000;
        }
    }
}
plugins {
    plugin.fpga fpga_plug;
}
context {
    uint pc;
}
decoder {
    fetch {
        bus = mem;
        pc;
    }
    context {
        uint instruction word;
    }
    operation oper {
        instruction_word = fetch.word;
        IPC;
    }
}
behavior {
    operation IPC {
        fpga_plug.ExecFunc();
        pc += 4;
    }
}
```

Figure 2. Architecture Description Language

Figure 2 shows a simplified architecture model with both tightly and loosely coupled model components mapped to an FPGA accelerator. The description consists of structural and behavioral specifications. For demonstration reasons, the instruction behavior only includes a program counter increment followed by a plugin function `ExecFunc()` invocation.

The declaration of the memory bus `mem` not only describes the main memory and peripheral mappings, but also specifies an embedded FPGA based accelerator device `fpga_dev`. Detailed access pattern sizes and alignment hints are given in the `access` section, that makes the bus interface available to the behavioral operations as named expression, e.g. `mem.byte[<address>]`. Through the `unit` attribute the data granularity (smallest addressable data unit) can be set.

Although the general execution flow is implicitly determined by the RUBICS core, the `fetch` environment has to provide the information about the proper instruction memory interface (`mem`) and the fetch address (`pc`) of the next instruction. The decoder may maintain its own global context `context`, which is especially favorable when decoding complex instruction sets.

The ADL makes the standard CLR data types available to the decoder and instruction behavior descriptions. Unique type conversions will be done automatically. A huge selection of support functions is available for specifying dedicated bit-level and floating point operations. Fixed point literals are handled with arbitrary length upon its use in a particular variable operation or assignment. This significantly simplifies constant propagation and reduces the number of required range checks. The architecture description will be translated into an internal Intermediate Representation (IR), which holds the information needed for the binary translation and the JIT compilation process.

IV. Binary Translation

The binary translation is the main task prior execution on the simulation host. After the target architecture and the application binary have been loaded and the Program Counter (PC) has been set to the appropriate start address, execution flow is transferred to the main simulation loop. According to the decoder specification in the IR, the instruction stream gets decoded and behavioral IR operation are issued and executed until the flow hits a break condition. A simplified simulation flow is outlined in Figure 3.

As behavioral operations are tied directly to particular address ranges, they can be cached to avoid redundant decode operations. In case of a cache-miss, a decode operation is invoked, which stores a new behavioral block to the simulation cache. The decode operation can be avoided in case of a cache-hit and the behavioral operation block is directly available for execution. Only instructions on consecutive addresses can be mapped to a single cache entry. The size of the behavioral operation block (dynamic block) is limited by application binary control flow transfer instructions (e.g. branches). Special handling of non-contiguous control flow is reflected by the `exit` keyword (end of dynamic block) inside the decoder specification. A sufficiently high dynamic block size is vital of a low cache lookup rate and thus for a high simulation performance.

In a first step, the binary translation creates a sequence of instruction tailored copies of the behavioral IR, which will then be optimized to eliminate redundant operations and variable access. The additional optimization effort (flow analysis) can easily be amortized, except for very short simulation runs. During the translation of the IR, native interface and plugin invocations are directly handled using native CLR calls for low overhead. A lookup-based memory delegator offers low latency access to multi-device bus interfaces with nearly constant time aperture access. Target memory blocks are directly mapped to virtual user address space of the simulation host by operating system functions utilizing copy-on-write pages. Furthermore, hot-spot compilation [8] is applied to the simulation process, which delays the translation of the behavioral IR copies into CIL bytecode until they have reached a certain execution count threshold. The final translation of the CIL bytecode into host machine instructions is transparently maintained by the CLR-internal JIT compiler.

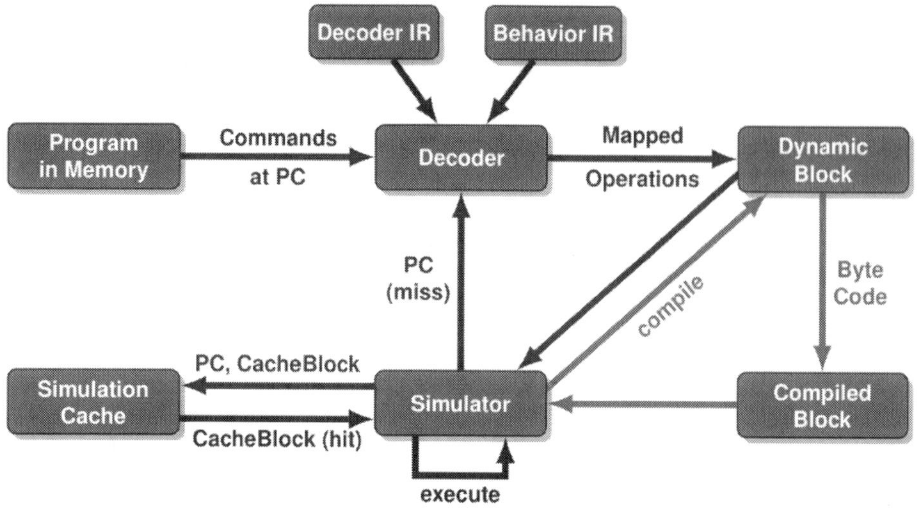

Figure 3. Simulation Cycle

V. Embedding Custom Hardware

For a reasonably complete behavioral processor description, the core architecture ADL model has to be extended by additional peripheral or plugin models. This is already supported by the RUBICS platform framework by its library concept. The behavior of a loadable library component can easily be specified using any CLR compatible programming language (C#, VB, etc.). Depending on the communication pattern and resource requirements, a migration of any RUBICS library component to an FPGA accelerator is basically possible. To achieve this, a synthesizable Register Transfer Level (RTL) model partition has to be manually created and described using a Hardware Description Language (HDL). The FPGA mapping decision is driven by the availability of such a HDL description (or the effort to create this description) and the potential performance gain including the communication overhead.

As FPGAs can only be accessed by the simulation host using a limited scale of available processor interfaces, inter-partition communication overhead directly relates to the simulation host platform. Although it would be possible to consider tightly coupled processor/FPGA host platforms, the best cost/performance trade-off can be achieved by integrating an inexpensive PCIe-based FPGA-board into a PC/workstation environment. Unfortunately, PCIe-based inter-partition communication heavily depends on the available PCIe transfer profiles, thus limiting the influence on communication latency and throughput. Therefore, only a streaming-based communication approach could be considered in this work.

Figure 4 illustrates the embedding of a custom behavioral model into the simulation process using FPGA hardware.

VI. Performance Analysis

In a particular case study, the FPGA hardware integration into the simulation host and its utilization as execution platform for a custom peripheral model can be demonstrated. The

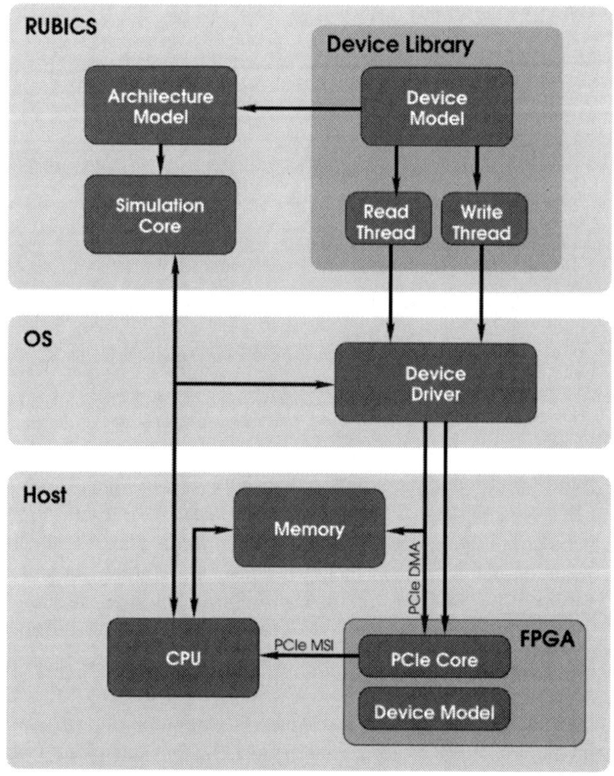

Figure 4. Simulation Environment with FPGA-Hardware

host system is composed of a fairly recent Intel Core-i5 6500 (SkyLake) with 16GB DDR4 memory. Through a standard PCIe expansion connector a Terasic DE5-Net FPGA board (Altera/Intel Stratix V FPGA) [9] is plugged into the main board. Only four PCIe-Lanes are used for communication. The system runs Debian Linux using an unpatched Kernel

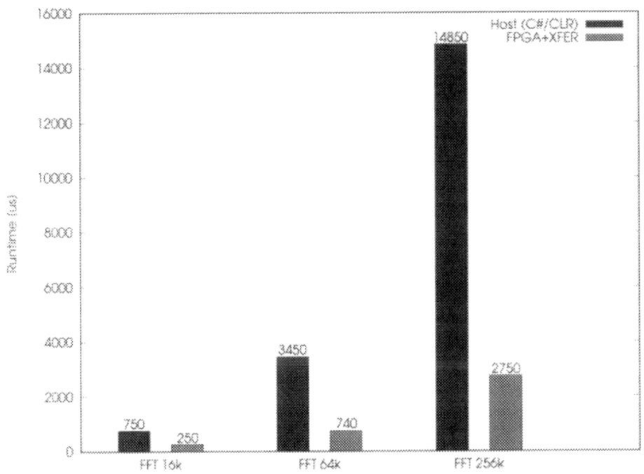

Figure 5. Simulation Runtime

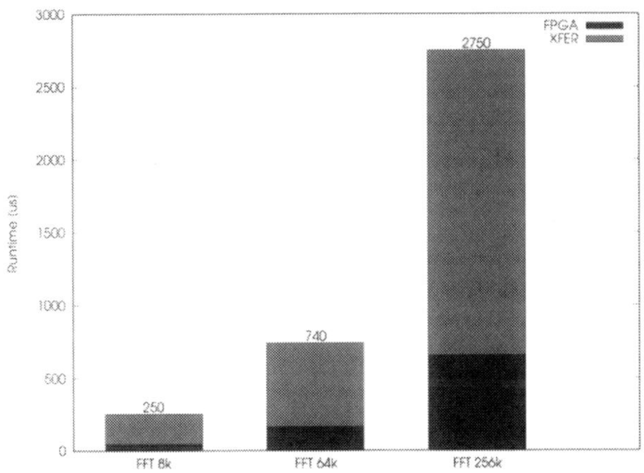

Figure 6. FPGA Calculation vs. Transfer

v4.10.1. All performance measurement were carried out on an ARMv7 Thumb2 instruction set model [10] in a RUBICS v0.6 platform framework on top of MONO CLR v4.8. The peripheral model chosen for FPGA mapping has been selected with main emphasis on implementation simplicity and interface fitness to the available PCIe IP-core. A decimation-in-frequency Fast Fourier Transform (FFT) model [11] with three different block sizes was evaluated using both a C#-based CLR thread as well as a coupled FPGA-based implementation. The description of the FPGA partition not only includes Verilog HDL RTL modules, but also structural component declarations required for automated FFT IP-core generation using QSys wizard of Quartus Prime v15.1. A XILLYBUS PCIe streaming controller IP-core [12] supplies the underlying communication infrastructure including a Linux OS device driver. Although the intended optimization goal was performance-oriented, the available FFT pipeline capabilities could not be fully utilized due to a maximum clock frequency of 250 MHz limited by the XILLYBUS PCIe-core.

Figure 5 summarizes the achievable overall simulation runtime reduction resulting from the FPGA accelerator using different FFT block sizes. A more detailed impression on particular calculation and transfer effort can be obtained from Figure 6. To neglect JIT amortization effects, the measurement results have been averaged over a total of 1000 FFT runs respectively. The overall simulation performance gain including transfer overhead reaches between 300% with an FFT block size of 16384 points and 540% with an FFT block size of 262144 points. The latter is the maximum FFT size that could be implemented using Quartus QSys wizard.

The FPGA resource consumption is dominated by the FFT component and reaches 25...30% of the available DSP and RAM blocks, whereas the remaining logic including XILLYBUS glue components utilizes only 2-4% of the chip capacity.

VII. Conclusion and Future Work

In this paper, we have shown the integration capabilities of application specific custom hardware models into the RUBICS behavioral simulation flow. An acceleration of the simulation process could be achieved by the utilization of coupled FPGA hardware on the simulation host. This approach is especially useful for complex behavioral models of peripheral components of processor-based SoC. Furthermore, the embedding of external models into the architecture description was demonstrated, which allows tight or loose coupling of external custom models to the core architecture. Through the selected migration of a custom FFT model partition to a loosely PCIe-coupled FPGA board a simulation performance improvement compared to the standalone mapping to the simulation host has been demonstrated. The achievable runtime-benefit increases with the mapping advantage of the FPGA compared to the host processor and the reduction of transfer overhead between the FPGA- and host-partitions. The selected FFT example does not fully comply these demands, thus resulting in a comparatively low performance gain. Especially the communication latency of the throughput-oriented XILLYBUS IP-core lowers the achievable overall simulation performance significantly. A definition of more realistic partitioning properties and goals would therefore be desirable. Beside the computational resource specification, this would also include precise knowledge about the request/response communication round-trip time. Also, the availability of a low-latency PCIe IP-core would be generally preferable for obtaining an increased overall integration efficiency of tightly coupled custom hardware models on FPGA. Furthermore, the communication latency can be entirely neglected by breaking the request/response scheme and avoid stalling the simulation progress while waiting for any hardware response. The case is most relevant to uni-directional fire-and-forget transfers like execution flow trace recording, which is subject of prospective investigations.

References

[1] "High speed cpu simulation using jit binary translation," 2007, URL: http://homepages.inf.ed.ac.uk/npt/pubs/mobs-07.pdf [accessed: 2017-03-21].
[2] M. Kaufmann, M. Häsing, T. Preußer, and R. G. Spallek, "The java virtual machine in retargetable, high-performance instruction set simulation," in Proc. 9th Int'l Conf. on Principles and Practice of Programming in Java (PPPJ). ACM, 2011.
[3] P. A. Wright, "Dynamic binary translation on the .net platform," Master Thesis, Victoria University of Wellington, New Zealand, 2014.
[4] D. Lockhart, B. Ilbeyi, and C. Batten, "Pydgin: generating fast instruction set simulators from simple architecture descriptions with meta-tracing JIT compilers," in IEEE Int'l. Symposium on Performance Analysis of Systems and Software (ISPASS), March 2015.
[5] F. Bellard, "Tiny code generator (tcg readme)," 2016, URL: http://wiki.qemu.org/Documentation/TCG/.
[6] S. Köhler, T. Frank, M. Häsing, and R. G. Spallek, "Rubics: Ein retargierbares framework zur modellierung von prozessorarchitekturen auf der basis von .net clr," in Dresdner Arbeitstagung Schaltungs- und Systementwurf (DASS). Fraunhofer Verlag, 2016.
[7] *ECMA-335: Common Language Infrastructure (CLI)*. ECMA International, June 2012, 6th edition.
[8] A. Aho, R. Sethi, and J. Ullmann, Compiler Construction. Addison–Wesley Publishing Company, 1988.
[9] DE5-Net User Manual v1.04, 2017, URL: http://www.terasic.com.tw [accessed: 2017-03-21].
[10] ARMv7-M Architecture Reference Manual, 2010, dDI 0403D, ID021310, URL: http://www.arm.com.
[11] J. W. Cooley and J. W. Tukey, "An algorithm for the machine calculation of complex fourier series," Mathematics of Computation, April 1965.
[12] "An fpga ip core for easy dma over pcie," 2017, URL: http://xillybus.com.

Towards an Implementation of Data Analytics for Smart Grid Security

Jacobo Blanco*, Silvio La Porta*, Niamh O'Mahony*, Rohan Chabukswar†,
Alie El-Din Mady† and Menouer Boubekeur†
*EMC Research Europe, Cork Ireland
Email: {jacobo.blanco,silvio.laporta,niamh.omahony}@emc.com
†United Technologies Research Center, Cork Ireland
Email: {chabukr,madyaa,boubekm}@utrc.utc.com

Abstract—**Given the recent increase in frequency, sophistication and success of cyber-attacks against critical IT infrastructure, such as the Smart Grid, the urgent need for advanced cyber-security solutions is clearly evident. This paper presents a security information analytics (SIA) framework, using various data analytics methods to detect anomalies in metered data, that may indicate attacks. The implementation of the SIA tool has been applied to a live micro-grid test-bed for the modeling of normal behaviour and for performance analysis. Furthermore, the framework is scalable, allowing additional analysis tools and resilient control solutions to be incorporated, further enhancing the reliability of the system.**

Keywords–Cyber-physical systems; Intrusion detection; Cyber-security

I. Introduction

Critical infrastructures have, traditionally, been operated as stand-alone systems, with dedicated communication networks, thus protecting them from the outside world. However, advances in Cyber-Physical Systems (CPS), like the smart grid, expose new vulnerabilities, which can be exploited by cyber-criminals intent on carrying out malicious attacks [1], [2]. Recent cyber-attacks on energy utilities demonstrate that cyber-criminals are increasingly targeting critical infrastructures and learning how interact with and use such systems.

For example, on December 23, 2015, hackers deployed malware into the systems of multiple regional power distribution companies in Ukraine, causing an outage that left around 700,000 customers without electricity. The attackers used BlackEnergy along with a destructive component called KillDisk to disrupt machines, thus increasing the time required to restore normal operational mode and remove evidence of an attack [3]. Whilst the first version of BlackEnergy was only a common trojan, able to execute different DDoS attacks[4], it was later reconfigured and extended by incorporating modules to target industrial control systems (ICS). The Sandworm Team, to whom the Ukrainian attack has been attributed [5], are known to have carried out previous attacks, which were reported to not only involve classic strategic espionage, but also to target SCADA systems [6], leveraging a supplementary module in BlackEnergy that scans an IP block for open ports used by SCADA control systems. Furthermore, recently surfaced malware, such as Havex, exhibits the capability to target control systems. Havex was originally used between 2011 and 2013 during the 'DragonFly' campaign [7] that targeted energy, gas and oil companies, in which one of the infection vectors used was the water hole technique – compromising SCADA software companies' websites by repacking malware with the legitimate software.

An important feature of the malware described above is its ability to capture screenshots and record operators' activities in the compromised machines, thus, remedying the attackers' lack of expert knowledge about the ICS. With knowledge of the system model, an attacker may successfully achieve an attack which will not be detectable to a system operator [8].

The evolution of attackers, attack methods and exploitable vulnerabilities clearly results in changing risks confronting smart grid security. The success of the attacks, detailed above, indicates that the security tools and applications, currently in use, are failing to protect critical infrastructures from advanced attackers. New tools and methodologies for both detecting and reacting to attacks are, thus, needed to fill the gap and limit the current threat landscape.

Much of the existing work on CPS security relies on the assumption that perfect knowledge of the physical system is available to the designer of the control and estimation system [2] or that the dynamics of the system can be modelled as discrete-time state transitions, using techniques such as Kalman filtering [9]. However, these methods are not always practical or accurate for complex systems with interdependencies between components, and can result in the use of over-simplified models which do not characterise the complexities and dynamics of the system well [9]. Furthermore, when the control system is based on a simplified system model, an attacker who can acquire sufficient knowledge of the system model may be able to generate an attack that will go undetected [8].

The smart grid already collects a vast amount of information that can be used to develop new security analytics tools to quickly and accurately detect cyber-attacks. These data allow the behaviour of the grid, under normal operating conditions, to be modelled. The detection of anomalies or deviations from normal behaviour, which may indicate attacks, is an important precursor to building resilient control systems, the final aim of which is to create critical infrastructures that repair or reconfigure themselves, in response to an attack. Apart from being able to spot obvious policy violations by applying *a priori* rules that compare measured data to thresholds or look for correlations across events, one possible feature in a consolidated security analytics tools could be assimilating diverse data sources to identify possible cyber-attacks that are invisible from the perspective of any one of these actions, but could be revealed by jointly considering several independent actions.

In this work, a framework for enhanced smart grid security is proposed, which enables anomaly detection by means of the joint implementation of various data analytics algorithms, including methods driven by expert system knowledge and statistical analysis, as well as data-driven techniques from machine learning. The algorithms process the available data, intelligently exploiting the inherent redundancies in the system. The framework, called a Security Information Analytics (SIA) tool, is designed to be flexible, in order to allow other methods and algorithms to be incorporated over time.

The remainder of this paper describes the approach followed to develop the SIA tool for the smart grid. The threats faced in smart grid security, along with requirements and constraints for security analytics, are highlighted in Section II. This is followed by an introduction to the Nimbus testbed, which was used to develop and validate the SIA tool, in Section III. The paper continues with a description of the internal architecture of the SIA tool in Section IV. The preliminary results are outlined in Section V and some conclusions are discussed in Section VI.

II. Smart Grid Security

A. *Smart Grid Threats*

The NESCOR failure scenarios [10] are an extremely valuable resource for anyone trying to understand and mitigate potential cyber physical attacks against a smart grid environment. Scenarios are organized in terms of impact and each scenario addresses attacker profile, attack method and exploited vulnerability, as they are relevant to that particular scenario. The scenarios are organized into six domains:

1) Automated Meter Infrastructure (***AMI***)
2) Distributed Energy Resources (***DER***)
3) Wide Area Monitoring, Protection, and Control (***WAMPAC***)
4) Electric Transportation (***ET***)
5) Demand Response (***DR***)
6) Distribution Grid Management (***DGM***)

In this work, the focus is on the security of the meters, due to their importance in the smart grid infrastructure, considering, primarily, the NESCOR scenarios that are related to meter forgery and mass-disconnection attacks:

- ***AMI.1*** Authorized Employee Issues Unauthorized Mass Remote Disconnect: an employee within the utility, having valid authorization, issues a "remote disconnect" command to a large number of meters.
- ***AMI.9*** Invalid Disconnect Messages to Meters Impact Customers and Utility: a threat agent obtains legitimate credentials to the AMI system and issues a disconnect command for one or more target meters or schedules a disconnection to occur automatically at a later time.
- ***AMI.10*** Unauthorized Pricing Information Impacts Utility Revenue: a threat agent sends out unauthorized pricing information, such as Time-of-Use (TOU) pricing. This may result in either a loss or increase in utility revenue until the invalid price is recognized. Such an attack leaves the electricity supplier open to legal challenges from its subscribers.
- ***AMI.14*** Breach of Cellular Provider's Network Exposes AMI Access: inadequate security implementation in the AMI monitoring and control backup system allows a threat agent to execute an attack on the AMI implementation during a business continuity or disaster recovery scenario. Access to these backup systems allows a threat agent to perform malicious activity.
- ***AMI.32*** Power Stolen by Reconfiguring Meter via Optical Port: Many smart meters provide the capability of re-calibrating the settings via an optical port, which can be misused by economic thieves, who offer to alter the meters for a fee, changing the settings for recording power consumption and often cutting utility bills by 50-75%. This requires collusion between a knowledgeable criminal and an electricity customer, and will become widespread because of the ease of intrusion and the economic benefit to both parties.

B. *Requirements and Constraints*

In order to detect attacks, such as those outlined above, as well as unforeseen attacks, including those in which the attacker has gained knowledge of the ICS, the SIA tool aims to incorporate various different methods and algorithms, in order to provide a reliable and robust security solution for the smart grid. The primary requirements for such a system include the following:

- Minimise the probability of an undetected attack.
- Minimise the delay between the start of an attack and its detection.
- Minimise the probability of false alarm.

The first two requirements aim to reduce the impact of attacks by ensuring that interventions can take place immediately, minimising any financial losses, damage to physical components or danger to human life. Arguably as important as the first two requirements, minimisation of the false alarm probability avoids costly unnecessary interventions and, also, ensures that alerts are not ignored by operators. Secondary requirements include intuitive interfaces for visualisation and querying of data, integration into existing work flows, and allowing both real-time response and long-term investigations to be easily executed. However, these secondary requirements are considered to be outside of the scope of this paper.

There are many constraints that must be overcome in order to implement robust and reliable security analytics tools that will meet the afore-mentioned requirements. The dataset generated in the smart grid is very large and disparate, requiring massively parallel processing for a real time implementation. As such, any algorithms that are used, must be suitable for distributed processing and computational efficiency is an important consideration. The measurement precision of meters is limited and varies between devices, this can limit the potential for anomaly detection. Furthermore, when jointly considering the measurements from multiple meters throughout the system between the readings from different meters, synchronization, or the lack thereof, is a factor that must be carefully considered, in particular, for time-varying systems.

III. Introduction to Nimbus Testbed

The Nimbus Microgrid is a low-energy test bed commissioned by United Technologies Research Center (UTRC) in Cork, Ireland [11]. Along with an electrical microgrid, the test bed incorporates the thermal heating system of the Nimbus and Rubicon buildings of the Cork Institute of Technology, to create a live-in laboratory for demonstrating building and climate controls.

A. Description

The Nimbus micro-grid (Figure 1) consists of the following components:

- A wind turbine
- A Li-Ion battery
- A combined heat and power unit
- A feeder management relay to couple the microgrid to the building grid
- A set of local loads

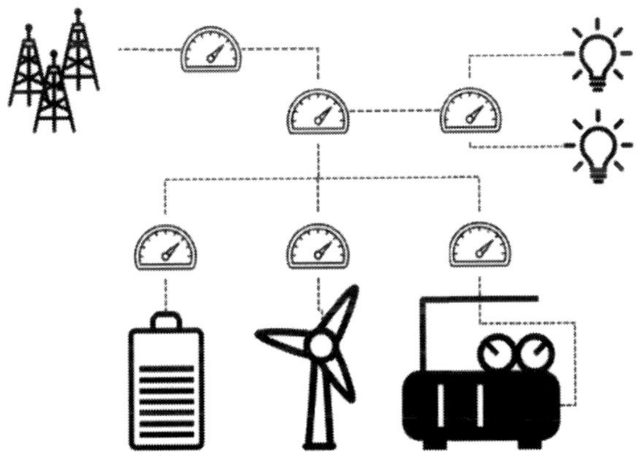

Figure 1. A simplified diagram of the Nimbus Test Bed

The microgrid and the connected thermal system are extensively monitored using a network of electrical meters and other sensors. These measurements, together with relevant information about gas and electricity power consumption measurements and prices, as well as thermal and electrical loads and weather and wind forecasts, are continuously available from the system and are collected into the data historian. The flow of information is outlined below.

B. Data Flow

1) **Measurement:** The primary points of data collection are the eight 3-phase electrical meters, each of which measures twenty-eight variables:
   - three phase-neutral and three phase-phase voltages,
   - four line currents (three phases and neutral),
   - total active (±), reactive (±), and apparent energy,
   - active, reactive and apparent power per phase,
   - total active and apparent power, and power factor,
   - frequency.

   The meter measurements make up the bulk of the collected data, accounting for a total of 224 variables. Furthermore, the battery, the combined heat and power unit, the wind turbine, the thermal storage tanks, and their associated inverters, all record the variables pertinent to each unit. These units also contain internal checks that generate alarms and warnings, which are communicated to the system.
2) **Collection:** The data variables listed above are communicated by the meters and system components to a programmable logic controller (PLC), which also logs other data from the system, such as the position indicators of all control valves and the status of breakers. It also acts as the conduit for the commands sent to the system, such as changes to the system mode and set points, commands to the breakers, as well as manual overrides. In total, 1252 variables are logged every second.
3) **Display & Logging:** The PLC communicates the data to the SCADA PC, which runs the human-machine-interface (HMI) tool shown in Figure 1, which displays the monitoring variables. The HMI also serves to display and acknowledge system alarms and warnings. The PC stores the variables into a database on the hard drive.
4) **Test Bed Middleware:** The Test Bed middleware is hosted on a PC on the same network as the SCADA PC. The middleware PC uses open platform communications (OPC) to periodically request the current variable values from the SCADA interface, which it parses and stores in another database on its hard drive. The middleware also acts the interface for any client (e.g., Matlab) to access the data using Simple Object Access Protocol.

IV. SIA Application

The SIA application is an interactive smart grid security analytics tool, implemented in R for the detection of anomalies in the Nimbus micro-grid. In this section, the architecture, algorithms used, and implementation of the tool are described in some detail.

A. SIA Architecture

The SIA application is composed of three main components: the security analytics engine, which tidies the SCADA data, runs the outlier algorithms, and makes a list of identified outliers; the web application, that visualizes the data and helps analysts to understand the security status of the grid; and a web API, an interface which can be used to feed security analytics intelligence into resilient control and remediation systems, to react to the threat or investigate the attack. This paper focuses on the security analytics engine.

B. Anomaly Detection Algorithms

There are five different methods of anomaly detection incorporated in the current implementation of the SIA tool and further methods will be added in ongoing work. The key idea behind the approach is to exploit redundancies, both in the data itself and in the outputs from the various methods, in order to improve the reliability of the anomaly detection.

The five currently implemented methods can be broadly categorized as *knowledge-based* or *data-driven*. The knowledge-based methods rely on expert knowledge of the micro-grid and its specific meters, or of the type of attack that might be carried out. For example, the voltage at any given meter is limited by the specifications of the equipment and the preconfigured value set by the test-bed operators. Similarly, a specific attack mode might cause multiple sensors to power off almost simultaneously; explicitly considering this type of attack can help it to be differentiated from a power fault. The *data-driven* category describes methods, such as machine learning, which rely on the data itself to learn the normal behaviour of the system, with no explicit assumptions made about the source of the data or the relationships between variables.

The SIA application is comprised of the five anomaly detectors described below. The single-variable outlier detector, rule-based outlier detector and dead sensor clustering algorithm are considered to be *knowledge-based*, whilst the smart detector and Kullback-Leibler distance are considered to be *data-driven*.

1) Single-variable outlier detector: This outlier detector is the simplest implemented in the analytic engine. The detector identifies if the value of a measured variable falls outside of a predefined range for that variable. The threshold can be defined by known specification limits on equipment or operational thresholds. In this case, the thresholds were defined by the specifications of the meters used in the NIMBUS test-bed.

2) Rule-based outlier detector: The rule-based detector exploits redundancies in the measured variables to find anomalies. Each meter measures multiple closely related variables, some of which are not physically independent. As an example, consider the six different voltages measured by an electrical meter: the magnitudes of three phase-to-neutral voltages and three phase-to-phase voltages. Since only five independent variables exist in the voltage system (three magnitudes and two relative phases), it is evident that there is one exploitable redundancy: each voltage vector needs to form a triangle with two others to create a closed system, as shown in Figure 2.

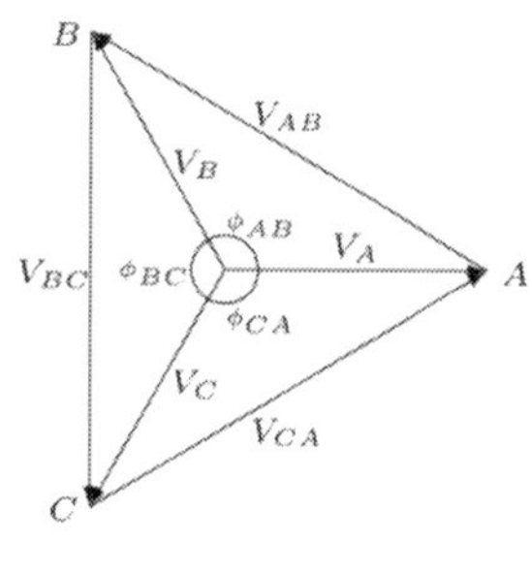

Figure 2. 3-Phase Voltage Phasors

Obtaining an equation from a redundancy requires expert knowledge. As an example, for Figure 2, Equation 1 sums the phases of the voltages:

$$\frac{1}{2\pi}\left[\cos^{-1}\frac{V_A^2+V_B^2-V_{AB}^2}{2V_AV_B} + \cos^{-1}\frac{V_B^2+V_C^2-V_{BC}^2}{2V_BV_C} + \cos^{-1}\frac{V_C^2+V_A^2-V_{CA}^2}{2V_CV_A}\right] = 1. \quad (1)$$

To account for measurement noise in the meter and other factors, such as sampling resolution and synchronization, historical data can be used to find the statistical distribution of the left hand side (LHS) of the equation. At any time, then, the value of the LHS for the current measurement can be compared to the historical distribution to calculate the probability of measuring that value. One or several thresholds can then be set on the probability that indicate the degree to which each redundancy check is violated.

In order to reduce false-positives, the number of violated equations is used as an outlier score. Namely, out of a total of twenty-one rules per meter, if less than three rules are violated, this is likely a false positive and can be safely ignored, however if more than six rules are violated the event is labelled as severe.

In order to remain portable, the system makes no assumptions about the variable output protocol or format. The equations are formatted using generic names for each variable. The rules are adapted to match the data format in use with a parsing routine. These rules can, then, be used directly with the input dataset.

3) Dead sensor clustering algorithm: This detector is designed to alert operators to the mass disconnection scenarios (***AMI.1***, ***AMI.9***, ***AMI.14***) discussed in Section II-A. This algorithm groups disconnected sensors using the time between disconnection. Multiple sensors in the same subnet work dropping within a few hours of each other likely points to an isolated hardware failure and poses a lower risk than a malicious attack. A much more severe event is a mass disconnection scenario where multiple related sensors receive a command to shut down within a few minutes of each other.

The dead sensor clustering procedure, illustrated in Figure 3, groups sensors into a cluster if they have disconnected within a time window which can be defined by the user. The time window is reset each time a sensor is disconnected and the cluster grows until no more sensors are disconnected within the time window. The cluster is defined as anomalous if the number of sensors associated with it is above a user-configurable threshold that should be defined in relation to the system size. This detector could be used to override a mass disconnection command and stop the attack at an early stage.

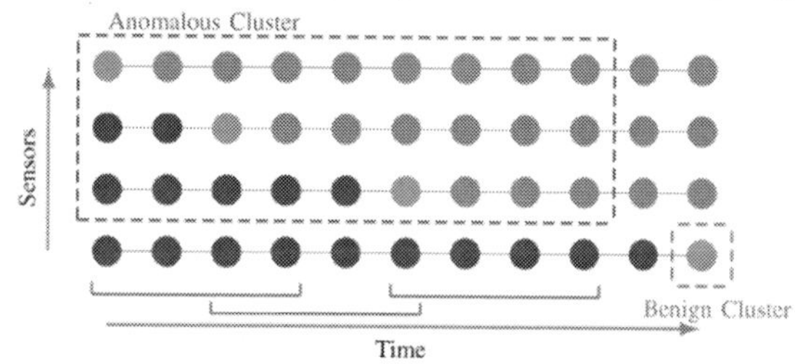

Figure 3. Diagram of the dead sensor clustering algorithm, showing the process by which disconnecting sensors are clustered together using a sliding time window. An orange node denotes a disconnected sensor, blue nodes denote connected sensors and grey nodes denote sensors that may be connected or disconnected. The time periods indicated in green represent the window. Here, a cluster with three or more sensors is considered anomalous.

4) Kullback-Leibler Distance: The Kullback-Leibler (KL) distance measures the difference between two distributions. In this case the symmetrized KL distance is used to determine by how much the daily measurements made by the sensors differ from a predefined baseline. Outliers are defined by those measurements which have a KL distance larger than a user-configurable value. In this work, the KL distance is calculated for each of the calculated rules, relating the redundant variables.

This detection algorithm serves to validate the results of the equations for an entire day against the baseline, and so it can not be used when running in real-time.

5) Smart Anomaly Detector: The so-called smart detector is a machine-learning (ML) algorithm that learns the normal behaviour of the system from the meter measurements to create a model. New measurements are, then, compared to the model and any instances which do not fit are classified as anomalous. In contrast to the rule-based anomaly detector, the smart detector produces a binary decision rather than a score.

ML algorithms are typically classified into supervised or unsupervised methods, depending on whether they require labelled data or not, respectively. Supervised methods typically work on data samples from two or more labelled classes, for example, normal and anomalous. The challenge with smart grids, and other anomaly detection exercises, is the lack of labelled anomalous data. In particular, it is very difficult to acquire known attack/fault data from smart grid installations and, even if such labelled anomalies were available, the case of new, unforeseen attacks or anomalies is not considered. One alternative is to assume that all data available represents normal behaviour, and to modify the supervised learning algorithm to work with a single class. Such algorithms are known as one-class ML, novelty detection, or anomaly detection algorithms in the literature. The algorithms learn the normal behaviour of the system, and then label any new data as anomalous if it does not fit with the model.

There are multiple anomaly detection ML algorithms in the literature, including variants of support vector machines (SVM), 1-Nearest Neighbour methods, parzen density estimation, and modified neural networks. In this work, a one-class support vector machine was used [12], [13], using the libsvm implementation [14]. Due to the diversity of electrical appliance behaviour, an individual model was trained for each meter in question. Some of the meters are connected to single-phase appliances while others to tri-phase industrial devices. As a result, some models include all variables used in the static rule-based detector, whilst others include a subset.

C. Combination of Anomaly Detector Outputs

The output from rule-based and smart anomaly detectors can be combined to reduce false-positives, by considering the overlapping subset of anomalous samples, detected by more than one detector. The single-variable detector is not included in the combination as it already provides an easily managable number of anomalies. In addition, this detector only examines a limited number of measurements, meaning the detection scope is much more restricted than the other detectors. This makes a combination with the single-variable detector inappropriate.

The combination is done by comparing the timestamps flagged as outliers by the smart anomaly detector and the rule-based detector. To get more information about which kinds of outliers are being detected by the smart detector, the overlap is examined as a function of the severity of the anomaly as defined in Section IV-B2.

V. RESULTS

The results of the various outlier detection algorithms are visualized in the web application portion of SIA. However, here we present the results of the rule-based and smart anomaly detectors only as they highlight some of the constraints and challenges in developing an effective smart grid analytics system.

A day worth of data collected at the Nimbus testbed using a stable time resolution of 15 seconds is used here. Note that this resolution is described as stable as this granularity does vary within the time range. The varying time resolution must be considered when comparing results of different algorithms and examining the severity of an outlier.

The Nimbus micro-grid is composed of 8 smart meters; in Figure 4 a typical output from the outlier detectors is shown for a single meter. Note that only the single variable and rule-based detectors are included here. To address ***AMI.32***, high-risk rules are defined and highlighted to the operator. These are a subset of rules which contain electrical currents. The current has been chosen as a potential at-risk variable for manipulation by agents wanting to reduce the cost of electricity.

The total number of anomalies flagged by the rule-based detector in a single day is 20840 over all 8 meters. This volume of outliers is clearly too high for effective remediation. This highlights the need to either improve the detection algorithms to improve their performance, or combine these results with complementary methods to reduce the false positives.

The former requires a deep and specialized understanding of the system to more accurately model meter behaviour. This approach is both time consuming, and reduced the ability of the system to be utilized in a different environment.

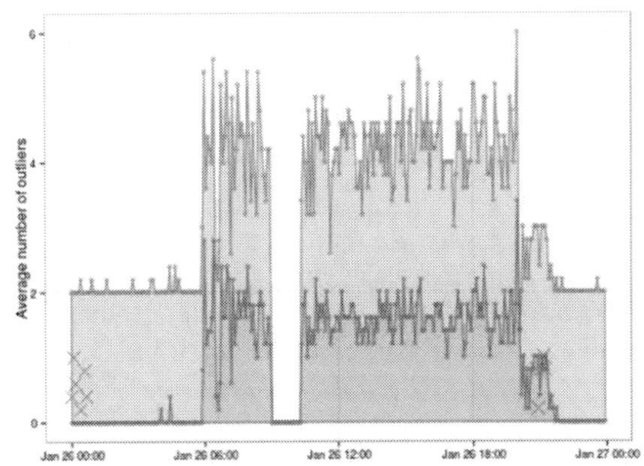

Figure 4. Number of outliers flagged as a function of time. Shown are the results from the rule-based and single variable detectors for a single sensors over a period of one day. The dotted distributions correspond to the number of outliers detected by the rule-based detector. The green distribution corresponds to all rules, while the red corresponds to so-called high-risk rules only. Anomalies detected by the single variable detector are marked by crosses.

Here, a combination of the rule-based detector and the smart anomaly detector results as described in Section IV-C is presented.

Examination of a days worth of data shows that a combination reduces the outliers by 70% compared to the rule-based detector alone. In addition, the combination filters out 80% of the low severity outliers while keeping over 93% of high severity outliers (Table I).

TABLE I. OVERLAP OF SMART AND RULE-BASED DECTORS BY SEVERITY

Severity	Overlap (%)
Low	17.7
Medium	56.2
High	93.7

VI. Conclusion and Future Work

The ever evolving security landscape presents a very real threat to critical infrastructure such as the smart grid. New technologies and modes of operation are required to protect the smart grid from increasingly sophisticated attacks. Exploiting data analytics is key in this effort. An overview of the design constraints for a security data analytics framework were presented along with a concrete implementation. The SIA application consists of an analytics engine designed to detect different attack and failure scenarios, and a web application interface to facilitate operations. Five anomaly detection algorithms were presented. These reflect both current approaches, relying on pre-existing knowledge and assumptions, and new approaches, that depend on data to create models with minimal domain-specific knowledge. Measurements from the microgrid are affected by multiple effects, which as a whole, limit the performance of the rule-based approach. In order to reduce false positives, a combination with an ML-based detector was carried out with some success. Remedying the limitations of the rule-based approach would require a greater understanding of the specific measurement components, and lead to an overspecification of algorithm. This would require significant work and reduce the applicability of such a model to other systems. Smart detectors which learn the behaviour of the system from the data can detect anomalies making minimal assumptions about the kinds of attack patterns, making the system more secure against future threats.

Acknowledgment

The research leading to these results has received funding from the European Union Seventh Framework Programme (FP7/2007-2013) under grant agreement no. 608224.

References

[1] D. Zhaoyang, "Smart grid cyber security," in Control Automation Robotics Vision (ICARCV), 2014 13th International Conference on, Dec 2014, pp. 1–2.

[2] A. Jones, Z. Kong, and C. Belta, "Anomaly detection in cyber-physical systems: A formal methods approach," in Decision and Control (CDC), 2014 IEEE 53rd Annual Conference on, Dec 2014, pp. 848–853.

[3] A. Cherepanov. BlackEnergy by the SSHBearDoor: attacks against Ukrainian news media and electric industry. [Online]. Available: http://www.welivesecurity.com/2016/01/03/blackenergy-sshbeardoor-details-2015-attacks-ukrainian-news-media-electric-industry/ (2016)

[4] J. Nazario, "Blackenergy ddos bot analysis," Arbor Networks, 2007.

[5] J. Hultquist. Sandworm team and the ukrainian power authority attacks. [Online]. Available: http://www.isightpartners.com/2016/01/ukraine-and-sandworm-team/ (2016)

[6] S. R. Symantec. Sandworm windows zero-day vulnerability being actively exploited in targeted attacks. [Online]. Available: http://www.symantec.com/connect/blogs/sandworm-windows-zero-day-vulnerability-being-actively-exploited-targeted-attacks (2014)

[7] S. S. Response. Cyberespionage attacks against energy suppliers, version 1.21. (2014)

[8] Y. Yuan and Y. Mo, "Security in cyber-physical systems: Controller design against known-plaintext attack," in Decision and Control (CDC), 2015 IEEE 54th Annual Conference on, Dec 2015, pp. 5814–5819.

[9] F. Pasqualetti, F. Dörfler, and F. Bullo, "Cyber-physical attacks in power networks: Models, fundamental limitations and monitor design," in Decision and Control and European Control Conference (CDC-ECC), 2011 50th IEEE Conference on, Dec 2011, pp. 2195–2201.

[10] National Electric Sector Cybersecurity Organization Resource (NESCOR), workgroup 1. National electric sector cybersecurity organization resource (nescor). (2014)

[11] V. Valdivia, S. O'Connell, F. Gonzalez-Espin, A. E. din Mady, K. Kouramas, L. D. Tommasi, H. Wiese, B. C. Villaverde, R. Foley, M. Cychowski, L. Hertig, D. Hamilton, and D. Pesch, "Sustainable building integrated energy test-bed," in Power Electronics for Distributed Generation Systems (PEDG), 2014 IEEE 5th International Symposium on, June 2014, pp. 1–6.

[12] B. Schölkopf, A. J. Smola, R. C. Williamson, and P. L. Bartlett, "New support vector algorithms," Neural Comput., vol. 12, no. 5, May 2000, pp. 1207–1245. [Online]. Available: http://dx.doi.org/10.1162/089976600300015565

[13] B. Schölkopf, J. C. Platt, J. Shawe-Taylor, A. J. Smola, and R. C. Williamson, "Estimating the support of a high-dimensional distribution," Neural computation, vol. 13, no. 7, 2001, pp. 1443–1471.

[14] C.-C. Chang and C.-J. Lin, "Libsvm: A library for support vector machines," ACM Transactions on Intelligent Systems and Technology (TIST), vol. 2, no. 3, 2011, p. 27.

Towards Secure Building Management System based on Internet of Things

Alie El-din Mady*, Ruben Trapero†, Antonio Skarmeta‡ and Stefano Bianchi§
*United Technologies Research Center, Cork Ireland
Email: madyaa@utrc.utc.com
†Cybersecurity Laboratory, Atos Research & Innovation, Spain
Email: ruben.trapero.external@atos.net
‡Universidad de Murcia, Murcia, Spain
Email: skarmeta@um.es
§Softeco Sismat, Genova, Italy
Email:stefano.bianchi@softeco.it

Abstract—**Energy management systems are used to control energy usage in buildings and campuses in order to provide reliable energy supply and maximize user comfort while minimizing energy usage. The heterogeneous, distributed, and dynamically evolving nature of energy management systems based on internet of things introduces new and unexpected risks that cannot be solved by current state-of-the-art security solutions. For this, new paradigms and methods are required in order to i) build security into the Information Communication Technology (ICT) system at the outset, ii) adapt to changing security conditions, iii) reduce the need to fix flaws after deploying the system, and iv) provide the assurance that the ICT system is secure and trustworthy at all times. This paper provides a holistic overview of designing a secure framework for Internet of Things (IoT) system, where the framework will be implemented as part of an ongoing H2020 project called ANASTACIA: Advanced Networked Agents for Security and Trust Assessment in Cyber-Physical System (CPS) based on IoT Architectures.**

Keywords–Cyber-physical systems; Intrusion detection; Cyber-security

I. INTRODUCTION

The aim of a modern Energy Management System (EMS) is to enhance the functionality of interactive control strategies leading towards energy efficiency and a more user friendly environment. Typically, the EMS operates several building systems, such as the supervisory control and data acquisition (SCADA), which controls the smartgrid of one or more buildings, and the Building Management System (BMS), which controls the building heating demand, security system, fire alarm system, etc. Heating, ventilation, and air conditioning (HVAC) is considered to be the highest source of energy consumption in the building operation, and the systems most affecting user comfort [1].

Historically, EMS systems were installed when potential security threats were only physical. In addition, having EMS connected on a segregated network reduces the risk of cyber and remote attacks. However, the evolving in building control requires connecting EMS to Internet of Things (IoT) to optimize accurately the user needs and building operations [2]. By connecting EMS to the building communication network, the possibility of EMS cyber-attack increases, which can lead to significant financial impact. The StuxNet cyber-attack supposedly targeting a nuclear-enrichment plant (by corrupting the measurements and actuator signals) in Iran [3], and BlackEnergy malware targeting several electricity distribution companies in Ukraine [4], are concrete examples of cyber-attacks. Thus, it is crucial to make the control of EMS to be resilient against cyber-crime.

The existing frameworks for EMS consider the system integration, connectivity and optimal control performance. The cyber-security in the EMS framework is mainly performed based on running tests and benchmarks to evaluate the possible cyber-attacks and their impact [5].

As part of an ongoing research in ANASTACIA project [6], this paper aims to propose a high-level framework architecture for Cyber-Physical System based on IoT, where EMS is an application of CPS. In this framework, we develop a trustworthy-by-design autonomic security framework with testing, validation and security optimization capabilities. ANASTACIA framework combines several elements from different domains: from IoT controllers to virtual functions accessible through Software Defined Network (SDN) interfaces, orchestration of security policies and enforcement of security preferences in heterogeneous scenarios.

In Section II, we present a CPS model used to show the usage of the developed security framework. Section III explains the the developed cyber security framework architecture. Section IV discusses a validation methodology to proof the efficiency of the developed framework. Finally, Section V provides a conclusion and future work.

II. CYBER-PHYSICAL SYSTEM MODEL

ANASTACIA CPS model provides a representation of how ANASTACIA framework can be integrated within a CPS. Figure 1 depicts the ANASTACIA system model. ANASTACIA is envisioned to enable trust and security by-design for CPS based on IoT and cloud architectures. In general terms, an IoT Infrastructure can be seen as a system with two well differentiated planes. The *Data Plane* is closer to the physical domain and is composed of IoT devices, the network that interconnect them and in general, the elements providing resources, such as servers or routers. On top of the Data Plane is the *Control Plane* that enables the management of the underlying devices. These include either IoT controllers that directly control the devices resources (sometimes even integrated in the same device) or Virtual Interfaces (i.e., VNFs) that are able to control/access to the Data Plane resources through the cloud.

IoT platforms are currently threatened by a myriad of external dangers. Advanced attacks targets IoT platforms by taking in account the existing vulnerabilities in devices

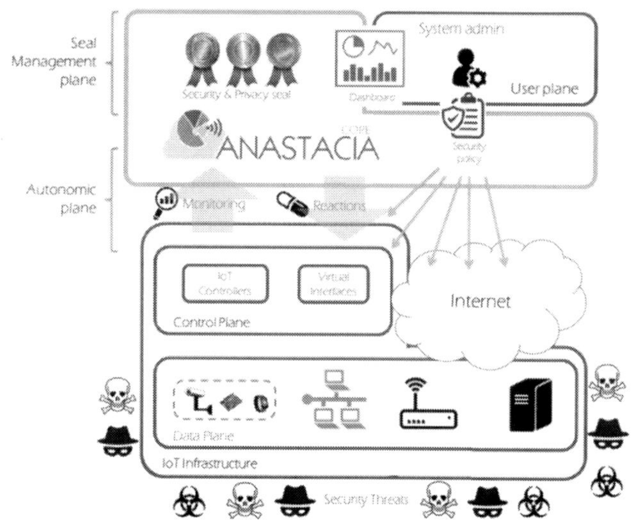

Figure 1. CPS Modeling

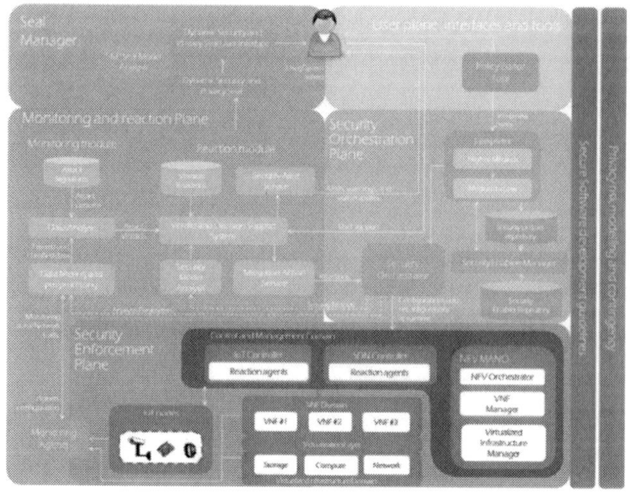

Figure 2. ANASTACIA Cyber-Security Framework Architecture

with poorly managed/configured security settings (i.e., default passwords) or even by using social engineering techniques that engage users to install malwares or disclose passwords. ANASTACIA is built on top of IoT platforms to protect them against such threats. ANASTACIA is conceived as a policy based framework where system admins, at the *User plane*, set a specific security policy that must be fulfilled within an IoT platform. This security policy is enforced within the IoT platform by orchestrating its resources (devices, services, etc.). The control of the fulfillment of the security policy is carried out by the ANASTACIA framework at the *Autonomic plane* by monitoring the IoT platform and detecting threats and ongoing attacks. Additionally, the ANASTACIA framework is able to create and trigger reactions that mitigate the effects of attacks, prevent against threats and guarantee the fulfillment of the security policy.

One of the most novel features of ANASTACIA is carried out at the *Seal Management plane*, built on top of the ANASTACIA framework. At this plane, a dynamic seal is created, representing the current level of security of the IoT platform.

III. CYBER-SECURITY FRAMEWORK ARCHITECTURE

The ANASTACIA system model (as presented in Figure 1) is structured as a set of layers that provide a broad view of the framework and stand out its integration within IoT infrastructures. ANASTACIA is envisioned as a framework built on top of an IoT infrastructure where network elements, physical and virtual network elements interact in the Data Plane. The interaction with these elements is done by using virtual interfaces with cloud computing networks for the usage of external resources (such as computing or storage). On top of that, the Control Plane manages the Data Plane by using APIs and by orchestrating Network Function Virtualization (NFV).

Figure 2 represents ANASTACIA framework, which extends the ANASTACIA system model by expanding the functions of the ANASTACIA core. The Autonomic Plane includes the components that provide the ANASTACIA framework with its intelligence and dynamic behavior. This plane can be divided into three sub-planes, which carry out specific activities within the framework as follows:

- **Security Orchestrator Plane** organizes the resources that support the *Enforcement Plane*, carrying out activities such as the transformation of security properties to configuration rules and aligning the security policies defined by the security interpreter with the provisioning of relevant security mechanisms. It has the whole vision of the underlying infrastructure and the resources and interfaces available at the *Security Enforcement Plane*.
- **Security Enforcement Plane** connects the ANASTACIA core with the IoT Platform, managing the interactions among objects and components for the enforcement of the security policy defined at the *User Plane*. This plane supports the enforcement of configurations and reactions triggered by the *Security Orchestrator Plane*, in order to preserve the expected security level. At this plane the agents that support the monitoring of IoT devices or the enforcement of reactions are instantiated, either if they are operating on remote or directly attached to the device.
- **Monitoring and Reaction Plane** connects to the IoT Platform through the *Security Enforcement Plane* in order to collect security-focused information related to the system behavior. At this plane, intelligent data-driven automated and contextual monitoring of activities at embedded devices, legacy systems and IoT devices by retrieving signals, event logs, traces, heartbeats signals, status reports or operational information. This plane also evaluates the fulfilment of the security policy by checking security models or threats signatures, detecting anomalies and creating reactions to mitigate such anomalies, in terms or reconfigurations and alerts to system administrators [1] [7].

Additionally, on top of the architecture the *User Plane* and the *Seal Management Plane* interact with the Autonomic plane:

- The User Plane includes interfaces, applications and tools that help system administrators to manage the IoT platform through the ANASTACIA framework. For example, at this plane system admins are able to edit the security policies that govern the underlying IoT platform.
- The Seal Manager is in charge of providing users with a real-time indicator of the overall security level.

The high level architecture can be used to identify the main activities to be carried out by the ANASTACIA framework, which is used to identify the specific components that are part of every identified plane. By analyzing several use-cases for EMS application, we can identify five main activities to be supported by the platform:

- **Security policy set-up** This is the initial process triggered once a security policy has been defined by the user. In this process the policy has to be configured in the platform in order to be enforced. The interpretation of the security policy claims, the configurations required to monitor the security controls associated to a policy or the definition of thresholds to identify policy violations, are some activities carried out by this process.
- **Security policy orchestration** Once the policy has been set-up, it is necessary to enforce the controls specified at the policy. The interfaces and IoT controllers must be orchestrated according to the security policy.
- **Security monitoring** In this process, the monitoring information is extracted from the devices through monitoring agents and according to the security controls interpreted from the security policy. In this activity, the monitoring data is filtered and aggregated in order to carry out its analysis and the detection of anomalies.
- **Security reaction** In this process, the detected anomalies are evaluated to design counter measures in order to mitigate the effects of attacks and potential threats.
- **Dynamic security and privacy seal** In this process, relevant information about detected threats, monitored information is evaluated to create a seal that determines the level of security guaranteed/offered by an IoT platform.

IV. ANASTACIA FRAMEWORK VALIDATION

In order to perform quick, scalable and automated testing over the architecture several interconnected virtual machines have been deployed covering the functionality for policy enforcement over IoT and SDN integration, specifically, the test has been realized for the isolation sensor use-case. As shown in Figure 3, the deployment includes the next seven virtual machines or isolated containers like docker:

1) IoT Application.
2) Micro Orchestrator.
3) SECURED Policy Interpreter.
4) ONOS SDN Controller [8].
5) OpenDayLight SDN Controller [9].
6) Open Virtual Switch.
7) Contiki emulator [10].

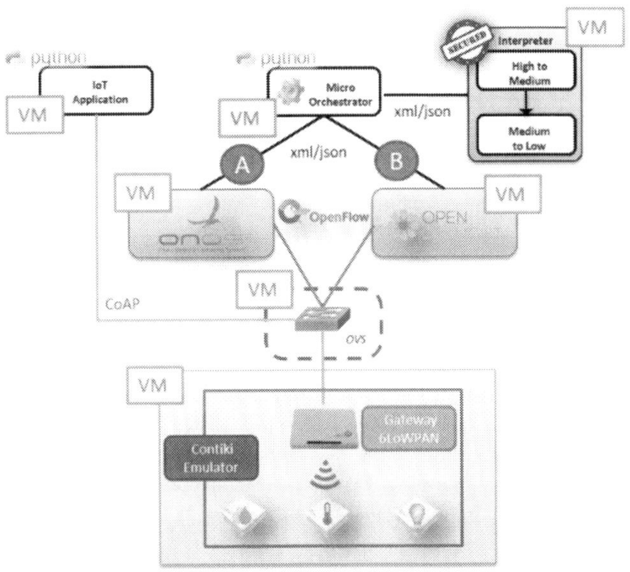

Figure 3. ANASTACIA Virtual TESTBED Deployment

The idea of the scenario is that the *IoT Application* can establish communication with a mote using a global IPv6 address and the communication can be interrupted through the enforcement of security policies applied by the *SDN controller*. To this purpose we have develop a little python script for the *IoT Application*, a python micro orchestrator and basic SDN plugins on the interpreter (for each of the mainstream controllers, this is *OpenDayLight* and *ONOS*). For the IoT application, the script sends sporadically CoAP request messages to the motes using global IPv6 addresses as source and destination. The CoAP message is received by the SDN Network (the OVS instance in this case) and forwarded to the virtual machine that contains the *Contiki* emulator. The *Contiki* emulator provides the capability to deploy a gateway between the 6LoWPAN network and the host virtual machine network, so the CoAP message is received by the Gateway and forwarded to the mote. During the communication, we decide to isolate the sensor, so we start in the *micro orchestrator* the policy enforcement. The *micro orchestrator* sends a refinement request to the interpreter and after the high to medium refinement process, the interpreter transforms the policy on a SDN configuration. At this point, we can to use *ODL-SDN* plugin or *ONOS-SDN* plugin in order to get the appropriate configuration for the selected platform. Once the policy refinement process has been finished, the *micro orchestrator* receives the SDN configuration file and invokes a specific call for the *SDN controller's* Northbound API according to the controller election. Specifically, for the sensor isolation use case we are installing a flow rule on the OVS indicating that all traffic containing the sensor's IPv6 address must be dropped.

We are currently working on the integration of the virtual IoT environment with the physical one; this means, allowing the connectivity from/to the emulator to leave the machine and be connected to a real SDN deployment. Therefore, the emulator could speak with real IoT devices or mimic them so that the SDN could redirect an attacker to a cloned scenario like a honeynet.

V. Conclusion and Future Work

The paper has presented a preliminary design of secure framework for cyber-physical system based on IoT. The design of the framework was derived by energy management system, which can be a critical CPS application considering safety critical infrastructure, such as hospitals, airports, etc. The novelty of the framework is based on the integrating and the coordination of serval security stages, leading to (semi) automatic security platform for CPS based IoT system. The future work under ANASTACIA project will focus on developing each component of the framework and validate it with different applications of CPS.

Acknowledgment

The research leading to these results has received funding from the European Union's Horizon 2020 research and innovation programme under Grant Agreement No. 731558.

References

[1] K. Paridari, A. Mady, S. L. Porta, R. Chabukswar, J. Blanco, A. Teixeira, H. Sandberg, and M. Boubekeur, "Cyber-physical-security framework for building energy management system," ACM/IEEE 7th International Conference on Cyber-Physical Systems (ICCPS), April 2016.

[2] D. Minoli, K. Sohraby, and B. Occhiogrosso, "Iot considerations, requirements, and architectures for smart buildings—energy optimization and next-generation building management systems," IEEE Internet of Things Journal, vol. 4, January 2017, pp. 269–283.

[3] J. P. Farwell and R. Rohozinski, "Stuxnet and the future of cyber war," Survival, vol. 53, 2011, pp. 23–40.

[4] O. Available. Blackenergy. [Online]. Available: http://www.securityweek.com/blackenergy-group-uses-destructive-plugin-ukraine-attacks (2015)

[5] S. Gold, "The scada challenge: securing critical infrastructure," Network Security, vol. 8, 2009, pp. 18–20.

[6] [Online]. Anastacia h2020 project. [Online]. Available: http://www.anastacia-h2020.eu/

[7] A. Mady, D. Mehta, D. M. Shila, and M. Boubekeur, "Towards resilient cyber security for embedded devices on internet," 2016 IEEE 3rd World Forum on Internet of Things (WF-IoT) (2016), vol. 0, Dec. 2016, pp. 1–2.

[8] [Online]. Open network operating system (onos). [Online]. Available: https://www.sdxcentral.com/projects/on-lab-open-network-operating-system-onos/

[9] O. (ODL). opendaylight sdn. [Online]. Available: https://www.opendaylight.org/

[10] Contiki. Contiki: The open source OS for the Internet of Things. [Online]. Available: http://www.contiki-os.org/

Anomaly-Based Intrusion Detection System for Embedded Devices on Internet

Deepak Mehta, Alie El-Din Mady, and Menouer Boubekeur

United Technologies Research Center
Cork, Ireland
Email: {mehtad,madyaa,boubekm}@utrc.utc.com

Devu Manikantan Shila

United Technologies Research Center
East Hartford, Connecticut
Email: manikad@utrc.utc.com

***Abstract*—Embedded devices connected to the Internet ranging from garage door openers, home thermostats, home automation systems to automobiles, are continuously exploited by remote attack vectors. According to OWASP Internet of Things project, these vulnerabilities are due to insecure web interfaces, insufficient authentication and authorization, insufficient transport layer protection, broken cryptography, insecure software/firmware updates, or poor physical security. As opposed to PowerPC systems, embedded devices lack resources to run advanced attack detection or anti-virus softwares. Moreover, embedded devices are often mass produced (thousand to millions) and share a static security footprint. Hence, a successful attack on a single device can be replicated across other devices with minimal effort. There exists a significant need towards developing a resilient cyber security methodology that provides scalable and efficient *intrusion detection and resilient architecture*. In this paper, we present an efficient hierarchical anomaly-based intrusion detection method and resilient policy framework that enables the system to detect suspicious activity and continue the operation with minimum functionality.**

***Keywords*–Cyber Security; Embedded devices; Internet of Things; Intrusion Detection; Resilient policy;**

I. INTRODUCTION

The continued rise of cyber attacks together with the evolving skills of the attackers, and inefficiency of the traditional security algorithms employed by the embedded devices to defend against advanced and sophisticated attacks, necessitate the development of novel defense and resilient techniques. Targeted aggressive attacks use well-researched and well-funded multi-vector tactics to introduce stealthy and persistent malware in connected embedded systems (i.e., Internet of Things) infrastructure systems. Examples include ThingBot, Ransomware [3]-[5], etc. The insecure composition of legacy devices with web interfaces (such as HTTP, PHP, etc.) [3] further enlarges the attack surfaces of these systems. Furthermore, vulnerabilities for embedded devices are discovered daily, which can be easily replicated to many other devices connected to the Internet. These factors highlight the importance of designing a scalable detection scheme that not only detect attacks but also minimize the attack impact and prevent spreading of attack over other similar embedded devices.

A handful of approaches exist along the tangents of attack detection for large scale systems and resilient algorithms for enabling minimal system services even under attack [6], [7], [8], [9], [10]. However, these approaches require high computational resources, which make it infeasible for embedded devices with limited resources. In addition, these approaches rely on operational data of the system, which in turn limits the ability to detect a wide variety of attacks.

This paper proposes an Intrusion Detection and Resilient Policy methodology for embedded devices connected to the Internet. In order to assist the development of the proposed approach, we have summarized various attack models for Internet connected embedded systems. This work aims to extend our preliminary proposal [1]. The paper is organized as follows: In Section II we first describe the overall methodology of hierarchical based intrusion detection and resilient policy for detection. In Section III we describe the details of our approach for anomaly-based intrusion detection system for embedded devices on internet. In Section IV we evaluate the developed methodology. Finally, in Section V we present conclusions and future work.

II. CYBER-PHYSICAL ATTACKS, DETECTION AND MITIGATION

A. Adversary models

We consider several different broad strategies an attacker may employ against Internet facing embedded devices [11]: a) *circumvention attack* finds exploits that does not depend on the security properties of the embedded device; b) *deputy attack* finds a way to exploit the vulnerabilities of a benign program in a malicious way; c) *brute force attack* attempts all possible cyber security keys until an exploit is found that succeeds; d) *dictionary attack* tries only some key space possibilities which are deemed most likely to succeed; e) *probing attack* uses probe packets to learn properties of the security method execution needed to construct an attack; f) *denial of service* attempts to make the IoT device unavailable; g) *backdoor attack* uses hardcoded credentials or passwords to gain access to the system; h) *code injection or reuse* attack uses vulnerable programs or coding errors to inject malicious code into the device.

B. Hierarchical based Intrusion Detection

This approach considers two level of Intrusion Detection System (IDS), as shown in Figure 1: local IDS and supervisory IDS. The local IDS is deployed on every embedded device, which uses various information, such as power consumption, memory usage and environmental data to learn and build a time series based statistical model. The resulting statistical model is used to detect any anomalous behaviors at the device layer and the anomalous findings are further reported to the supervisory IDS for decision making. The supervisory IDS, deployed at the gateway, learns and builds a data correlation model that captures the dependencies between all connected devices during the deployment phase (we assume normal operational behavior during the period of installation). When an anomaly is reported from the local IDS, the supervisory IDS uses the data correlation model to confirm the intrusion based on other devices behavior (e.g., the behavior of other correlated devices will not change when the device is attacked, which is used as an evidence). In order to prevent supervisory IDS from detecting attacks, an attacker has to learn the group of correlated devices and tamper them accordingly, which is a complex task. In the event of an attack, supervisory IDS will apply a resilient policy to: a) thwart attacks on other similar devices by trigerring a change in the configuration of the devices; b) isolates the attacked devices and continues to provide the same services via use of virtual sensors. In this paper we will focus on supervisory intrusion detection.

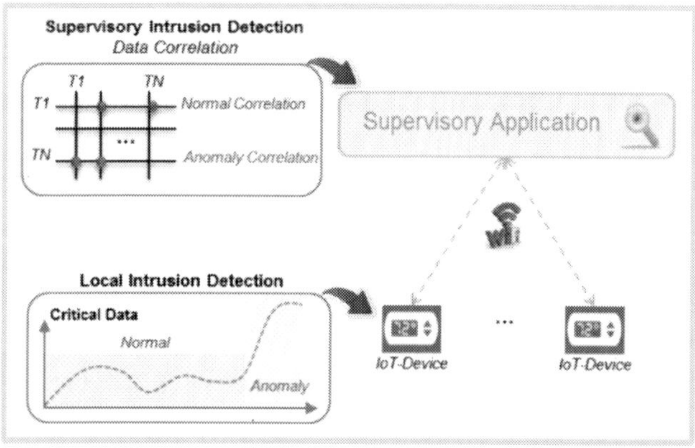

Figure 1. Hierarchical based Intrusion Detection

C. Resilient Policy

The supervisory IDS applies a resilient policy to initially isolate the attacked device from other devices. The supervisory IDS uses a combination of the data correlation model and the local statistical model to build a *virtual sensor* [10]. This virtual sensor uses prediction algorithms, such as Kalman Filtering to predict the actuation values supplied by the attacked device, and deliver the same services (e.g., actuation values) without the help of the attacked device. Moreover, the supervisory IDS also triggers a change in system configuration (e.g., a defense depending on the attack detected) to the correlated devices to prevent spreading of attack to other devices.

III. Supervisory Intrusion Detection

The core function of any IDS is to gather and analyse information in order to identify any intrusion. When the context is cyber-physical system or Internet of Things, IDS should not only monitor cyber-related metrics (e.g., network activity, CPU speed, log files) but also physical processes/measurements that govern behaviour of physical devices. IoT or sensor data consists of a continuous stream of data (aka time-series) where the time interval between successive updates could vary from milliseconds to minutes. The data produced, usually pertains to the information about the physical state of a system, i.e., temperature, pressure, voltage, power consumption, flow rate, speed, acceleration, etc. The goal is to detect intrusion not only in cyber space but also in physical space. For example, the data reported by an IoT sensor could be far from its normal behaviour or an actuator could behaves in a highly erratic manner.

The existing intrusion detection techniques can be broadly classified into two categories: *knowledge-based* and *anomaly-based* [12].

- A knowledge-based IDS uses a database of patterns/signatures (a footprint specified in terms of data packets, number of failed attempts, upper and lower bounds physical measurements etc.) of previously known attacks and system vulnerabilities. Periodically, the current signature is checked with the database to identify and prevent the same attacks in the future. The advantages of knowledge-based intrusion detection system is that it is highly affective towards well known attacks and has low false positive rate. The disadvantages are that it cannot identify new attacks and the database would need frequent updates.
- The anomaly-based [13] intrusion detection system builds a profile (or a data-model) of the *normal* behaviour using either statistical or unsupervised machine learning methods. It then uses the normal profile to flag any deviations from that profile as alerts. The advantages of anomaly-based IDS is that it can identify new attacks, but the disadvantage is that it is prone to high false positive rate.

Both approaches have been extensively studied. A reader is referred to [12] for more details.

In the following sections, we shall describe a novel approach for supervisory intrusion detection. More precisely, we will exploit the relationship between a set of given time-series for detecting anomalies. This could either be used on its own or and it could be used as an additional feature of another algorithm to improve its efficiency.

A. Correlation-based Anomaly Detection

Problem Setting. We are given a database of unlabelled n time series $T = \{t^1, t^2, \ldots, t^n\}$ containing both normal and anomalous sub-sequences. The assumption is that the majority of them are normal. The problem is to detect anomalous subsequence within a given time-series by exploiting a set of corresponding sub-sequences of other time-series when possible.

The overall methodology of the proposed anomaly-based intrusion detection is shown in Figure 2. It first transforms the input data by aggregation and discretization prior to learning the model that represents the normal behaviour of the signals. The parameters of the model are then tuned to improve the overall performance of the method. We shall now describe each step in detail.

Transformation: Aggregation and Discretization

The aggregation step transforms a sequence of k consecutive values of one (or more) time-series by a representative value using a chosen aggregation function.

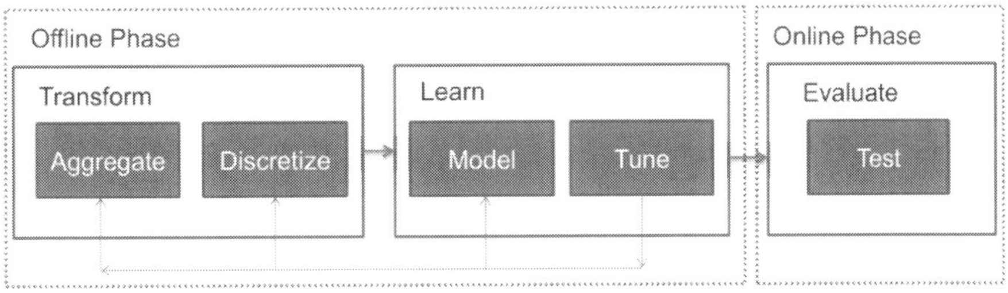

Figure 2. Overall Methodology for Anomaly-based Intrusion Detection

Given a training database of n series, $T_{train} = \{t^1, \ldots, t^n\}$, we transform it into $n \times (n-1)$ time-series denoted by $S = \{s^{pq} | p \leq n \wedge q \leq n\}$. Each time-series s^{pq} is a sequence of values, i.e., $\langle s_1^{pq}, \ldots, s_{m-k+1}^{pq} \rangle$, where each s_i^{pq} is an aggregation of sub-sequences $\langle t_i^p, \ldots, t_{i+k}^p \rangle$ and $\langle t_i^q, \ldots, t_{i+k}^q \rangle$ with a representative value when sliding a window of size k by one step at a time. The two sub-sequences are aggregated using normalised cross-correlation function (NCC). The cross-correlation function (aka. cross-covariance function) provides a measure of similarity of two sub-sequences, which is computed as follows:

$$\begin{aligned} s_i^{pq} &= NCC(\langle t_i^p, \ldots, t_{i+k}^p \rangle, \langle t_i^q, \ldots, t_{i+k}^q \rangle) \\ &= \frac{\sum_i^{i+k} t_i^p \times t_i^q}{\sqrt{\sum_i^{i+k} (t_i^p)^2 \times \sum_i^{i+k} (t_i^q)^2}} \end{aligned} \quad (1)$$

The normalized cross-correlation scoring is straightforward to interpret. It returns a value between +1 and -1 inclusive, where 1 means the two sub-sequences are exactly the same, 0 means they are very different from each other, and -1 they are exactly opposite. An example of positive correlation and no correlation between different pairs of sensors reporting temperatures is shown in Figure 3. The aggregation function is not restricted to NCC. Any reasonable function can be used instead.

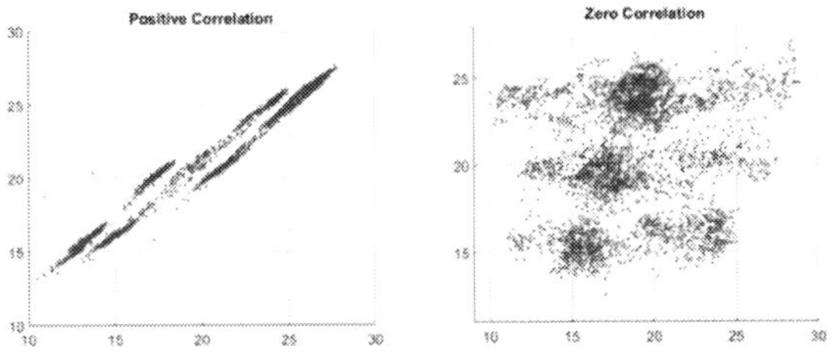

Figure 3. Example: Positive correlation (left) and No correlation (right) between temperatures readings of sensors

The next step is the discretization of a given time-series, where the goal is to transform the time-series from a sequence of continuous values to a sequence of discrete intervals by dividing the amplitude range of the input time-series. There are several ways in which the intervals can be chosen. The simplest way is to create equal bin size and a more sophisticated approach is to use clustering. In this paper we have implemented the former approach. Each interval could be represented by a unique number or by an alphabet. We introduce a parameter d to denote the number of discrete intervals. Furthermore, let α_i^{pq} denotes the ith discrete-interval associated with the transformed time-series s^{pq}. Discretization can decrease the dimensionality of the data and it can increase the efficiency of the algorithm for anomaly detection. A good overview on discretization is provided in [14].

Learning Model and Tuning. The goal of this step is to learn a data-model that captures the normal behaviour and tune the parameters of the model in order to maximise the detection of the anomalies while minimising the false positive rate. In the following, we describe how we generate a model for a given signal.

Let f_i^{pq} denotes the frequency of the discrete-interval α_i^{pq} observed in the time-series s^{pq}. We also introduce a parameter λ to denote the minimum percentage of non-anomalous sub-sequences within any time-series. Recall that the initial assumption was that most of the sub-sequences are normal but very few might be anomalous. The general idea is to select a set of discrete intervals that combined together represent normal portion of the time-series, which should be at least λ percentage of the m subs-sequences of window-size k within a time-series.

Let N^{pq} be the set of discrete intervals that are normally observed within time series s^{pq} with respect to the parameter λ. The subset of the discrete intervals classified as normal, i.e., $N^{pq} \subseteq \{\alpha_1^{pq}, \ldots, \alpha_d^{pq}$, is computed as follows:

- The sum of the frequencies of discrete intervals covered by N^{pq} must be greater than a given threshold, i.e., $\sum_{\alpha_j^{pq} \in N^{pq}} (f_j^{pq}/m) \geq \lambda$.
- If the ith discrete interval is classified as normal ($\alpha_i^{pq} \subseteq N^{pq}$) then any j^{th} interval occurring more than the ith interval ($f_j^{pq} \geq f_i^{pq}$) must also be classified as normal ($\alpha_j^{pq} \subseteq N^{pq}$).
- Minimise the number of discrete intervals classified as normal subject to the above two constraints.

For a given time-series (signal or sensor), the above step is repeated with respect to each other signal. The data-model that captures the normal behaviour of a time-series is encoded as a Boolean matrix where each row correspond to another time-series and each column corresponds to a discrete interval. An example of a Boolean matrix model for a time-series t^5 is shown in Table I. The last 4 columns denote the number of discrete intervals, i.e., $d = 4$. Each row corresponds to the set of discrete intervals that are classified as normal (when the value is 1) with respect to the qth time-series which belongs to the set $\{t^1, t^2, t^3, t^4\}$.

The anomaly score of a given window of a time-series is computed by first checking whether the correlation associated

TABLE I. AN EXAMPLE OF A BOOLEAN MATRIX MODEL.

$(p = 5)$	q	1	2	3	4
N^{51}	1	1	0	0	1
N^{52}	2	1	0	0	1
N^{53}	3	0	0	1	1
N^{54}	4	0	1	0	0

with the sub-sequence of another time-series falls in a discrete interval classified as normal. This is done with respect to each corresponding sub-sequence of other time-series. The anomaly score of the window is the number of discrete-intervals associated with other time-series falling in the normal category. We also introduce anomaly threshold, denoted as ϕ, as another parameter. The anomaly score is compared with the threshold, and if it is greater than the threshold than the window is classified as anomalous. In the final step, the following parameters are tuned:

1) The aggregation step introduced the parameter k to denote the length of the window.
2) The discretization step introduced the parameter d to denote the number of discrete intervals.
3) The modelling step introduced the parameter λ to denote the percentage of the number of sub-sequences assumed to be normal within a time-series.
4) The final parameter is the attack-threshold denoted as ϕ.

IV. EVALUATION.

In this section we present preliminary results. For the evaluation purpose we experimented with two sets of data:

1) The historical data for thermostat temperatures, where 12 sensor data have been used. This data is collected at the demo-site at Cork Institute of Technology (CIT), where the demo-site has an energy management system controls a small size smart-grid covering several buildings [2].
2) Real-CPU, memory, and temperature data obtained from three TI CC3200-LAUNCHXL IoT devices, considering CPU usage, memory stack size and temperature value. This data was collected from a simple demo for internet connected thermostat demonstration. the devices was using WiFi to communicate with a centralized server to send the temperature values and receive any actuation instructions.

We divided the data into training data and test data.

Training Parameters. For training purpose we restricted the values of the parameters as defined before. The size of the window was restricted to the set $\{10, 20, 40\}$. The number of discrete intervals was chosen from the set $\{10, 20\}$. The maximum percentage of the sequences assumed to be normal was chosen from the set $80\%, 85\%, 90\%, 95\%, 100\%$. The attack score threshold was chosen from the set $0.01, 0.02, 0.05, 0.1, 0.15, 0.2, 0.5$. During the training phase, the parameters of the model for representing the normal behaviour was tuned from the above combination of parameter space.

Attack Model. To test the performance of our approach we injected the attack by perturbing the test data, which relied on three parameters: (1) *disturbance magnitude* reflects the percentage of the amplitude changed in the original value. The set of percentage values that were used are $\{25\%, 20\%, 15\%, 10\%, 5\%\}$. Both increase and decrease was allowed. (2) *attack window size* denotes the size of the window chosen for injecting perturbation. (3) *disturbance behaviour* defines whether the changed introduced over a window was fixed or variable.

The results for the two sets are summarised in the following confusion matrices:

TABLE II. CONFUSION MATRIX FOR THERMOSTAT SENSORS

	detected	not detected
intrusion	94.5%	6.5%
no intrusion	7.6%	92.4%

TABLE III. CONFUSION MATRIX FOR TI IOT DEVICES

	detected	not detected
intrusion	99.8%	0.2%
no intrusion	4.6%	95.4%

The results clearly show that the good performance of the proposed approach. Most of the attacks that were not detected were those where the amplitude changes was very close to the original values. The data for the TI IoT devices had hardly any noise so any deviation from the normal behaviour was detected as intrusion, which explains the good performance of the approach.

V. CONCLUSION

In this paper, we have proposed an Intrusion detection methodology for IoT embedded devices. The methodology is based on a hierarchical design in order to distribute the computational resources over the IoT devices and increase the methodology scalability. Our approach is based on observing the devices performance and its correlation to similar devices. Experimental results shows that the efficiency of the proposed approach for detecting suspicious activities.

In future we plan to investigate the application of this technique with more rich dataset in particular related to the manufacturing domain. Currently we have assumed that the data is consisting of continuous domains. Therefore, in future we would like to extend this technique to consider events and categorical data. Also, There are many variants of our approach that also deserve future investigation.

ACKNOWLEDGEMENT

The research leading to these results in part has received funding from the European Unions Horizon 2020 research and innovation programme under Grant Agreement No. 731558.

REFERENCES

[1] A. Mady, D. Mehta, D. M. Shila, and M. Boubekeur, "Towards resilient cyber security for embedded devices on internet," 2016 IEEE 3rd World Forum on Internet of Things (WF-IoT) (2016), pp. 12, Dec. 2016.

[2] V. Valdivia et al., "Sustainable building integrated energy test-bed," Power Electronics for Distributed Generation Systems (PEDG), 2014 IEEE 5th International Symposium on, pp. 16, 2010.

[3] S. Haider, D. Manikantan Shila, and M. van Dijk, "Security agents for embedded intrusion detection," Circuit Cellar Magazine, Mar. 2015.

[4] B. Donohue, "Beware the thingbot," www.blog.kaspersky.com, Jan. 2014.

[5] "OWASP Internet of Things project," www.owasp.org/index.php, 2014.

[6] A. A. Cardenas, P. K. Manadhata, and S. P. Rajan, *Big data analytics for security*, IEEE Security & Privacy, pp. 74-76, Dec. 2013.

[7] A. Valdes and K. Skinner, *Adaptive, Model-Based Monitoring for Cyber Attack Detection*, Recent Advances in Intrusion Detection Volume 1907 of the series Lecture Notes in Computer Science pp 80-93, 2000.

[8] F. Pasqualetti, F. Dörfler, and F. Bullo, *Attack Detection and Identification in Cyber-Physical Systems–Part I: Models and Fundamental Limitations*, arXiv preprint arXiv:1202.6144, 2012.

[9] H. Fawzi, P. Tabuada, and S. Diggavi, *Secure Estimation and Control for Cyber-Physical Systems Under Adversarial Attacks*, Automatic Control, IEEE Transactions on, pp. 1454-1467, Jan. 2014.

[10] K. Paridari et al., *Cyber-Physical-Security Framework for Building Energy Management System*, In 2016 ACM/IEEE 7th International Conference on Cyber-Physical Systems (ICCPS), 2016.

[11] D. Evans, A. Nguyen-Tuong, J. Knight, *Effectiveness of moving target defenses*, Moving Target Defense, 2011.

[12] R. Mitchell and I.-R. Chen, "A survey of intrusion detection techniques for cyber-physical systems," ACM Comput. Surv., vol. 46, no. 4, pp. 55:1–55:29, Mar. 2014.

[13] C. Varun, A. Banerjee, and V. Kumar, *Anomaly detection: A survey*, ACM computing surveys (CSUR), 2009.

[14] D. Cheboli, *Anomaly Detection of Time-Series*, Phd Thesis, 2010.

Physics-Based Methods for Distinguishing Attacks from Faults

Gregory Provan Riccardo Orizio

School of Computer Science
University College Cork
Cork, Ireland
Email: g.provan, r.orizio@cs.ucc.ie

***Abstract*—Cyber-physical systems (CPSs) are a key framework for analysing a range of systems, from power plants to automobiles. One recent trend has been using this framework for security analysis. This article uses physics-based methods for distinguishing attacks from faults. We frame a CPS as a discrete-time linear system that can switch between various modes. By encoding faults and attacks each as specific modes, we build CPS models that incorporate the impact of a range of types of fault and attack. We then use this CPS model to isolate (and distinguish between) a fault and an attack. We illustrate our approach on a hydraulic benchmark system.**

***Keywords*–model-based security; model-based diagnosis; state identification.**

I. Introduction

The study of Cyber-Physical Systems (CPSs) [1] is attracting great interest, due to the significance of the applications that a CPS can model. For example, CPSs can model nuclear power plants, air-traffic control systems, smart cities, etc.

Recently, researchers have been focusing on identifying and defending against attacks on a CPS, e.g., [2], [3], [4], [5]. A broad range of approaches have been used for attack modeling and detection, none of which is fully comprehensive in terms of the range of attacks that can be identified [2], [3].

This article focuses on using physics-based models to isolate attacks on a system. We assume that a CPS is an instance of a hybrid system, in that the system can operate in a variety of distinct behaviours, which we call modes. For example, an aircraft can be in take-off or cruise mode, or it can operate in one of several faulty modes. We use system mode identification approaches [6], together with appropriate attack models, to compute an attack on a system.

In our approach, we create a first-principles physics-based model of the CPS and its control system. We explicitly create modes depicting the impact of faults on the CPS. We assume that an attacker may inject data into the CPS to mimic faults that occur naturally. As a consequence, we also include physics-based attack models.

Our objective is to analyze which faults can be distinguished from attacks using limited sensors in the CPS (most real-world systems have limited sensors available). This analysis enables us to understand the strengths and limitations of physics-based CPS attack analysis.

Our contributions are as follows:

- We describe an observer-based framework for isolating faults and attacks, and a method for distinguishing between them;
- We show that physics-based methods can distinguish attacks on sensors from sensor faults, but that actuator attacks cannot be distinguished from actuator faults;
- We illustrate our approach on a well-known hydraulic benchmark.

We organize the paper as follows. We introduce a running example in Section II. Next, Sections III and IV present the formal framework for our work. We present our empirical studies in Section V, and summarize our results in Section VII.

II. Running Example

We illustrate our concepts using a three-tank system, as shown in figure 1.

A. Nominal Model

We denote the tanks as T_1, T_2, and T_3. They all have the same area $A_1 = A_2 = A_3 = 3$ [m^2]. We assume that $g = 10$ and the liquid is "pure" water with density $\rho = 1$.

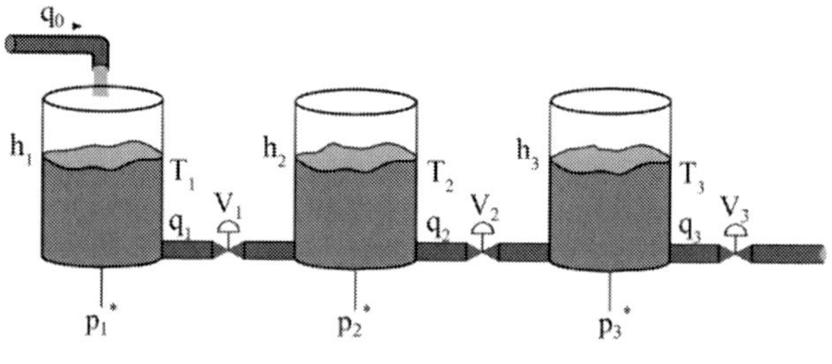

Figure 1. Diagram of the three-tank system.

Tank T_1 is filled from a pipe q_0 with a constant flow of 0.75 [m^3/s]. It drains into T_2 via a pipe q_1. The liquid level is denoted as h_1. There is a pressure sensor p_1 connected to T_1 that measures the pressure in Pascals [Pa]. The system has valves V_1, V_2, V_3 as shown in figure 1.

For this system we control the inflow q_0 and valve positions, i.e., our input vector $u = \{q_0, V_1, V_2, V_3\}$. We can measure the tank pressure values, i.e., the measurement vector is $y = \{p_1, p_2, p_3\}$. Our control task is to maintain set-point heights in each of the tanks. The diagnostic task is to compute the true value of V_i, given p_i, for $i = 1, 2, 3$.

We define our nominal model as follows. Starting from Newton's (and Bernoulli's) equations and manipulating them (the actual derivation is irrelevant in this paper) we derive the following Ordinary Differential Equation (ODE) that gives the level of the liquid in T_1:

$$\frac{dh_1}{dt} = q_0 - q_1 = \frac{q_0 - k_1 s(h_1, h_2)\sqrt{|h_1 - h_2|}}{A_1}, \quad (1)$$

where $s(h_1, h_2)$ denotes $\text{sign}(h_1 - h_2)$. In eq. 1, the coefficient k_1 is given by $k_1 = \nu_1 \kappa_1$, which is the product of the valve V_1 setting, $\nu_1 \in [0, 1]$, where 0 denotes a closed valve and 1 an open valve, and the outflow parameters κ_1, which include the cross-sectional area of the tank A_1, the area of the drainage hole, $\sqrt{2g}$, and the friction/contraction factor of the hole. We emphasize the use of k_1 because, later, we will be "diagnosing" our system in term of changes in k_1. Consider a physical valve V_1 between T_1 and T_2 that constrains the flow between the two tanks. We can say that the valve changes proportionally to the cross-sectional drainage area of q_1 and hence k_1.

We define the water levels of T_2 and T_3, denoted as h_2 and h_3 respectively, as:

$$\frac{dh_i}{dt} = \frac{k_{i-1} s(h_{i-1}, h_i)\sqrt{|h_{i-1} - h_i|} - k_i\sqrt{h_i}}{A_i}, \quad (2)$$

where i is the tank index ($i \in \{2, 3\}$).

We assume that $\kappa_1 = \kappa_2 = \kappa_3 = 0.75$.

Finally, we can compute from the water level a pressure given by

$$p_i = \frac{g\, h_i\, A}{A} = g\, h_i \quad (3)$$

where i is the tank index ($i \in \{1, 2, 3\}$).

We assume that the initial water level in the three tanks is zero.

B. Fault Model

In the following we define valve (actuator) faults; other faults, e.g., leaks or sensor faults, can be defined analogously.

We assume an additive valve fault, where the actual valve position for valve i, given commanded position ν_i and fault Δ_{ν_i}, is

$$\nu_i = \begin{cases} \max\{0, \nu_i + \Delta_{\nu_i}\} & \text{if } \Delta_{\nu_i} \leq 0 \\ \min\{1, \nu_i + \Delta_{\nu_i}\} & \text{if } \Delta_{\nu_i} > 0 \end{cases} \quad (4)$$

where $\Delta_{\nu_i} \in [-1, 1]$.

C. Attack Model

For our attack model, we assume that an attacker cannot monitor the system, but can inject false data.

We first consider injecting a fake sensor reading. Hence, for pressure sensor p_i ($i = 1, 2, 3$), which can output nominal values in the range $[0, p_i^{max}]$, an attacker can inject a fixed value of $p_i^a \in [0, p_i^{max}]$.

If an attacker injects a fake actuator value $\nu_i \in [0, 1]$ ($i = 1, 2, 3$), then valve i will be commanded to this "fake" position.

There is a difference in the physical behaviours of these two attacks. Whereas the actuator attack alters the system itself, the sensor attack has no impact on the physical behaviour unless the control system changes in response to the fake sensor value.

III. Cyber-Physical Systems with Faults and Attacks

This section provides the theoretical basis for our models and attack detection procedures. We first define a discrete-time state-space model for a Cyber-Physical System (CPS) that is subject to faults and attacks.

A. Cyber-Physical Systems

The nominal (or ideal) system model is given by

$$\begin{aligned} x_{k+1} &= A_\gamma x_k + B_\gamma u_k + w_k; \\ y_k &= C_\gamma x_k + v_k; \end{aligned} \quad (5)$$

where $x_k \in \mathbb{R}^n$ is the state of the system, $x_0 \in \mathbb{R}^n$ the initial state of the system, $u_k \in \mathbb{R}^l$ the control input, and $y_k \in \mathbb{R}^p$ the measurement at time instance k. We assume that a system can operate in a mode $\gamma_i \in \Gamma$. Each mode determines the physical behaviours of CPS. We capture the mode using a matrix with subscript γ, e.g., A_γ. The unknown process and measurement noise are $w_k \in \mathbb{R}^n$ and $v_k \in \mathbb{R}^p$, respectively. We define our matrices as follows: $A_\gamma \in \mathbb{R}^{n \times n}$ is the system matrix, $B_\gamma \in \mathbb{R}^{n \times l}$ is the control input matrix and $C_\gamma \in \mathbb{R}^{p \times n}$ the measurement matrix.[1]

For example, for the tank system our state vector is $x = \{h_1, h_2, h_3\}$, our input $u = \{q_0, V_1, V_2, V_3\}$, and $y = \{p_1, p_2, p_3\}$, our output. The output equation is given by

$$y_k = \begin{bmatrix} g & 0 & 0 \\ 0 & g & 0 \\ 0 & 0 & g \end{bmatrix} x_k \quad (6)$$

We assume that we control the system using a state (Luenberger) observer based on a set of equations with observer matrix L. Using the observed system with observed state and measurement, $\hat{x}_k \in \mathbb{R}^n$ and $\hat{y}_k \in \mathbb{R}^p$, respectively:

$$\begin{aligned} \hat{x}_{k+1} &= A_\gamma \hat{x}_k + B_\gamma u_k + w_k; \\ \hat{y}_k &= C_\gamma \hat{x}_k + v_k; \end{aligned} \quad (7)$$

we obtain the observer equations:

$$\begin{aligned} \hat{x}_{k+1} &= A_\gamma \hat{x}_k + B_\gamma u_k + L_\gamma (y_k - C_\gamma \hat{x}_k); \\ r_k &= y_k - C_\gamma \hat{x}_k; \\ u_k &= -K_\gamma \hat{x}_k, \end{aligned} \quad (8)$$

where $r_k \in \mathbb{R}^p$ is the residual $y_k - \hat{y}_k$. We assume the control matrix $K_\gamma \in \mathbb{R}^{l \times p}$ and observer matrix $L_\gamma \in \mathbb{R}^{n \times p}$ are chosen so that the closed-loop system and error dynamics are stable.

[1] We assume that the initial conditions for all systems (e.g., x_0, $\tilde{x}_0$ are known.

In the following, we assume that the actual input and measurement values, $\tilde{u}_k$ and $\tilde{y}_k$ respectively, can differ from the values of u_k and y_k due to data loss, noise in the network, faults, or due to a malicious attack $a_k \in \mathbb{R}^m$ on the system.

B. Fault Model

In this article we consider (a) sensor faults, where the sensor will either generate erroneous output or no output, and (b) plant/actuator faults. In the following we will specify additive fault models for these two fault classes. We define an additive fault vector $\boldsymbol{f}$, which we incorporate in a fault model as follows:

$$\begin{aligned} x^f_{k+1} &= A_\gamma x^f_k + B_\gamma u_k + B_f f_k + w_k; \quad (9)\\ y_k &= C_\gamma x^f_k + C_f f_k + v_k; \end{aligned}$$

where x^f_k is the faulty state vector at time k, B_f represents the influence the fault has on the state and C_f the influence of the fault on the measurement (sensor) data.

$$\begin{aligned} \tilde{x}_{k+1} &= A\tilde{x}_k + Bu_k + L(\tilde{y}_k - C\tilde{x}_k); \quad (10)\\ r_k &= \tilde{y}_k - C\tilde{x}_k;\\ u_k &= -K\tilde{x}_k, \end{aligned}$$

where we have: $\tilde{x}_k \in \mathbb{R}^n$ is the state of the observer, $u_k \in \mathbb{R}^l$ the calculated control input, $\tilde{y}_k \in \mathbb{R}^p$ the measurements received over the network and $r_k \in \mathbb{R}^p$ is the residual. We assume the control matrix $K \in \mathbb{R}^{l \times p}$ and observer matrix $L \in \mathbb{R}^{n \times p}$ are chosen so that the closed-loop system and error dynamics are stable.

The values of $\tilde{u}_k$ and $\tilde{y}_k$ can differ from the values of u_k and y_k due to data loss, noise in the network, faults, or due to a malicious attack $a_k \in \mathbb{R}^m$ on the system.

C. Attack Model

We propose an attack model that specifies two types of attack: attacks on the system's actuators (or state), a^x_k, and attacks on the system output, a^y_k. Introducing the attack vector $a_k = [(a^x_k)^T (a^y_k)^T]^T$ to the plant and observer leads to

$$\begin{aligned} x_{k+1} &= A_\gamma x_k + B_\gamma u_k + B_a a_k + w_k; \quad (11)\\ y_k &= C_\gamma x_k + D_a a_k + v_k; \end{aligned}$$

where B_a represents the influence the attack has on the state by either a physical or an actuator attack and D_a the influence of the attack on the measurements by falsifying sensor data.

$$\begin{aligned} x_{k+1} &= A_\gamma x_k + Bu_k + B_a a_k + w_k; \quad (12)\\ y_k &= C_\gamma x_k + v_k;\\ \tilde{x}_{k+1} &= A_\gamma \tilde{x}_k + B_\gamma u_k + L_\gamma (y_k + D_a a_k - C_\gamma \tilde{x}_k);\\ r_k &= y_k + D_a a_k - C_\gamma \tilde{x}_k;\\ u_k &= -K_\gamma \tilde{x}_k; \end{aligned}$$

Due to the separation of the attacks into attacks on the states and the measurements, the attack matrices often take the structure

$$B_a = [B^x_a, \mathbf{0}] \text{ and } D_a = [\mathbf{0}, D^y_a]; \quad (13)$$

where $\mathbf{0}$ is the zero matrix with dimensions appropriate to the attack vector.

D. Extended System Model

We combine the plant and the observer to get an extended system. We define $\mathcal{X}_k = [x^T_k \tilde{x}^T_k]^T$ as the extended system state, the attack a_k as the input and the residual r_k as the system output

$$\begin{aligned} m_{k+1} &= A_e m_k + B_e a_k + \begin{bmatrix} w_k \\ Lv_k \end{bmatrix}; \quad (14)\\ r_k &= C_e m_k + D_e a_k + v_k \quad (15) \end{aligned}$$

with

$$\begin{aligned} A_e &= \begin{bmatrix} A & -BK \\ LC & A - BK - LC \end{bmatrix}, \quad B_e = \begin{bmatrix} B_a \\ LD_a \end{bmatrix} \quad (16)\\ C_e &= [C \quad -C] \text{ and } D_e = D_a. \quad (17) \end{aligned}$$

The initial state is given by $\mathcal{X}_0 = [x^T_0 \tilde{x}^T_0]^T$. Since K and L stabilize the plant and the error dynamics, A_e is stable as well. The residual r_k is used to determine how much the real system state deviates from the estimated state given by the observer, so we can use r_k to detect faults or attacks on the system.

IV. Distinguishing Faults from Security Breaches

This section focuses on methods for distinguishing faults from security breaches. We assume that a stealthy attacker will attempt to mask attacks as natural events, e.g., faults. In that case, we use the physics of the fault evolution and/or onset to isolate true faults.

A. Model-Based Isolation

We address this problem using a model-based framework. We assume that our system can be in one of q possible modes, where a mode characterizes a system behaviour. We can define modes corresponding to nominal, fault, and attack conditions.

We assume that we can specify the behaviour of each mode using a physical model of that mode. We denote model i using ψ_i. Our family of models $\Psi = \{\psi_1, ..., \psi_q\}$ consists of subsets of models denoting nominal, fault, and attack modes, $\{\Psi^N, \Psi^f, \Psi^a\}$ respectively. Model i generates a behaviour $\boldsymbol{\xi}_i$ (with measurement $\hat{\boldsymbol{y}}_i$) given initial conditions x_0. A behaviour over interval $[0, ..., T]$ is a state sequence $\{x_0, ..., x_T\}$.

Definition 1 (Mode Estimation): Our mode estimation task, given an anomalous observation $\tilde{y}$, is to compute the model whose behaviour most closely matches the observation $\tilde{y}$, i.e.,

$$\psi^* = \arg\min_{\psi_i \in \Psi} \parallel \tilde{y}_i - \hat{y}_i \parallel, \quad (18)$$

where $\parallel \tilde{y}_i - \hat{y}_i \parallel$ is a difference norm at instant i

We assume that we compute a residual vector $r = \{r_1, ..., r_q\}$, with residual i associated with mode i. Residual r_i is "activated", i.e., $r_i > \delta_i$ for some tunable threshold δ_i, iff the system is in mode λ_i.

Definition 2 (Mode Identifiability): Given a model Ψ with a set of modes $\Lambda = \{\lambda_1, ..., \lambda_q\}$, mode i is identifiable (i.e., can be distinguished from mode j, for $i \neq j$) if (a) λ_i generates a behaviour ξ_i that is distinguishable from ξ_j for all $i \neq j$, and (b) there exists a residual r such that $r_i > \delta_i$ iff the system is in mode λ_i.

This notion of mode identifiability enables us to detect attacks, since an identifiable system guarantees that attacks can always be isolated. The ability to distinguish fault- and attack-modes depends on the fidelity of the models and the availability of appropriate sensor data.

B. Example: Sensor/Actuator Attack Detection

We assume a system in which we have the correct measurement y, the simulated measurement $\hat{y}$, and an attacker who injects a false measurement $\tilde{y}$ for a subset of the sensors. We can compute residuals for the "true" system as $r_i = \| y_i - \hat{y}_i \|$, and the system under attack as $r_i^a = \| \tilde{y}_i - \hat{y}_i \|$.

We compare r with r_a to distinguish faults from attacks. If $r_i = r_i^a, \ \forall i > 0$ then the fault and attack are indistinguishable via physics-based analysis. Distinguishing faults from attacks also depends on the models assumed for faults from attacks. In this article we restrict our attention to attacks that fix the sensor/actuator at an anomalous value at some $k > 0$ and remains at that value.

Sensor Attack: We assume that, given a physical fault (e.g., stuck actuator or tank leak) a sensor will report the physical deviations from nominal conditions. For example, a tank leak in tank T_2 will lead to lower-than-expected tank height for T_2, such that the deviation will increase over time. In this article we look at residuals, but also rates of change of outputs y_k and residuals r_k, i.e., $\dot{y}_k$, $\dot{r}_k$, respectively.

Actuator Attack: If we restrict our fault model to "stuck" actuators, e.g., a valve that gets stuck open, then our attack model can exactly mimic a "stuck" actuator, and hence this class of attack cannot be distinguished from a "stuck" actuator fault.

V. Experimental Results

In the following we will show some tests and results achieved on the three-tank system, starting from the data simulation of the system itself in various conditions through the analysis and fault detection of these data.

A. Simulations

We based our experiments on our own simulated data of the three-tank system. In order to correctly simulate faults and attacks we set three different simulation modes for the system: normal, faulty and attack.

The faulty simulation included a random delta value for each valve, either positive or negative, in order to reproduce a positioning problem differing from the normal value. Each delta value is independent from each other, plus the final valve position will still respect the [0,1] interval constraint.

The attack simulation influences either the valve settings, the sensor measurements or both. The principle of each attack is the same: the attacker sets a fixed value to one or more of the system's components, overriding the correct value. The difference between the two attacks relies on the fact that a valve attack immediately influences the system behaviour, forcing more (or less) fluid to go through the system. On the other hand, attacking a sensor could not be as effective in the case of a non-feedback system.

We run our simulations on a 50 and 500 seconds period, extracting data from our sensors every 2 seconds.

B. Analysis procedure

In order to detect faults and attacks on our system, we used residuals and first derivative studies of the sensor data. Relative errors and deeper derivative studies were performed, but we were not able to extract good results from them.

We were able to identify incongruences in the data when the residuals were over a predefined tolerance. On the other hand, the gradients were able to give an idea of how the data would evolve in time, allowing us to identify absolute tendencies of data.

This approach has been proven to be a good way to find injected sensor data. When sensor data are attacked, we obtain the relation

$$\dot{y}_k = -\dot{r}_k, \tag{19}$$

where $\dot{y}_k$ and $\dot{r}_k$ denote the first derivative of the sensor output and the residual, respectively.

The fact that we are limited of having only the sensor data allows us to detect when a fault or attack occurred but they are not enough to identify which valve had a problem and if the problem was an attack or a random fault of the system.

C. Experiment I - Attacks on sensors

The objective of our first experiment was to identify whether a sensor has been attacked or not.

Thanks to the first derivative analysis of the normal behaviour and the residuals we were able to identify in which cases the data were crafted by an attacker.

Figure 2 shows the data generated by an attacked sensor. We can clearly see how that equation 19 holds, i.e., the residual function is a y-mirrored version of the normal behaviour.

Each sensor attack is correctly detected by our procedure, either alone or in conjunction with other attacks.

D. Experiment II - Attacks on Actuators (Valves)

This experiment addresses detection and isolation of actuator attacks, i.e., valves whose control setting are set to be incorrect.

We started analysing only one attack per simulation. In each simulation we were able to detect that an attack has occured, but we could not precisely locate on which valve. Besides we found that our procedure observed attacks on

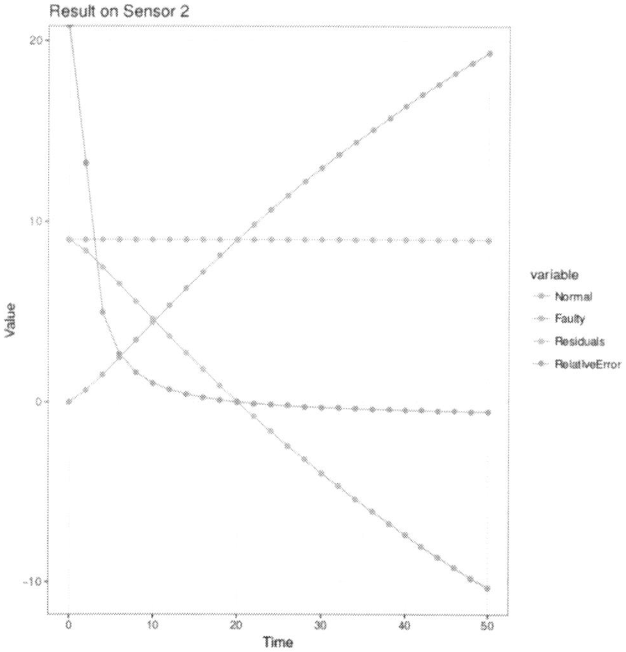

Figure 2. Injected data on the second sensor of our system. The graph shows the normal and faulty behaviour and their related residuals and relative errors.

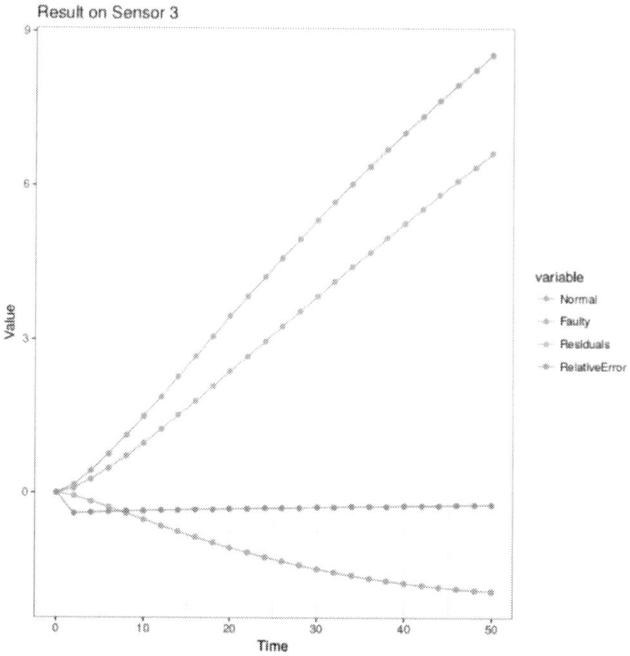

Figure 3. Data of the third sensor related to test 535.

different valves even if the attack was performed only on one: this is due to the complexity and synergies of the system itself which we were not be able to capture with only data from the pressure sensors.

Figure 3 shows the data of an attacked valve, while Table I shows which faults were detected for each experiment:

Test	Valve 1	Valve 2	Valve 3
155	✓	X	X
355	✓	X	X
755	✓	X	X
955	✓	X	X
515	X	✓	X
535	X	✓	X
575	X	✓	X
595	X	✓	X
551			✓
553			✓
557			✓
559			✓

TABLE I. Results of our procedure. The test number shows the valve settings for each valve (i.e. 155: v1 = 0.1, v2 = 0.5, v3 = 0.5). The nominal setting is 555. A valve is marked when our procedure identifies a problem with it. ✓ denotes a correct diagnosis, and X denotes an incorrect diagnosis.

We also tested combination of attacks: attacks are still detected, but is even more difficult to identify on which valves the attack was done. The results of our tests are shown in Table II.

Test	Valve 1	Valve 2	Valve 3
544	X	✓	✓
158	✓	X	✓
658	✓	X	✓
958	✓	X	✓
745	✓	✓	X
247	✓	✓	✓
432	✓	✓	✓
632	✓	✓	✓
638	✓	✓	✓
678	✓	✓	✓

TABLE II. Results of our procedure on multi valve attacks.

E. Experiment III - Attacks on both Sensors and Actuators (Valves)

The goal of this experiment was to combine the previous experiments and see how simultaneous attacks impact the system and if we were still able to identify which parts of the system have been attacked. We presume to be able to correctly detect sensor problems and the presence of valve errors, but cannot identify the faulty valves, as happened also in experiment II.

As expected and shown in Table III we are able to identify the attacks on the sensors but not on the valves.

VI. Related Work

This article extends the work of [7], who describe a framework for detecting security breaches in networked control systems. [7] make the simplifying assumption that anomalies due to security breaches and to other sources are *a priori* separable, so the task of identifying security breaches becomes trivial. In real situations, this assump-

Test	Valve 1	Valve 2	Valve 3	Sensor
s1_325		✓	X	1
s2_553	X		✓	2
s3_148	✓	✓		3
s12_558			✓	1-2
s23_647	✓			2-3
s31_348		✓		1-3
s123_666				1-2-3

TABLE III. Results of our procedure on multi valve attacks. The test number, other than showing the valve settings, shows also which sensors are attacked.

tion does not hold, and we focus on methods for distinguishing faults from security breaches.

VII. Conclusion

This article has proposed a physics-based approach for modeling a CPS and using this model to distinguish faults from attacks. We have shown on a hydraulic system the capabilities of this approach. We have also shown that not all attacks can be identified via this physics-based approach. To extend this approach, deeper studies on sensors data synergies are needed in order to extract some more information about possible valve faults/attacks.

Acknowledgment

The authors would like to thank SFI for funding this work under grants SFI grants 12/RC/2289 and 13/RC/2094.

References

[1] E. A. Lee and S. A. Seshia, Introduction to embedded systems: A cyber-physical systems approach. MIT Press, 2016.

[2] R. Mitchell and I.-R. Chen, "A survey of intrusion detection techniques for cyber-physical systems," ACM Computing Surveys (CSUR), vol. 46, no. 4, 2014, p. 55.

[3] D. I. Urbina, J. A. Giraldo, A. A. Cardenas, N. O. Tippenhauer, J. Valente, M. Faisal, J. Ruths, R. Candell, and H. Sandberg, "Limiting the impact of stealthy attacks on industrial control systems," in Proceedings of the 2016 ACM SIGSAC Conference on Computer and Communications Security. ACM, 2016, pp. 1092–1105.

[4] S. Lakshminarayana, T. Z. Teng, D. K. Yau, and R. Tan, "Optimal attack against cyber-physical control systems with reactive attack mitigation," in Proceedings of the Eighth International Conference on Future Energy Systems. ACM, 2017, pp. 179–190.

[5] T. Darure, J.-J. Yamé, and F. Hamelin, "Model-based fault-tolerant control of vav damper lock-in place failure in a multizone building," in Control, Automation, Robotics and Vision (ICARCV), 2016 14th International Conference on. IEEE, 2016, pp. 1–6.

[6] S. Paoletti, A. L. Juloski, G. Ferrari-Trecate, and R. Vidal, "Identification of hybrid systems: a tutorial," European journal of control, vol. 13, no. 2-3, 2007, pp. 242–260.

[7] D. Umsonst, H. Sandberg, and A. A. Cárdenas, "Security analysis of control system anomaly detectors," in American Control Conference (ACC), 2017. IEEE, 2017, pp. 5500–5506.

International Academy, Research,
and Industry Association (IARIA)
412 Derby Way
Wilmington, DE 19810

CURRAN ASSOCIATES INC.
proceedings
.com

ISBN 978-1-5108-5138-2

9 781510 851382